CONVEYANCING 2012

CONVEYANCING 2012

Kenneth G C Reid WS

Professor of Scots Law in the University of Edinburgh

and

George L Gretton WS

Lord President Reid Professor of Law in the University of Edinburgh

with a contribution by Alan Barr of the University of Edinburgh
and Brodies LLP

Avizandum Publishing Ltd
Edinburgh
2013

Published by
Avizandum Publishing Ltd
25 Candlemaker Row
Edinburgh EH1 2QG

First published 2013

© Kenneth G C Reid and George L Gretton, 2013

ISBN 978-1-904968-59-7

British Library Cataloguing in Publication Data
A catalogue record for this book is available from the British Library.

Typeset by Waverley Typesetters, Warham, Norfolk
Printed and bound by Bell & Bain Ltd, Glasgow

CONTENTS

PREFACE

This is the fourteenth annual update of new developments in the law of conveyancing. As in previous years, it is divided into five parts. There is, first, a brief description of all cases which have been reported, or appeared on the websites of the Scottish Courts (www.scotcourts.gov.uk) or of the Lands Tribunal for Scotland (www.lands-tribunal-scotland.org.uk/records.html), or have otherwise come to our attention, since *Conveyancing 2011*. The next two parts summarise, respectively, statutory developments during 2012 and other material of interest to conveyancers. The fourth part is a detailed commentary on selected issues arising from the first three parts. Finally, in Part V, there are three tables. A cumulative table of decisions, usually by the Lands Tribunal, on the variation or discharge of title conditions covers all decisions since the revised jurisdiction in part 9 of the Title Conditions (Scotland) Act 2003 came into effect. Then there is a cumulative table of appeals, designed to facilitate moving from one annual volume to the next. Finally, there is a table of cases digested in earlier volumes but reported, either for the first time or in an additional series, in 2012. This is for the convenience of future reference.

We do not seek to cover agricultural holdings, crofting, public sector tenancies (except the right-to-buy legislation), compulsory purchase or planning law. Otherwise our coverage is intended to be complete.

We gratefully acknowledge help received from Ross Gilbert Anderson, Douglas Ballantyne, Alan Barr, Sandy Grant, Eoghainn MacLean, Roddy Paisley, Roy Shearer, Sarah Skea, Andrew Steven, Neil Tainsh, Michael Upton and Scott Wortley.

Kenneth G C Reid
George L Gretton
30 March 2013

TABLE OF STATUTES

TABLE OF ORDERS

TABLE OF CASES

PART I

CASES

CASES

MISSIVES OF SALE

(1) Scotia Homes (South) Ltd v McLean
2012 GWD 6-111 affd 2013 GWD 1-35, Sh Ct

Since the onset of the recession, there have been many cases of buyers on missives seeking to back out of the transaction. This and the following case are examples. In this case the argument for the buyers was that the missives were too indeterminate to be enforceable because they did not adequately identify the property.

Mr and Mrs McLean concluded missives to buy 'that flatted dwellinghouse being Plot 44 of your development at Langtoun Maltings, Kirkcaldy, on the terms and conditions contained in your pro-forma offer annexed'. This contained the words 'plot' and 'dwellinghouse', and both were defined. 'Plot' was defined as 'the dwellinghouse together with any garden ground, car parking space and/or garage pertaining exclusively thereto known by the Plot number specified in the schedule'; 'dwellinghouse' was defined as 'the dwellinghouse (and garage, if applicable) of the house type specified in the Schedule and shown on the Company's site layout plan (which plan is demonstrative only and may be varied by the Company as circumstances require) erected or to be erected by the Company as part of the Development and where the context so admits or requires such fixtures and fittings therein as are included in the sale'. Elsewhere the offer referred to the property as 'FT 12 (Second Floor)'. At this stage the unit had not yet been built. The 'site layout plan' existed, but was not physically copied into the missives. It, or at least some version of it, had been seen by the buyers before missives were concluded. But this plan did not give details of the individual unit. Finally, clause 14 of the offer to sell said:

> It is expressly declared and agreed that the Contract forms the agreement entered into between the Company and the Purchaser and no reliance has been or will be placed by either the Company or the Purchaser in any manner or way whatsoever upon any representation, warranty or undertaking given by or on behalf of either the Company or the Purchaser whether written or verbal which is not specified in or does not form part of the Contract.

When the unit had been completed the buyers declined to go ahead. The developer remarketed the unit, and resold at a lower price. It raised this action to recover the shortfall. There were two defences. One was that the contract had been induced by misrepresentation, in that the sales representative had said that the unit would have three bedrooms whereas in fact it had only two. The other was that the missives were void by reason of uncertainty. Both defences failed when the case was before the sheriff (A G McCulloch). Only the second was appealed to the sheriff principal.

It is well-established by authority that the standard of description required in missives is not particularly exacting. But this case seems to be the first in which the question was considered in relation to a flat that, at the time of the missives, did not yet exist. The sheriff principal (R A Dunlop QC) agreed with the sheriff and held in favour of the developer (paras 39 and 40):

> An agreement may be complete although it is not worked out in meticulous detail – see for example McBryde on *Contract* 3rd edn para 5.13 ff. While initially attracted by the proposition that a two dimensional plan was inadequate to describe a three dimensional subject I have come to the view that an absence of any express provision stipulating a dimension for the elevation of the flat is in the circumstances of this case immaterial and a matter of detail. As counsel for the respondents pointed out, the building regulations enjoin a minimum elevation which would provide an objective basis for the implication of a reasonable elevation and in such circumstances it ceases to be impossible to work out what the contract means. Accordingly it cannot be said that on this ground the contract is 'void from uncertainty'.
>
> Insofar as concerns the other points of criticism made by counsel for the appellants with regard to the provisions referring to garden ground, car parking space and/or garage I agree with the submission of counsel for the respondents that there was no agreement that there was or required to be any garden ground, car parking space and/or garage included in the subjects of sale. It is right to acknowledge that the contract is not well written, no doubt due in part to the fact that it is a pro-forma intended for use in respect of different properties throughout the development, but in my view clause 1.1(m) can be construed as meaning that if, contingently, the development came to be built in such a way that objectively such garden ground, car parking space or garage did at completion 'pertain exclusively' to the flat in question then the appellants could require that it be granted to them. Conversely, if it did not, then the appellants could not enforce a claim to such rights as they had not from the start stipulated for them. If, contrary to this view, there is a distinction to be made in relation to car parking, as the sheriff has made, then in my view the same considerations as I have discussed in the preceding paragraph would apply so as to entitle the appellants to a reasonably located car parking space, the contents of which could be supplied by evidence if needed.

As for clause 14, quoted above, it was held, on the basis of the case law on 'entire agreement clauses', that it did not exclude consideration of the site layout plan. One might add that since it was expressly referred to in the missives, it could hardly be ousted by the general wording of clause 14. Be that as it may, the value of the site layout plan seems minimal, given that it was unilaterally variable by the developer.

By way of postscript, there might, as with so many builders missives, be a question of compatibility with the Unfair Terms in Consumer Contracts

Regulations 1999, SI 1999/2083: see G L Gretton and K G C Reid, *Conveyancing* (4th edn, 2011) para 30-02.

(2) Pinecraven Construction (Guernsey) Ltd v Taddei
[2012] CSOH 18, 2012 GWD 8-155

The pursuer, the developer of residential housing at Trimontium Heights, Dingleton Road, Melrose, made an offer to sell to the defenders, dated 13 April 2007. The offer was open for acceptance by 27 April 2007. On 26 April 2007 the buyers sent a qualified acceptance. On 2 May 2007, the pursuer accepted the qualification and held the bargain as concluded. The price was £445,000 and the buyers paid a deposit of £5,000 at or soon after conclusion of missives. In June 2008, when the house was not yet finished, the defenders wrote to the pursuer intimating that they did not wish to proceed with the purchase. The pursuer remarketed the property, resold at a lower price (£320,000), and in this action sought to recover (i) the shortfall, plus (ii) interest and incidentals amounting to £14,105.

The defence was that missives had never been validly concluded. The offer of 13 April had required acceptance by 27 April. That had not happened, for the letter of 26 April had not been an acceptance, merely a qualified acceptance. Not surprisingly, this argument failed, and the Lord Ordinary (Kinclaven) found in favour of the pursuer. A qualified acceptance is in the eyes of the law a rejection coupled with a new offer. Thus the letter from the defenders' agents of 26 April was an offer to buy. It did not contain a deadline for acceptance, and so was open for acceptance within a reasonable period. It was accepted after six days, which was a reasonable period. Accordingly missives had been validly concluded on 2 May.

(3) Persimmon Homes Ltd v Bellway Homes Ltd
[2012] CSOH 60, 2012 GWD 15-304

This was a sequel to *Persimmon Homes Ltd v Bellway Homes Ltd* [2011] CSOH 149, 2011 GWD 35-720 (*Conveyancing 2011* Case (11)). Bellway concluded missives in May 2006 to sell development land in the Glasgow area to Persimmon, the price being £4,160,000. Bellway was bound, under the missives, to carry out certain preliminary works ('the seller's works'), such as the construction of roads and footpaths. The missives then continued:

> In the event that the Seller has failed to complete all of the Seller's Works ... by the Long Stop Date ... then the Seller will be obliged to offer to sell to the Purchaser another residential development site within Central Scotland of comparable size and value to the Subjects. Upon settlement of the transaction contemplated by the missives in respect of the said other residential development site the missives to follow hereon (of which this offer forms part) shall be terminated.

The longstop date was 15 December 2007. As 2007 progressed it became apparent that Bellway would not be able to do the works by the agreed date.

Bellway offered Persimmon a site in Airdrie but this was rejected. Persimmon then rescinded the missives and sued for damages for breach of contract in the sum of £1,789,948. (Although the point is not discussed in the opinion, we take it that matters rested solely on the missives, ie that the transaction never settled.) A proof established that, whilst the Airdrie site was of 'comparable size', it was not of 'comparable value' to the Glasgow site. Accordingly it was held (in the 2011 case) that the defender was in breach of contract. Although that had been decided after proof, a further debate was held. The main issue at this stage of the litigation was whether Persimmon had rescinded prematurely, in that they had not adopted an ultimatum procedure. As the Lord Ordinary (Drummond Young) put it (para 6):

> [T]he ultimatum procedure had not been used, and accordingly the defenders were still entitled to offer an alternative site that met the requirements of condition 12. Consequently, the critical question was whether the missives had been properly rescinded by the pursuers' agents' letter of 12 June 2009.

But the Lord Ordinary noted that an ultimatum is not needed in a case where it would be pointless, in the sense that the party in breach would not comply anyway. And here it was clear that Bellway would not have complied with an ultimatum. Hence Bellway's argument was rejected.

(4) EDI Central Ltd v National Car Parks Ltd
[2012] CSIH 6, 2012 SLT 421

This was an appeal from the Outer House decision reported at 2011 SLT 75 (*Conveyancing 2010* Case (5)). The issue was whether the pursuer had used 'all reasonable endeavours' to make possible a development in central Edinburgh. The decision of the Lord Ordinary that the pursuer had indeed used all reasonable endeavours was upheld, and his analysis of the law approved.

(5) Richal v Seed
2012 GWD 39-767, Sh Ct

Missives were concluded, on 9 June 2010, for the sale of a house at Auchnagatt, a small village in rural Aberdeenshire. The date of entry was scheduled for 6 August, but at the end of July the missives were formally varied to change it to 5 August. Settlement duly took place on that date. But it then emerged that the sellers had, on 15 July, received a notice from the local authority that there was now a 'proposed local development plan' which, if implemented, could result in substantial development taking place on adjoining farmland. The buyer was unhappy. Did she have a remedy against the sellers? The missives were based on the standard Aberdeen missive clauses, and thus provided as follows:

(i) So far as the Seller is aware the Property is not affected by … any proposals, applications or re-development plans affecting the Property or any adjacent or neighbouring property which could reasonably be considered to be detrimental to the Property.

(ii) Without prejudice to the foregoing, the Seller warrants that he has not been served with nor received any neighbour notification notice issued in terms of planning legislation by any third party. If such notice is served on or received by the Seller prior to the date of settlement, the Seller will immediately forward the notice to the Purchaser's Solicitor. If the proposals contained in the notice would have a materially detrimental effect on the Property the Purchaser will be entitled to resile from the Missives without penalty due to or by either party.

The buyer argued that the sellers were in breach of both (i) and (ii). As to (i), the relevant date of awareness was conclusion of missives, and while it was true that missives had been concluded in June, well before the issue of the notice, she argued that the missives had been re-concluded on 30 July, and so the relevant date of awareness was now that date. As to (ii), there would, argued the buyer, have been a breach by the sellers even if the missives had never been re-opened, because the local authority notice had been sent to the sellers on 15 July, and so should have been immediately intimated to the buyer, in which case she would have had the option of pulling out of the contract.

The sheriff held in favour of the buyer and ordered a proof as to the quantum of loss. The sellers appealed, without success, to the sheriff principal (Derek Pyle). Taking the second issue first, the sellers argued that the notice sent to them had not been a 'neighbour notification notice', ie a notice informing a neighbour of a planning application. This narrow interpretation of the phrase did not commend itself to the sheriff principal. One reason was that 'neighbour notification notice' is in fact not a technical term used in the planning legislation to refer to the notice to be given to neighbours about planning applications. He also stressed the word 'any'. This seems a sensible approach. From the standpoint of average clients, it makes little difference precisely what the planning notice is. What is important is that it flags up a significant possibility of development in an adjacent property.

To win, the sellers needed to succeed on both issues. In fact they lost not only on (ii), just discussed, but also on (i), though here the sheriff principal admitted to finding the point difficult. The wording of the letter of 27 July was:

> On behalf of and as instructed by our clients Mr and Mrs Michael Seed we hereby reopen the missives concluded between our respective clients ... and amend the missives as follows: Entry and actual occupation shall be as at 5th August 2010. Except as varied hereby we confirm and ratify the terms and conditions of said missives.

This was met by a formal letter of agreement dated 30 July. The sheriff principal criticised the wording of the quoted letter on the ground that it bears to be in unilateral form ('we hereby ... amend') and no doubt he was right to do so, though at the end of the day nothing seems to turn on the point. More substantively, he said (para 13):

> It was a matter of concession by the appellants' solicitor, both before me and before the sheriff, that the warranty was of the planning situation as at the date of conclusion of the missives ... The effect of the later letters was to create a new date for the conclusion

of the bargain to sell the property. Thus the natural consequence of amending the date of entry was to create a new date as at which the warranty was given.

Warranties in missives sometimes specify the date to which the warranty refers: for instance the standard warranty about the central heating is usually worded so as to refer to date of entry. But sometimes no date is specified. This might be an issue to be considered when standard-form missives are being reviewed. If a warranty is tied, whether expressly or by implication, to an event date rather than to a calendar date, that date may prove, as here, a moveable feast.

(6) McSorley v Drennan
[2012] CSIH 59, 2012 GWD 25-506

An owner contracted to sell only part of the property he owned, but the disposition by mistake transferred the whole property, ie there was an over-conveyance. By the time that the problem came to light, the buyers had resold. In this action the original seller sued the first buyers for damages. The decision of the sheriff principal (*Conveyancing 2011* Case (14)) has now been reversed by the Inner House. See **Commentary** p 162.

(7) Northern Hydroseeding Ltd v McDonald
2012 GWD 14-289, Sh Ct

This was a dispute about Auldbrig Filling Station, Bridgend, Tullibody, Alloa. The story is one of muddle on both sides, a proposed but abortive sale, and a claim by the owner for compensation for the period that the defender was in occupation.

The defender approached the owner (the pursuer) with a view to buying the filling station. He did so in the name of 'the Motor Vehicle Protection Association', which is referred to in the case as an unincorporated association. (The precise identity did not matter for the purposes of the litigation, but it seems more likely that 'the Motor Vehicle Protection Association' was simply the defender himself, using a trading name. It is not easy to see how it could have been an unincorporated association. If it was a trading association consisting of himself and one or more others, it would presumably have been a partnership.)

Negotiations about a sale continued for some time but eventually came to nothing. But at a stage when it looked as if a sale might happen (late November 2006), the pursuer gave possession of the filling station to the defender. This was all the more remarkable since it happened without any documentation as to the basis of the transfer of possession. In January 2007, however, the pursuer and defender signed a three-month lease. This designed the tenant as the 'Motor Vehicle Protection Association Ltd'. There was no such company. Since solicitors were involved, this ongoing muddle about the identity of 'Motor Vehicle Protection Association' and 'Motor Vehicle Protection Association Ltd' is perhaps surprising.

After the three-month period had elapsed the defender continued to occupy and trade from the property for about three years. To begin with he paid rent, but eventually stopped doing so. In 2010 the pursuer obtained decree to remove the defender. The present action was to obtain compensation for the occupation of the property during the period that the defender was not paying rent. The defence was that there had been a contract of sale and that he was in lawful possession under that contract. Since there was admittedly no written contract the defender had to argue factual agreement coupled with personal bar. The sheriff (John Mundy), after proof, **held** that there had been no agreement and accordingly the pursuer was entitled to compensation for the defender's occupation of the property, the sum being calculated as a reasonable rental figure, minus sums already paid. The sum awarded was £37,050 plus interest.

(8) Morris v Morris
2012 GWD 10-184, Sh Ct

This was a family law case but has some conveyancing interest. A married couple parted. A separation agreement was signed under which the husband agreed (i) to convey to the wife his one-half share of the matrimonial home (at 6 Jedburgh Road, Dundee) and (ii) to pay off the whole sum secured over the property (roughly £135,000), which failing damages. Although he tendered a disposition of his *pro indiviso* share, he did not pay off the secured loan. The wife raised an action of specific implement. The defence was that the defender lacked the means to pay, and that accordingly the court should decline to grant decree of specific implement. What it was precisely that the defender was seeking is not clear to us. Perhaps it was for decree of damages instead of decree of specific implement, though it is not explained how it would have benefited the defender to be ordered to pay £135,000 to the pursuer instead of the same sum to Lloyds TSB plc. At all events the sheriff (John Mundy) held that the defender had no relevant pleadings to support his case, and decree of specific implement was granted. The terms of the decree were:

> decree ordaining the defender to implement clause 3 of the Minute of Agreement between the parties dated 25 and 31 August 2010 and registered in the Books of Council and Session on 2 September 2010, and that by: (a) the defender executing and delivering to the pursuer a declaration of the defender's present solvency within a period of 28 days from this date; and (b) the defender paying to Lloyds TSB plc … the full sum required to redeem the secured loan owed by the parties in terms of mortgage account number 50000084209484 (including without prejudice to the foregoing generality any early redemption charges or penalties due on the date of settlement) and that within a period of 28 days from this date. …

The general principle is that specific implement cannot normally be granted for payment of money. As far as we can see, this issue was not discussed in the case. If the defender were to fail to obey the order to pay off the secured loan, the question would arise as to what the pursuer could do next. Assuming that the decree could not be enforced by imprisonment, it would seem that she would have to revert to her alternative crave for damages. Some of the procedural issues involved are discussed in W W McBryde and G L Gretton, 'Sale of heritable property and failure to pay' 2012 SLT (News) 17, albeit in relation to actions by sellers against buyers.

COMMON PROPERTY

(9) Serup v McCormack
18 April 2012, Scottish Land Court

More than a decade ago now, the House of Lords decided in *Clydesdale Bank plc v Davidson* 1998 SC (HL) 51 that *pro indiviso* owners are not able to grant a real right of lease to one of their number. Controversial in law and inconvenient in practice, the decision was based on the view that a person cannot be both an owner of property and also the holder of a subordinate real right, for the latter, as the lesser right, would inevitably be absorbed by the former. '[I]t is not possible for a person to have two real rights in the same property at the same time. This is because of the principle of *confusio*, by which the lesser right is absorbed into the greater right and is extinguished' (per Lord Hope at 56C).

In *Serup v McCormack* the issue arose in a different way. At the time the lease was created, landlord and tenant were entirely distinct; but in due course the tenant became a *pro indiviso* owner of the property and hence one of the landlords. Was the lease then extinguished? It was **held** that it was. No doubt, as counsel for the (former) tenant argued (paras 28 and 30), some of the views in *Clydesdale Bank* were expressed rather broadly (para 39). It was in fact possible, the court accepted, for one and the same person to have two real rights in the same property at the same time (eg where there is a servitude in favour of a neighbour, and that neighbour also happens to have a lease of the servient property), and it seemed wrong to regard a sole tenancy as less valuable than a modest *pro indiviso* share. Nonetheless the position was ruled by *Clydesdale Bank*, and the effect of that decision could not be avoided by arguing for the different approach sometimes taken in respect of servitudes.

Given the position adopted in *Clydesdale Bank*, the decision comes as no great surprise, and indeed was anticipated in our discussion of that case at the time: See *What Happened in 1997?* p 61. It was perhaps in recognition of the tenant's difficulties that her counsel resorted, enterprisingly, to decisions from two other mixed jurisdictions: *Perera v Samarakoon* (1922) 23 NLR 502 (Ceylon/Sri Lanka) and *Atkins v Johnson* 535 So 2d 1063 (1988) (Louisiana). In relation to the former, counsel was able to cite modern Scottish authority – *Axis West Development Ltd v Chartwell Land Investments Ltd* 1999 SLT 1416; *Moncrieff v Jamieson* [2007] UKHL 42, 2008 SC (HL) 1; and *Compugraphics International Ltd v Nikolic* [2011] CSIH 34, 2011 SC 744 – to the effect that 'it was appropriate to have regard to foreign law for guidance in relation to land rights such as servitudes, at least where such law was based on Roman Dutch principles' (para 11). In the event, this adventurous approach made no difference.

(10) Duncan v Duncan
2012 SLT (Sh Ct) 47, 2012 Hous LR 57

The parties, who were in the process of divorcing, owned a house in common. When the wife raised an action for sale of the house (17 Stevenson Street, Grangemouth) and division of its proceeds, the husband countered by requesting the court to use its discretion, under s 19 of the Matrimonial Homes (Family Protection) (Scotland) Act 1981, to refuse or postpone the order. Section 19, however, applies only to matrimonial homes, and the husband had failed to aver either that the house was such a home or facts from which such an inference could be drawn. Decree was accordingly granted, the sheriff (T McCartney) emphasising (at para 11) that a house was not a matrimonial home merely because it was co-owned by a husband and wife or occupied by the husband.

SERVITUDES

(11) Jones v Gray
[2011] CSOH 204, 2012 GWD 2-18

In an action seeking to establish a servitude of way by prescription it was **held** sufficient for the pursuers to aver that possession was open and as of right; at least in the urban setting in question this led to an inference that the use was known to the owner of the (servient) property, and such knowledge did not need to be the subject of express averment. Further, it was accepted by both parties that, for prescription, possession required to be 'continuous' rather than 'constant'. A proof before answer was allowed.

(12) Livingstone of Bachuil v Paine
[2012] CSOH 161, 2012 GWD 35-707

In a petition for interdict against taking access through the petitioner's property, on the Isle of Lismore, the first respondent averred that, as 'uninfeft' proprietor of a croft, he had a servitude right of way which had been established by prescription. Access rights over the same route had been contested in 1899 by predecessors of the parties, at which time the access was allowed to continue on the basis of a public right of way. That public right, it was accepted, had now ceased to exist (because the route no longer led to a public place), but an alternative defence in 1899 had been based on servitude and, while the sheriff had not found it necessary to decide the case on that point, the decision was at any rate evidence of use of the route by the owner of the croft. Since 1899, or so the first respondent averred, the route had been in constant use. The petitioner disputed both the extent and the quality of the use, arguing in particular that use in modern times had been of consent and not as of right, and so was not sufficient to establish a servitude by prescription.

The present stage of the litigation concerned the relevance of the respondents' pleadings. The Lord Ordinary (Lord Turnbull) allowed a proof before answer but under exclusion of averments relating to (i) certain aspects of use in earlier years and (ii) the argument that, following the 1899 decision, the present litigation was *res judicata*. In addition, he found that the second respondent, who was the tenant of the first, had no title to defend on the basis that she neither owned the benefited property nor held a lease with an express right to the servitude. This final issue is a difficult one on which the authorities are rather unclear.

(13) Harton Homes Ltd v Durk
2012 SCLR 554, Sh Ct

No servitude of access could be implied in a split-off conveyance where (i) an alternative access was available and (ii) the access sought had not been in use prior to severance. See **Commentary** p 168.

(14) Innellan Golf Club v Mansfield
12 July 2012, Dunoon Sheriff Court

When a reservoir was feued to Argyll County Council in 1892 there was granted a servitude right of access along the line of a conduit. As this route was impossible or virtually impossible to use with vehicles, the defender, the present-day owner of the reservoir (now disused), began to construct a new access road over land belonging to the pursuers. The pursuers challenged the defender's right to do so. The defender failed at first instance, following a proof (see Opinion of Sheriff C A Kelly issued on 14 October 2009) but appealed to the sheriff principal (B A Kerr QC). By this stage the defender's argument was (i) that, on the authority of *Louttit's Trs v Highland Railway Co* (1892) 19 R 791 and *Bowers v Kennedy* 2000 SC 555, he was entitled to have an access route to his property and one which moreover was sufficient to allow effectual use of his property, (ii) that since the reservoir could not be repaired without the use of vehicles, vehicular access was required, (iii) that the 1892 route could not be used for vehicles, meaning that the reservoir was in effect landlocked, and (iv) that the only suitable access route was the one which the defender had identified.

It was **held** that the defender had failed to prove that his preferred access was the only suitable one. That was sufficient to dispose of the case. But in any event the sheriff principal doubted, surely correctly, whether the reservoir could properly be regarded as landlocked. In that case there could be no question of an access right on the basis of *Bowers v Kennedy*.

For a valuable analysis of this decision, and the broader issues that it raises, see Jacqueline Fordyce, 'The plight of the landlocked proprietor' 2012 SLT (News) 243.

(15) Jackson v Elliott
29 June 2012, Kilmarnock Sheriff Court

The pursuer's land was adjacent to a road belonging to the defenders. The road was subject to a servitude of way in favour of the pursuer created in 1991: this was 'a heritable and irredeemable servitude right of access both pedestrian and vehicular over the access road from the A77'. In 1991 the road was used to access the pursuer's fields by means of two agricultural gates. Much later, when the fields in question had been sold to the defenders, the pursuer sought to open up an access to the road at a different point in order to reach other fields which he still retained. This involved the destruction of a fence and hedge which, it was held after a proof, was the property of the defenders. As it happened, the pursuer was able to access his fields directly from the A77. The question was whether he was entitled to open up a second access via the private road in the manner in which he had attempted.

It was **held** that the pursuer could not open such an access. Unlike in *Alvis v Harrison* 1991 SLT 64, where the access right was conceded to extend over the verges, there was nothing in the wording of the servitude to suggest that access could be taken at whatever point the pursuer chose. The servitude was over the road and not over the verge. Nor could the pursuer's actions be justified as a right ancillary to the main servitude. In *Moncrieff v Jamieson* [2007] UKHL 42, 2008 SC (HL) 1 it was explained that, for an ancillary right to arise, not only must it be necessary for the comfortable use of the servitude but it must also have been in the contemplation of the parties at the time of the grant of servitude. In 1991 no one could have foreseen that the pursuer might wish to take access in this way.

(16) Campbell v Watling
20 June 2011, Dunoon Sheriff Court

Circumstances in which **held**, after a proof, that a servitude of way had not been lost by negative prescription or abandonment but that, on the contrary, the access route had continued to be used with vegetation and foliage being cut back where needed to make this possible. Quite properly, it was accepted that servitudes prescribe under s 8 of the Prescription and Limitation (Scotland) Act 1973 ('extinction of other rights relating to property by prescriptive periods of 20 years') and not, as is sometimes suggested, under s 7 ('extinction of obligations by prescriptive periods of 20 years'). See David Johnston, *Prescription and Limitation* (2nd edn, 2012) para 7.14(3).

REAL BURDENS

(17) Russel Properties (Europe) Ltd v Dundas Heritable Ltd
[2012] CSOH 175, 2012 GWD 38-749

The pursuer owned most of the non-residential units in a mixed residential and commercial development. The defender owned a pub in the same development. All units derived their titles from the East Kilbride Development Corporation which, until 2004, had been feudal superior. The titles did not confer enforcement rights on co-feuars. The pursuer sought to enforce a real burden in the defender's title, initially by interim interdict. **Held**: that the burdens were not part of a common scheme, and accordingly that the pursuer had no title to enforce under s 53 of the Title Conditions (Scotland) Act 2003. See **Commentary** p 113.

VARIATION ETC OF TITLE CONDITIONS BY LANDS TRIBUNAL

(18) Rennie v Cullen House Gardens Ltd
29 June 2012, Lands Tr

An application for a title variation to allow an extension to one of the 14 houses in a historic building (Cullen House, at Cullen, Banffshire) was opposed by the residents' company which owned certain of the grounds and which, under the burdens as re-written in 2005 following the abolition of the feudal system, had the power to give or refuse consent. The company members were the owners of the 14 houses, and they had decided by a large majority to refuse consent. No individual owner opposed the application: instead their views were represented by the company. This was challenged by the applicant on the basis that the company could oppose only in respect of the property which it owned, being the relevant benefited property for the purposes of factor (b) in s 100 of the Title Conditions (Scotland) Act 2003 (the extent of benefit to the benefited property). And as it happened, the proposed extension, being in an enclosed courtyard, was invisible from the gardens.

The Tribunal accepted the logic of this argument but circumvented it by recourse to factor (j) ('any other factor which the Lands Tribunal consider to be material'). This would allow the Tribunal 'to have regard to the opposition by the community of owners' (para 35). Anxious, apparently, that this should not set a precedent, the Tribunal continued:

> We should make clear that this does not imply that there is any general entitlement of managers or owners' associations to oppose applications such as this. Further, if ownership of some benefited property gives such bodies title, the strength and materiality of their interest will depend on the particular circumstances.

The point being made in the first of these two sentences seems to be that representations can only normally be made to the Tribunal by, as the Act puts it (s 95(b)), 'any person who has title to enforce the title condition'. Whether that would include a body which had derivative title, ie could enforce not as owner of a benefited property but only as representing such owners, is not discussed.

The burden was one of a package of conditions designed to preserve the amenity of a magnificent Grade A listed building which had been sensitively restored and converted in the 1980s (factor (f)). This was 'an entirely reasonable aim at this location' (para 58). The resulting 'close protection' was achieved 'by giving control to the owners, not in the form of individual veto, but through a vote in the community company' (para 41). The applicant had made considerable efforts to design a sensitive extension and, following a review by Historic Scotland, had been given listed building consent. Not all owners were opposed. There was no evidence that the values of any of the houses would be affected. Nonetheless, the extension would 'eat into' an enclosed courtyard to an unacceptable degree, protruding some 14 metres and occupying one sixth of its area (para 50). This was not to say that a much more modest extension might not be permissible: unusually, the Tribunal ventured the view that 'an extension of around two metres, to similar design and standard, obtruding obviously considerably less into the courtyard, might be reasonable' (para 66). But the extension as currently proposed would have too serious an effect on the amenity of the courtyard. The application was refused. (The case had much in common with *Scott v Teasdale*, 22 December 2009, Lands Tribunal (*Conveyancing 2009* Case (32)) and reached the same result.)

(19) MacDonald v Murdoch
7 August 2012, Lands Tr

When in 1997 the owners of Ashburn House, Auchintore Road, Fort William, carved out and sold a plot of ground, the disposition bound the owners and their successors not to build on the remaining garden, and to insert a real burden to this effect in any subsequent conveyance of the garden. Later Ashburn House and garden were disponed to the applicants. It is unclear that any burden actually was imposed in that disposition. Certainly the applicants' title sheet appears to have referred to the 1997 disposition (para 3). The Tribunal noted that, while neither of the parties to the 1997 disposition now owned the respective properties, 'it is long established that validly created title conditions of this nature are praedial and not personal, burdening and benefiting properties and not simply the contracting parties' (para 23). Indeed so. But as the 1997 disposition was a conveyance of the benefited property and not of the burdened, it could not, under the law then in force, create a real burden: see *Jolly's Exx v Viscount Stonehaven* 1958 SC 635. For that to happen it would have been necessary for the condition to be repeated in the later disposition of the burdened property (ie the garden of Ashburn House). If that was not done, the condition did not bind the applicants (although it might be possible to run an 'offside goals' argument to the effect that the applicants, knowing of the obligation to insert a real burden in their disposition, are bound to accept the imposition of such a burden).

Be that as it may, the application was considered on the basis that the burden was valid. The application was for variation of the burden to the extent of allowing the erection of a one-and-a-half-storey house on the garden at Ashburn House. This would be facing the house (Beechwood) which had been built on the 1997 plot and interfere with its views over Loch Linnhe. Unsurprisingly, the application was opposed by Beechwood's owner.

As usual, the decision turned largely on the Tribunal's assessment of the impact of the proposed new building – or, to express matters more legalistically, on the value to the respondent of maintaining the burden unaltered (factor (b) in s 100 of the Title Conditions (Scotland) Act 2003). The Tribunal explained that (para 17):

As with other cases under this jurisdiction and involving proposals to build in garden ground, contrary to an existing title condition, this case comes down largely to our assessment of the plans and elevation drawings lodged as productions and most importantly our impression at the site inspection of the effect of the proposed dwelling on the benefited proprietor's property.

Usually, the Tribunal expects some degree of fortitude on the part of neighbours and allows building work to go ahead. But it has a (commendable) weakness for open outlooks and fine views – see eg *Faeley v Clark* 2006 GWD 28-626 (*Conveyancing 2006* Case (29) and *Fyfe v Benson* 26 July 2011, Lands Tribunal (*Conveyancing 2011* Case (30)) – and although in this case it felt that 'the attractive views to the west would be largely unaffected' (para 28), nonetheless it concluded that:

> the general amenity of Beechwood, if the proposal proceeded, would be transformed from a general feeling of openness to the west and north, albeit with the more distant rear of Ashburn House in clear view, to one of being as the respondent argues 'hemmed in'. It was that very threat that the condition was designed to safeguard.

The Tribunal considered but rejected the idea that the loss to the respondents could be made good by financial compensation (para 30):

> Sometimes compensation is appropriate in situations such as this where a new house is proposed contrary to a title restriction, even where the benefited proprietor has made clear his opposition. In this case we have considered that the impact of the proposal on the amenity of Beechwood would have such an impact on its amenity that it would not be reasonable simply to compensate the respondent with a monetary award.

The application was therefore refused.

(20) McCulloch v Reid
3 April 2012, Lands Tr

About ten years ago Roundhill farmhouse and steading, near Strathaven, was sold as five separate units. The applicants were owners of one of those units comprising the farmhouse itself.

Under the split-off disposition, of 2001, there was a prohibition on using the courtyard at the rear 'for the purpose of vehicle access, passage or parking'. The applicants sought variation of this burden to the extent of allowing parking for two private cars. The application was opposed by the owners of two of the houses in the steading, which faced on to the courtyard.

The application was refused. Although 'it might seem on the face of it like a modest request to allow a small amount of private parking' (para 21), the Tribunal thought that, given the extensive area for parking already available at the front of the applicants' property, any benefit for the applicants (factor (c)) would be slight, 'beyond personal preference and convenience' (para 25). On the other hand, not only was 'protection against everyday car use at this location … a significant amenity benefit' (para 22) for the respondents (factor (b)), but the burden was 'a very specific and clearly expressed burden, one of a number of detailed conditions inserted in the titles in the course of splitting up the buildings' so that to allow the application 'would significantly change the agreed parking arrangements which were incorporated into the applicants' title' (para 22).

(21) Trigstone Ltd v Mackenzie
16 February 2012, Lands Tr

In 1949 an extensive Victorian villa ('Tusculum') at York Road, North Berwick, was converted into six flats. A part of the garden was assigned to each. A charter of novodamus prohibited the erection of any buildings other than summerhouses or glasshouses. In 1977 and again in 1979 the Tribunal varied the conditions to allow the erection of bungalows at the extremities of the garden, against payment of compensation. (The first decision is reported as *Ness v Shannon* 1978 SLT (Lands Tr) 13.) The applicants now proposed to demolish one of those bungalows and replace it with a four-storey-plus-attic block of flats. The application was opposed by all the other owners which meant, as the Tribunal noted, that it would fail if it seemed unreasonable in respect of any one of the respondents – even if it was reasonable in respect of all of the others (para 29).

Although s 100 of the Title Conditions (Scotland) Act 2003 sets out a number of different factors, the Tribunal helpfully acknowledged what is becoming apparent as its practice, namely that 'in cases such as this three factors normally receive particular weight, viz the purpose of the title condition [factor (f)], the extent of benefit conferred by it [factor (b)] (in this case, where there is a particular proposal, the benefit involved in being able to prevent the proposal from proceeding), and the extent to which the burden impedes enjoyment of the burdened property [factor (c)]' (para 28). (A similar statement is given in *MacDonald v Murdoch* (above) at para 18.)

The Tribunal further emphasised that 'we require to consider the issue objectively, which is important because parties in such cases, quite under-standably, usually approach them from their own personal points of view' (para 29). The context for these remarks was the fact that the respondents, in their evidence and argument, to a large extent 'failed to see the woods for the trees' and placed considerable weight on factors – a small loss of light in the winter, marginal impact on privacy by overlooking, and issues involving parking, rubbish, and emergency access – which were 'bordering on the trivial' (para 32).

The purpose of the burden (factor (f)) was to protect the amenity of the flats and gardens. It was true that the burden was a 'substantial impediment' to the applicants' enjoyment of their property (factor (c)), bearing in mind 'that "enjoyment" in this context includes development, for profit, to the extent permitted by public planning' (para 39: on this point see G L Gretton and K G C Reid, *Conveyancing* (4th edn, 2011) para 16-11). On the other hand – a point which the Tribunal often makes in the context of factor (c) especially in cases where the application is being refused – the existence of the burden 'was, or should have been, a known feature of ownership' (para 46) – in other words, the applicants bought with their eyes open. (Compare here the statement in *Whitelaw v Acheson* 28 September 2012 (below), a case in which the application was granted, that 'the applicant bought the house knowing of the title conditions but also knowing that she had a legal right to ask the Tribunal to change them' (para 14).) The decisive factor, however, was the effect of the proposed building on the respondents (factor (b)), for its mass would have a 'considerable impact on the southerly aspect from some flats' (para 12). The application was refused.

Three other matters may be mentioned. First, the Tribunal said that (para 43):

[I]n this particular case we do consider the respondent's concerns about the effect of granting this application on possible future development reasonable and of some weight. The answer to 'precedent' arguments is often simply that no precedent would be set and any future applications would simply be considered on their own merits, but sometimes one particular proposal can be seen as something of a test for others. We should certainly not pre-judge any future applications, but in this case, in addition to the history, in which permission for one bungalow was quickly followed by permission for another, there is actual evidence which, we think, particularly justifies a concern that there might be an attempt to do something similar [with one of the other properties].

On the other hand, the Tribunal was not impressed by the fact, urged by the respondents, that the house was now in a conservation area: 'we do not see that public planning consideration as adding anything: we are in effect considering a more particular, and stronger, private conservation provision' (para 35).

Finally, in deference to the evidence on valuation, the Tribunal noted that, had it granted the application, it would have awarded compensation under s 90(7)(a) (in respect of loss to the owner in consequence of the variation) reflecting a loss of value of 2.5% for two of the flats (£9,375) and of 5% for a third (£22,500).

(22) Whitelaw v Acheson
29 February and 28 September 2012, Lands Tr

This was an application to vary burdens in a feu charter of 1885 to the extent needed (i) to allow a change from residential use to use as a therapy and wellbeing centre and (ii) to allow an extension to be built at the side and back. The property in question was a Victorian villa at 201 Colinton Road, Edinburgh, and the application was opposed by the owners of the villa next door (number 199).

The application was granted in part. In relation to (i), the Tribunal varied the burden so as to allow 'use of the subjects for psychotherapy by way of counselling, including group counselling, and by way of one-to-one forms of therapeutic treatment including (without prejudice to the generality) head hand and face massage and the technique known as "Reiki" but excluding body massage'. See **Commentary** p 119.

In relation to (ii), the applicant had planning permission for a substantial extension, 'unashamedly modern and contemporary in appearance' (29 Feb para 19), which would lie between numbers 201 and 199, presenting a solid wall

to the latter, about two metres from the boundary fence. Although the view
at the back of number 199 was 'already adversely affected by the dominant
impact of the unsightly sports centre [Craiglockhart Tennis and Sports
Centre]', the proposed extension, modern and non-domestic in nature, 'would
have a much more immediate and intimate impact', putting at risk 'the charm
of the related properties and the spacious domestic outlook' (29 Feb para 40).
But the real problem, the Tribunal thought, was not one of aesthetics (29 Feb
para 41):

> We think it rare that the amenity of a residential property could be said to be
> significantly adversely affected by the nature of a building or extension in adjacent
> subjects except where such a building would have an adverse impact on light or
> view. Personal opinions of style or design are irrelevant and structures which have
> planning permission can be taken to be acceptable from the viewpoint of the general
> public. However, the significance of the extension in the present case is not simply
> the visual impact but the fact that it appears to us to signal a very obvious change
> from a domestic to a commercial environment. This will detract from the domestic
> ambience of the respondents' home. The extension goes beyond what might have
> been expected by way of extension to 201 as a dwelling.

Thus the effect on the benefited property of the extension being built would
be substantial (factor (b)). If an extension was to be allowed, it should be at the
rear and not the side. On the case being continued, the applicant put forward
a new proposal for a rear extension; and having rejected a building project for
which planning consent existed, the Tribunal now accepted one for which there
was no such consent (although the prospects of obtaining consent were thought
to be good) – thus emphasising by example the different roles played by public
and private law. The fact that the extension was designed primarily for people
with physical disabilities was a point in its favour because 'any steps taken to
improve the experience of people with physical handicaps are to be encouraged'
(28 Sept para 7). The Tribunal, however, imposed a reduction in size, on the basis
that the larger the extension the more people would use the premises and hence
the greater the potential disturbance caused by the footfall. It was necessary to
keep the extension within reasonable limits.

A postscript. The Tribunal said that (29 Feb para 3):

> We were provided with bundles which included references to over 30 decided cases.
> However, as parties were broadly agreed as to the proper approach to be taken by
> the Tribunal, no purpose is served in detailing these authorities.

This is typical: while parties often cite cases, it is rare for the Tribunal to take
any notice of them, or at any rate to make reference to them in its opinions. In
the Tribunal's view, often repeated, applications almost always turn on their
own particular facts and circumstances, and there is nothing to be gained from
looking at past decisions. As the Tribunal said in another case from 2012, *McNab
v Smith* (below, paras 46 and 47), 'No two cases are the same, however similar
they might appear on paper. There is therefore a very limited amount to be learnt

from other cases.' Be that as it may, however, past decisions provide a helpful guide to the approach which the Tribunal is likely to take to different types of case, and to the arguments which are most likely to find favour.

(23) Patterson v Drouet
2013 GWD 3-99, Lands Tr

Under the deed of conditions, liability for maintenance in an eight-flat tenement in Glasgow was allocated in accordance with gross annual value. In the normal course of things, the value ascribed to the two ground-floor flats would have fallen steeply when their use changed from commercial to residential, but this effect was blocked by s 111 of the Local Government Finance Act 1992 which, following the abolition of domestic rates, froze all valuations as at 1 April 1989. Although all the flats (with a minor exception) were now in residential use, the two flats on the ground floor picked up three quarters of the cost of maintenance.

An earlier application to the Lands Tribunal had stalled on grounds of competency: see *Patterson v Drouet* 20 January 2011 (*Conveyancing 2011* Case (17A)). This new application was made under the procedure introduced by s 91 of the Title Conditions (Scotland) Act 2003 which allows community burdens to be varied in respect of the entire community on the application of the owners of at least a quarter of the units. The application was to vary the burden by substituting floor area as the basis of liability. This would almost triple the liability of the owners of the upper flats. Nonetheless, the Tribunal granted the application and refused an award of compensation. See **Commentary** p 137.

(24) McNab v Smith
15 June 2012, Lands Tr

The applicant owned East Hills Farm, Lochwinnoch, and the respondent West Hills Farm. Only the latter was a working (dairy) farm. Access to both was by a private road running north from a public road. The initial stretch belonged to the respondent and the rest to the applicant; each had a servitude of vehicular access over the part owned by the other. One of the respondent's fields ran the entire length of the road and could be accessed from the road at four points – gates A–D – of which gates C and D were in the northerly stretch of road belonging to the applicant. The respondent used that stretch for the passage of his 60 cows into his field. This involved moving the cows approximately 140 metres along the applicant's road around 100 times each grazing season – around 16 times per month for half the year. Each movement took between 10 and 15 minutes. For as long as the road had a grass verge it was possible to pass in a car, the cows taking refuge in the verge, but in 2003–04 the road was upgraded by the applicant and the grass verges replaced by cobbles and field stones. The disagreements between the parties dated from that time, resulting in 'considerable discord' and 'protracted court litigation' (para 1).

The application was for the discharge of the servitude, failing which its restriction. In hearing the evidence the Tribunal made use of its powers under r 24(1) of the Lands Tribunal for Scotland Rules 2003, SSI 2003/452, to appoint an agricultural expert Assessor. Among the matters on which he was doubtless of assistance was the question of the 'poaching' affecting the gates, 'ie wet, muddy conditions which are inconvenient, causing the cows discomfort and potentially diseases such as mastitis and also requiring time to be taken cleaning them before milking' (para 18).

As usual, the Tribunal proceeded mainly by weighing the respective merits of factor (b) (benefit to benefited property) and factor (c) (impediment to enjoyment of burdened property). In relation to factor (b), while the right to use the road, and so to take access by gates C and D, was 'not crucial to the respondent's business' (para 62), gate C was less susceptible to 'poaching' than the lower gates, and there was also merit, when using the northerly part of the field, in having the cows pass by road rather than by trampling through the southerly part of the field. As for factor (c), the applicant was exposed to the inconvenience of a herd of dairy cattle moving along the only vehicular access to her house – though admittedly, even if successful in the application, she would continue to be so exposed in respect of the stretch of road belonging to the respondent. She was also exposed to the possibility – as it turned out, the actuality – of conflict resulting from competing users.

The Tribunal concluded that the servitude should be discharged but on the basis of payment of compensation for the respondent's loss (Title Conditions (Scotland) Act 2003 s 90(7)(a)), on which topic the parties were invited to seek agreement or, failing agreement, to make submissions. Although the normal measure of compensation has been the reduction in value of the benefited property, the Tribunal indicated that this might be a case where the measure ought to be the cost of carrying out the various works, such as drainage, which would be necessary if the respondent were to be reliant solely on gates A and B.

(25) Cope v X
19 November 2012, Lands Tr

Access to the respondent's house, near Blairgowrie, was by a road through land belonging to the first and second applicants. In particular the road ran close to the second applicant's house. The applicants built a new road but the respondent declined to use it, preferring the old. The purpose of the application was to vary the servitude so that it gave access rights over the new road only.

Among the topics raised by the respondent's evidence were an alleged failure by the applicants to negotiate, and alleged obstruction on the old road caused by suckers from a blackthorn hedge (which caused punctures) and poultry manure. The main issue, however, as almost always, was the balance between factor (b) (the extent to which the existing servitude conferred benefit on the benefited property) and factor (c) (the extent to which it impeded enjoyment of the burdened property).

On factor (c), the Tribunal accepted 'that having a road running through the curtilage of a dwelling is a factor of material consideration' but thought that privacy was not much affected (para 31).

The consideration of factor (b) turned on three main issues: (i) the risk of danger from sharing a road with agricultural vehicles, (ii) the possible extra cost of maintenance in respect of the new road, and (iii) the risk that the new road would be more difficult to use in winter. The first issue arose only because the new road had been built *before* the application so that the respondent now had the old road more or less to herself (para 29). But the new road, the Tribunal found, was generally wide enough for two cars to pass and even agricultural equipment would usually be able to pass a stationary car drawn into the side. Accepting that 'many drivers are not confident reversing' (para 36), the Tribunal thought that reversing would not often be required. Overall the Tribunal was satisfied 'that use of the new road will present no significant problems' (para 35).

On the second issue, the Tribunal found that the new road had been properly constructed. Although the evidence was unclear, it seemed likely that the respondent would have to spend 'a little more' on maintenance but this would not be 'a sum of any great significance' (para 56).

Finally, in relation to winter use the Tribunal, while accepting that 'the new road will not always be passable in wintery conditions' (para 58), thought that – based on 'our own experience on Perthshire roads' (para 62) – the same must also sometimes be true of the old road. As the new road was straighter and shorter, it would be easier to clear of snow using a tractor. In any event, 'we are not persuaded that the comparative dangers in winter have been shown to tip the balance to any significant extent against the new road' (para 65).

(26) Hossack v Robertson
29 June 2012, Lands Tr

This was a dispute between neighbours at West Shore Street, Ullapool. The respondent took access from his house, which lay to the east of the applicants' house, to his yard, which lay to the west, by means of a one-metre wide path across the applicants' back garden. The route of this pedestrian servitude had been fixed by the Tribunal in an earlier application in 1999 which in turn had followed on from a litigation which reached the Second Division: see *Robertson v Hossack* 1995 SLT 291. The current application was for re-routing the servitude to the end of the back garden so as to allow the applicants to build a conservatory. The resulting route would be two metres longer.

The Tribunal had little difficulty in deciding to grant the application. While the new route would involve 'some inconvenience' to the respondent (para 19) in respect that it was slightly longer (factor (b)), the existing route imposed a 'very considerable' burden (para 20) on the applicants by preventing a reasonable use of their land, namely the building of a conservatory (factor (c)).

(27) Stephenson v Thomas
21 November 2012, Lands Tr

'If an access right through another's property is replaced by a direct access of comparable standard, that will usually (as decisions cited by the applicants illustrated) be a change of circumstances pointing strongly to the reasonableness of discharge' (para 43). The issue in this case was whether the replacement access was indeed of comparable standard and whether, as a result, the original access was of any remaining benefit to the respondents.

The facts were a little unusual. When, in 1990, the property now belonging to the respondents, at Cairndow, Argyll, was split off from the land now belonging to the applicants there was granted to the disponees a servitude of vehicular access over a defined route in a corner of the retained property. As the properties were separated by a burn, this involved crossing a bridge. The bridge, however, was 'of amateurish construction' (para 15). Even in 1990 it was in a 'rickety state'. And as the disponees promptly opened up a different access to the main road, the bridge was barely used and had long since deteriorated to the point of being unusable.

Recently, however, and despite having used the new road for a number of years, the respondents had begun to have safety concerns because the access point to the main road was near a bend. They sought to assert the original route and, when this met a dusty response from the applicants, raised an action of declarator and interdict in the sheriff court. This was defended on the basis that the servitude had been extinguished by negative prescription or abandonment. Rather than pursue that defence, however, the applicants sought to remove the problem with the present application for discharge. This was made possible by the fact that the Tribunal has jurisdiction to discharge 'purported' title conditions (Title Conditions (Scotland) Act 2003 s 90(1)(a)). The sheriff court action was sisted pending the Tribunal's decision.

As the route of the servitude was well away from any building, it could not be said to impede to any extent the applicants' enjoyment of their property (factor (c)). The case therefore turned on whether a servitude which provided a means of access which had not been used for many years could be said to confer any benefit on the respondents (factor (b)). The argument that it did rested on the respondents' declared intention to begin using the route in preference to a replacement route which they now found to be dangerous. But apart from the sheriff court action, there was little to show that this intention would mature into action. No proper steps had been taken to cost the rebuilding of the bridge and the carrying out of other measures which would be needed if the route was to be usable; and in any event it was uncertain that planning permission and a road opening permit would be forthcoming.

Finding the case to be 'evenly balanced' (para 54), the Tribunal contemplated continuing the proceedings to see whether the respondents did indeed follow through and re-open the access route. In the end, however, the respondents were given the benefit of the doubt and the application was refused, subject to the warning that 'if the respondents do not advance their proposal within a reasonable timescale, the result of a further application to the Tribunal might be expected to be different' (para 59).

(28) Stirling v Thorley
12 October 2012, Lands Tr

Typically, applications stand or fall on an assessment of the impact of the applicants' proposed development on the respondents' property – or, to align this approach with the factors set out in s 100 of the Title Conditions (Scotland) Act 2003, on factor (b) (benefit to benefited property). The present case, however, turned mainly on factor (c), on the extent to which the condition impeded – or, in the Tribunal's assessment did not impede – enjoyment of the burdened property.

In the mid-1990s the owner of the Braidwood estate at Silverburn, near Penicuik, Midlothian, sold a house and also a steading development which was developed into three further houses. Access from the public road was by a driveway retained, along with much other land, by the disponer, and a servitude was granted in the dispositions. The applicants were the successors of that disponer while the respondents were the owners of the four houses. The applicants had detailed planning permission to build a house on a site which took up around half of a large turning area (of approximately 30 square metres). As the respondents' servitude extended to the turning area, the application was for an appropriate variation of the servitude.

Even after the proposed development, the turning area would still be large enough to allow even quite large vehicles to turn, although no longer using forward gear only (a 'banjo turn'). And while it would become trickier for large vehicles to manoeuvre in or near the steading courtyard, and there would be less room to load and unload or to use as a passing place, the overall effect on the benefited properties (factor (b)) would be relatively modest. 'There is some benefit', the Tribunal concluded, in maintaining the servitude unaltered 'but it should not be exaggerated' (para 52). That modest benefit, however, must be set against the even more modest impediment which the servitude presented to the burdened property (factor (c)). While planning policy in rural areas dictated that the applicants build near other houses, there seemed to be no reason to build in a manner which took up quite so much of the turning area. A smaller degree of encroachment would have been possible and might well be favourably received by the Tribunal. But as the application stood, it fell to be rejected.

The decision seems to mark a return to a practice, once in favour but then rather departed from, of treating factor (b) as qualified by factor (f). (See G L Gretton and K G C Reid, *Conveyancing* (4th edn, 2011) para 16-10.) On this approach, for which there is no express warrant in the legislation, the Tribunal asks in relation to factor (b), not what benefit would be lost if the application were to be granted, but what benefit *which was within the original purpose for which the condition was imposed* would be lost. A benefit, however significant, is then disregarded if it is not found to be within the original purpose. (Inconsistently, the same approach has not, or not yet, been applied in respect of factor (c).) In the present case, the Tribunal found the purpose of the servitude to be to provide access and turning space; it was not to prevent development on the burdened property. It followed, said the Tribunal, that 'while we can understand the respondents' ... resistance to the addition of a house on this site, we do not think that we should give any weight to that consideration which – as it seemed to us – was an important motive in the respondents' opposition to the application' (para 37). Later, in the context of a discussion of factor (b), the Tribunal repeated that 'we do not think that the impact, if any, on amenity and views should carry any weight in this case' (para 52). As it happens, the Tribunal would not have found that amenity was adversely affected by the proposed house (para 38). But the approach seems wrong in principle. Whether a benefit was intended or not, its removal will be no less painful for the proprietor in question, and no less relevant in the Tribunal's assessment of what is reasonable.

(29) Trodden v Cogle
20 January 2012, Lands Tr

An application for variation of the route of a servitude was settled shortly before a contested hearing. It took three years for the settlement to be fully implemented, by the grant of a deed of servitude, and a further two before the respondent made the present application for expenses. Expenses, of course, generally follow success (see Title Conditions (Scotland) Act 2003 s 103(1). What was unusual in the present case was that the Tribunal, not having in the end heard the case, was not in a position to pronounce on the merits.

The Tribunal accepted that the respondent was entitled to something by way of expenses. He had been successful at least in the sense that part of the original application, for a determination as to validity and enforceability under s 90(1)(a)(ii), had been incompetent and swiftly dropped. (The provision applies only to real burdens, not servitudes.) Moreover, at 31 pages, the applicant's pleadings were 'unreasonably long' for what was in the end quite a simple case (para 8). Although the respondent to some extent 'joined in this verbosity', the adjustment of such complex pleadings had caused the respondent additional expense. On the other hand, the respondent should not be given his full expenses, partly because the Tribunal could not adjudicate on the merits and partly because the respondent had delayed two years in making his claim despite the fact that the parties had envisaged an immediate claim. Accordingly, the award of expenses would be restricted to one third.

(30) Gibson v Anderson
3 May 2012, Lands Tr

For burdens of more than 100 years old, the burdened proprietor has the option of using the 'sunset rule' procedure set out in ss 20–24 of the Title Conditions (Scotland) Act 2003. A notice of the proposed termination is given to the benefited proprietors and, unless one at least expresses opposition by applying to the Tribunal for renewal of the burdens, the burdens are terminated on registration of the notice. Thus not only are the benefited proprietors, for once, put to the cost and labour of initiating a Tribunal application, but if they choose to do so they must bear the onus of proof of showing that renewal would be a reasonable outcome (para 33). In all other respects, the application proceeds in the same way as one initiated by the burdened proprietor, and the Tribunal must have regard to the usual factors, set out in s 100.

Notification normally involves sending to the benefited proprietors 'a copy of the proposed notice of termination' (s 21(2)). The required form of a notice of termination is set out in sch 2 of the Act. Among the information to be given is the identity of the burdened property (s 20(4)(a)). Note 2 of sch 2 sets out how:

> Describe the property in a way that is sufficient to identify it. Where the property has a postal address the description should include that address. Where the title has been registered in the Land Register the description should refer to the title number of the property or of the larger subjects of which the property forms part. Otherwise it should normally refer to and identify a deed recorded in a specified division of the Register of Sasines.

In the present case the notice described the burdened property as being 6 Barnshot Road, Colinton when in fact it was only part of that property, being an additional area of ground which had been separately disponed in 1898. In seeking renewal of the burden the applicant sought to found on what was agreed to be a mistake, but without putting forward a view as to what the consequence of that mistake ought to be. In fact, assuming the mistake to be material, the only consequence, as the respondents pointed out, would be to make the whole application incompetent. This is because, by s 90(1)(b), a person can only apply to renew a burden 'in respect of which intimation of a proposal to execute and register a notice of termination has been given under section 21 of the Act'. If, therefore, the notice was too flawed to count as valid intimation, the statutory basis for making the application would be removed. For the applicant, therefore, success in his argument would be self-defeating at least in the short term, although a finding of invalidity might in the end lead the Keeper to refuse to register the notice of termination.

All too aware of where the argument would lead, the Tribunal declined to deal with it. The issue, it said, was irrelevant (para 7):

> because once an order is made under our jurisdiction there is no Notice which could have any present or future effect: the issue of termination is no longer determined by notice at the hands of the burdened proprietor but by the Tribunal, which exercises its jurisdiction under Section 90(1) and either renews, or varies, or discharges the burden. Once the Tribunal has determined such an application, the issue thus becomes academic.

But in any case there was no jurisdiction to deal with the matter; the contrast here was with certain notices under the Abolition of Feudal Tenure etc (Scotland) Act 2000 where express jurisdiction had been conferred.

While understandable, this approach does not readily convince. The Tribunal's jurisdiction to hear the application rests on the giving of intimation under s 21 of the Act: no intimation, no jurisdiction. Suppose that there was alleged to have been no intimation at all, or a notice of termination that was blank, or crammed full of incorrect information. Could the Tribunal really hear the application without further inquiry?

The merits of the case were more straightforward. Allermuir House in Colinton, Edinburgh, built around 1879 by the distinguished architect, Sir Robert Rowand Anderson, has a fine southerly view of Allermuir Hill in the Pentlands. In 1898 Anderson disponed a strip of land between his house and the hill, to be used as part of the garden of another house. The disposition prohibited the erection of 'any buildings or other erections other than a greenhouse, stable or outhouse to be used in connection with the house' and restricted to a single storey. The respondents, who now owned the house and strip, had outline planning permission to build an additional, two-storey house on their plot which would involve building to some extent on the strip. As this would be contrary to the burden, they served a notice of termination. In response, two of the benefited proprietors applied, separately, to the Tribunal for the burden to be renewed. The present application was by the owners of Allermuir House; the other, which raised different issues and is to be considered separately, was by the respondents' next-door neighbour.

The applicants sought to improve their position by conceding a variation of the burden to the effect of allowing *any* building on the strip provided it was limited to a single storey. It was not enough. The height restriction was, the Tribunal thought, 'a considerable impediment' to the realisation of the strip's development value (factor (c)). It was true that the purpose of the burden was to preserve the view for Allermuir House (factor (f)); and it was also true that, relatively little intrusive development having taken place since 1898 (factor (a)), the view remained largely intact. But while a large building on the strip would indeed cause serious injury to the view, the Tribunal was prepared to say, based on a site visit and its own expertise, that 'a house not exceeding 6.5 metres high – more accurately, a part not exceeding 6.5 metres high – and extending only, say, one quarter of the distance across the burdened strip, would intrude to a very much lesser degree and in a way which would to a large extent blend in with the other features of the lower part of the protected view as it is at present' (para 42). This would not prevent the respondents from building on the *rest* of the strip to the extent of one storey, and of course there was no limitation as to the height of the building insofar as it was built on their main plot, to which the burden did not apply. (At this stage the respondents had no precise plans for the house.) The burden was thus varied accordingly, and the application to renew refused.

Two other matters may be mentioned. First, although the application was, by definition, concerned with an elderly burden, the Tribunal considered that factor (e) (the age of the burden) 'should not be considered in any different way in this type of application' (para 33). In relation to that factor, while the Tribunal thought that 'old burdens should not be preserved unnecessarily', it was 'satisfied that this burden has not simply become obsolete by the passage of time' (para 46).

Secondly, and in relation to the evidence led about the architectural significance of Allermuir House, the Tribunal explained that (para 34):

> the architectural importance of Allermuir House and any public interest in the work of its architect are not factors of any weight in this application. If there were anything in the nature of some form of public obligation, or even regular practice, of showing the house to the public and the view of the hill played a part in that, these things might have some relevance, but the evidence in our view fell short of that. The house is no doubt of considerable interest to architectural historians, but in the issue of the reasonableness of exercising the Tribunal's jurisdiction in relation to this title condition, we think that it has the character of a private property.

ROADS AND PUBLIC RIGHTS OF WAY

(31) Morston Whitecross Ltd v Falkirk Council
[2012] CSOH 97, 2012 SLT 899

How wide is a public road? Is it the entire area that lies, as it were, from fence to fence? Or might it only be part of that area, in which case there is a strip of land at the side of the road which is not subject to the public right of passage? The question is important in cases where a person owning land beside a road wishes to open up a new access to it over the strip. If the strip is part of the road, then it is open to public use; but if it is not, the developer must negotiate with the owner to acquire the necessary rights. The issue has been litigated a number of times in recent years: see eg *Elmford Ltd v City of Glasgow Council (No 2)* 2001 SC 267 (discussed in *Conveyancing 2000* pp 51–52) and *Hamilton v Nairn* [2010] CSIH 77, 2011 SC 49 (*Conveyancing 2010* Case (44)). Nonetheless, as Lord Malcolm emphasised in *Morston Whitecross*, a new case on the same topic, the issue 'is a matter of fact for the court to determine by reference to the relevant circumstances on the ground' (para 16).

The dispute concerned a section of the A801 at Whitecross, near Linlithgow, which was constructed by the local authority and adopted as a public road in the early 1970s. The section in question was built on an embankment which sloped down at either side to a fence (para 15). On the eastern side, but not on the western, the embanked land extended to an additional width of 38 feet prior to the downwards slope and the fence. It appears that this additional area was acquired with a view to possible future dualling of the road, an eventuality which in the event had not (yet) occurred. It was this additional area which was in dispute. The pursuer, who owned adjacent land, sought a declarator that it was part of the public road. This was resisted by the defender council, which was hoping for a price for what would then be a ransom strip.

In the landmark case of *Hamilton v Dumfries and Galloway Council (No 2)* [2009] CSIH 13, 2009 SC 277 (discussed in *Conveyancing 2009* pp 156–63) it was held that public rights in respect of roads – or in other words public rights of way – could be established (i) by positive prescription, (ii) by grant, express or implied, or (iii) by statute. When a new road is made and listed, the public rights are generally taken to be created by implied grant. It is then simply a matter of identifying the area of ground to which that implied grant refers. In the words of Lord Malcolm, 'the question to be resolved is this – has the disputed ground been dedicated to public passage?' (para 22). (For the question of whether 'dedication' is, strictly, the correct concept here, see *Hamilton v Nairn* [2009] CSOH 163, 2010 SLT 399 at para 22 per Lord Glennie.) And that, added Lord Malcolm, 'is more a matter of impression than deduction' (para 20).

In order to place the present facts in context, Lord Malcolm postulated the examples of (a) where additional ground ran through an extra-wide tunnel or over an extra-wide bridge, or (b) where there was no embankment so that the additional ground simply lay beside a carriageway built at ground level. In the first case, 'the tunnel or bridge would, in all probability, create the impression that all of it had been dedicated to public passage, even though it was wider than required for the current use' (para 26); in the second case, the ground was unlikely to be considered as part of the road. The present facts fell 'somewhere between' these two cases (para 26).

The proper test, Lord Malcolm thought, was 'the use, character and function of the land at the time' of construction and listing and not the 'future intentions' of the local authority in relation to the possible construction of a second carriageway (para 27). Bearing that in mind (para 23):

> It might help to imagine standing on the disputed area of the embankment in the early 1970s and asking, has this been dedicated to public passage? To the west one would see the barriers with the carriageway beyond. To the east there would be the top of the slope of the embankment with fields beyond. One would be standing on a relatively large expanse of flat grassland, which was being put to no use whatsoever. For myself I consider it doubtful that one would conclude that the land had been dedicated to public passage.

The link of the disputed ground to the carriageway was simply 'too tenuous to justify categorisation as part of the public road' (para 24). The court found for the defender.

EXECUTION OF DEEDS

(32) Ahmed v Mohammed
[2012] CSOH 137, 2012 GWD 29-590

The pursuer and the second defender were married but separated. They co-owned a flat in Glasgow, and the second defender continued to live there with the children of the marriage after the separation. Eventually the house was sold and disponed to the first defender (who was the second defender's brother). In this action the pursuer sought declarator (i) that a signature on the disposition which purported to be his was forged and (ii) that the disposition was incapable of transferring his one half *pro indiviso* share to the first defender. (The first defender's 'position on record is that he acted in good faith throughout the course of the transaction involving the sale of the flat to him. The pursuer did not seek to prove otherwise' (para 5).)

Although it was accepted that someone signed the disposition in front of the solicitor who acted in the sale, it was disputed whether that person was the pursuer. The cursive signature on the disposition bore no resemblance to the signature by block capitals normally used by the pursuer. Further, it emerged at the proof that the solicitor did not sufficiently establish the identity of the person who signed, not least because a driving licence had been forged.

The temporary judge (M G Thomson QC) was satisfied in respect of (i) (ie as to the forgery) but, due to the restricted nature of the proof and the fact that the first defender was not represented at it, was not willing, at least at this stage, to grant (ii) (ie declarator as to the absence of legal effect).

It may be that the real object of the litigation was to obtain indemnity from the Keeper, for, assuming that the first defender was in possession and innocent, there could be no question of rectification of the Register, and the pursuer's claim would be for indemnity for non-rectification under s 12(1)(b) of the Land Registration (Scotland) Act 1979. It may be added that the case does not mention that Act, and a question might arise as to its consistency with its provisions.

(33) Nicol's Legal Representative v Nicol
[2012] CSOH 115, 2012 GWD 25-539

Another case in which it was found, after proof, that the signature of the granter had been forged. The deed was a will, and the signature was forged by the principal beneficiary, who was the deceased's mother.

COMPETITION OF TITLE

(34) Trustees of Calthorpe's 1959 Discretionary Settlement v G Hamilton (Tullochgribban Mains) Ltd
[2012] CSOH 138, 2012 GWD 29-599

Both parties held ostensible title to the same property. The pursuers were the grantees of a disposition recorded in the Register of Sasines in 1991; the defender was the grantee of a disposition registered in the Land Register in 2008 under exclusion of indemnity. The action was one for reduction of the 2008 disposition and rectification of the Land Register. It was **held** (1) that the granter of the pursuers' disposition had no title to the property (2) that, while the pursuers may have had possession, the description in their disposition was contradictory and so not *habile* for the purposes of prescription, and (3) that accordingly, the granter of the defender's disposition had owned the property at the time of the grant, with the result that the owner was now the defender. There were therefore no grounds for reducing the defender's disposition. See **Commentary** p 152.

(35) Drumpellier and Mount Vernon Estates Ltd v Meehan
[2012] CSOH 154, 2012 GWD 37-743

The pursuer and the defenders were in dispute as to the ownership of 'the extensive lands of Drumpellier and Langloan' (para 1) in Lanarkshire. As both parties could muster some sort of a title, one might have expected the issue to turn on which had possession; positive prescription would then do the rest. In the event, this issue was considered only at the margins. Instead, the court undertook the heroic labour of considering the validity of titles which stretched back for 200 years.

The pursuer's titles were found to bear to involve the transfer of the *dominium utile* (para 14). The defenders' title rested, indirectly, on a disposition of 1911 which read, in part (para 24):

> We Mrs Anna Stirling Widow of Thomas Mayne Stirling of Muiravonside … and Mark Bannatyne Solicitor Glasgow the remaining trustees appointed by and acting under the Trust Disposition and Settlement granted by the said Thomas Mayne Stirling … and with relative Codicil … and as such Trustees standing heritably vest in the *dominium directum* or superiority hereinafter disponed for certain good causes and considerations but without any price being paid therefore Do hereby give Grant and Dispone to and in favour of Thomas Willing Stirling … All and whole the lands of Drumpellier and Langloan … together with our whole right title and interest as Trustees foresaid present and future in the lands and others above disponed in the first and second places.

As the disposition purported to convey the lands themselves, as opposed to any particular estate in the lands, it was capable of conveying (a) the *dominium utile*, (b) the superiority, (c) both *dominium utile* and superiority, held as unconsolidated estates, or (d) mixed estate, ie *dominium utile* as respects part of the land and superiority in respect of the rest.

Applying the principle that ambiguous words of description can be explained by reference to the rest of the deed (*Orr v Mitchell* (1893) 20 R (HL) 27), the Lord Ordinary (Woolman) concluded that only the superiority was conveyed. This was because (i) the narrative clause referred to the granters as owning only the superiority interest, (ii) those narrative words were tied into the dispositive clause through the words 'together with our whole right title and interest as Trustees foresaid', (iii) the feu duties were assigned, and (iv) the warrandice clause was worded in such a way as to indicate transfer of the superiority (eg it excepted the feus). Taken together, this was sufficient to counter certain other, rather minor, indicators in the deed which might suggest transfer of the *dominium utile*. As the defenders thus had no right to the property – superiorities having been abolished in 2004 – it must follow that the pursuer was entitled to decree of reduction to the extent that the defenders' deeds gave rise to a conflict of title.

It might perhaps be argued that the Lord Ordinary over-states the effect of the factors he identifies. Number (ii), a standard provision, looks more like words of style than an attempt to tie the narrative clause into the dispositive. Numbers (iii) and (iv) seem equally consistent with a mixed estate. Nonetheless, taking the factors as a whole it certainly does seem that only the superiority was to be conveyed.

That conclusion would not, of itself, prevent the 1911 disposition, or a deed based on it, from being used as a foundation for prescription. For provided that it was at least a *possible* interpretation of the deed that it conveyed the *dominium utile*, it would not matter that a far more plausible interpretation was that it did not. See eg *Auld v Hay* (1880) 7 R 663. As the defenders did not aver possession, however, this issue did not arise and was not discussed (see para 35).

(36) Pocock's Tr v Skene Investments (Aberdeen) Ltd
[2012] CSIH 61, 2012 GWD 27-562

The facts as averred by the pursuer – as yet there has been no proof – were as follows. In July 2000 Mr David George Pocock concluded missives to buy the basement and ground-floor flat at 5 Queen's Gardens, Aberdeen, from Skene Investments (Aberdeen) Ltd. Mr Russell Taylor acted as solicitor for Mr Pocock. In due course the price (£207,125) was paid and a disposition in favour of Mr Pocock was granted. Mr Pocock then decided that title should be taken in the name of Howemoss Properties Ltd, a company of which he was a director. Apparently seeking to avoid the SDLT that would be payable if Mr Pocock simply registered his own disposition and granted a new one to Howemoss, Mr Pocock arranged with Mr Taylor to doctor the former. The first page of the disposition was discarded, and was replaced with a new first page in which the grantee was now stated as being Howemoss Properties Ltd, rather than Mr Pocock. The second page, which bore the signatures, remained. This doctored disposition – now utterly invalid, despite appearances to the contrary – was then sent off to the Keeper for registration.

A series of transactions then followed. Howemoss Properties Ltd granted standard securities – ultimately as many as four – to Woolwich plc. Later, in 2002, the house was divided into two flats and each was sold separately, Mr Pocock signing the dispositions as a director of Howemoss. In the ordinary course of events, the acquirers (and their lenders) would have been protected by the statutory guarantee of title. But they were unlucky. To the initial (and unknowable) misfortune of the fraudulent disposition were added two further pieces of ill luck. In the first place, it turned out that the Keeper had not registered any of the dispositions or standard securities, including the initial disposition in favour of Howemoss Properties. There was thus no Midas touch. At first this may have been no more than the delay that often attends what may have been a first registration; but latterly the Keeper refused to register because the fact of forgery had started to come to light. And then, in a second piece of ill luck, Mr Pocock was sequestrated.

Meanwhile a judicial factor had been appointed to Mr Taylor and in June 2004 she alerted Mr Pocock's trustee in sequestration to the problems with the original disposition. A protracted period of investigation, consultation, and discussion with the Keeper followed. In September 2007 the trustee's solicitor wrote to the solicitors acting for Mr Torr, the purchaser, some five years' earlier, of the ground-floor flat, explaining what had happened to the original disposition and warning of possible litigation. This, however, did not prevent Mr Torr from granting a standard security to Abbey National plc in February of the following year. What checks on title were made on behalf of Abbey are not clear (para 10).

The present action was one by Mr Pocock's trustee in sequestration, seeking to prove the tenor of the original deed, and seeking declarators and reductions in respect of the various deeds granted since the initial disposition by Skene Investments had been delivered. His argument was devastatingly simple. The only deed of the set which was valid and effective was the very first, the disposition by Skene Investments (Aberdeen) Ltd to Mr Pocock. Although that deed no longer existed, for it had been cannibalised to make the second disposition, its terms could be proved. Its effect was to make Mr Pocock the unregistered holder – the uninfeft proprietor, as one used to say – of 5 Queen's Gardens. Nothing that had happened since had changed that position. As the disposition to Howemoss Properties Ltd was void, so also were all deeds which followed on from that disposition, and since there had been no registration, the statutory guarantee of title did not exist. The acquirers, therefore, had no title to the flats for which they had paid. Nor had their lenders. At best they had a damages claim against Mr Pocock. But Mr Pocock was insolvent and their claim would simply join the claims of other unsecured creditors. Meanwhile the trustee could complete title to the house in his own name, unencumbered by any of the standard securities.

The acquirers and their lenders put forward three main defences. First, as fraudster, Mr Pocock was personally barred from founding on the invalidity of the falsified disposition. Secondly, a trustee in sequestration cannot profit from the fraud of the bankrupt. And thirdly, the four-year delay between finding out about the fraud and raising the present action amounted to *mora* on the part of the trustee in sequestration. At first instance the first two defences failed but proof before answer was allowed in respect of the third: see [2011] CSOH 144, 2011 GWD 30-654 (*Conveyancing 2011* Case (40)).

Abbey appealed, and the trustee cross-appealed. The former argued that the position as to *mora*, taciturnity and acquiescence was so clear that the defence should be upheld without a proof; the latter argued that no relevant defence was disclosed by the averments, which should not therefore be admitted to probation. The appeal court, an Extra Division, found for the trustee. As Lady Paton explained, giving the Opinion of the Court (para 36):

[T]he steps taken by the pursuer amounted to investigation, consultation, the seeking of appropriate advice, warnings to both the Keeper and to a current heritable proprietor (Mr Torr), and the raising of an action. For this reason alone we find

Abbey's averments of taciturnity and acquiescence to be inadequate and irrelevant. Furthermore we agree with senior counsel for the pursuer that the pursuer was entitled responsibly to seek information and advice before raising a court action with all its consequences.

(It should perhaps be noted that the nullity of his title meant that Mr Torr was not truly a 'heritable proprietor'.)

Abbey's other ground of appeal concerned the defence of profiting from the bankrupt's fraud. By his delay, Abbey argued, the trustee must be taken to have adopted the forgery. Here again the court was not persuaded that a relevant defence had been averred (para 38):

> [T]he crucial element illustrated by decisions such as *Mackenzie v British Linen Bank* [(1881) 8 R 8)] and *Muir's Exrs* [*v Craig's Trs* 1913 SC 349] is that a person who knows about the forgery, and knows that a third party is being misled into relying upon the forgery, says or does nothing to alert the third party to the problem. In effect therefore it is necessary for Abbey to aver and prove that the pursuer knew not only that the disposition was falsified, but also that Abbey were intending to lend Mr Torr money in reliance upon that falsified disposition, and yet did nothing to prevent Abbey from relying upon the falsified disposition. ... Furthermore, the pursuer's actings as outlined in paragraphs [7] to [11] above, and in particular the letter dated 5 September 2007, do not disclose a picture of an adoption of forgery. On the contrary, the pursuer had taken active steps to warn Mr Torr's agents that his disposition was from a non-owner and that court proceedings challenging that disposition would be raised. It is impossible, in our opinion, to view that as an adoption of forgery.

As Ken Swinton has pointed out, the facts of this case help make the argument for separate representation for purchaser-borrowers and their lenders: see 'An argument for separate representation: *Pocock's Tr v Skene Investments*' (2012) 80 *Scottish Law Gazette* 58.

(37) Glencoe Developments Ltd v Sneddon
[2012] CSOH 43, 2012 GWD 13-244

This was the latest in a series of litigations concerning the troubled affairs of Glencoe Developments Ltd. (See *Sneddon v MacCallum* [2011] CSOH 59, 2011 GWD 13-292 and *Kirkham v McDonald* [2012] CSOH 6, 2012 GWD 4-59.) The company was a single-purpose vehicle formed to hold land at Onich, Fort William. Of the four £1 shares of issued capital, two were held by Margaret Sneddon and two by Stewart MacCallum (apparently on behalf of David Kirkham). At an EGM held on 20 June 2011 the company purported to pass a resolution authorising the transfer of the land to Andrew Sneddon (Mrs Sneddon's husband), and in the event the disposition was granted to Campbell Sneddon (Mrs Sneddon's son) and registered in the Land Register. Later Mrs Sneddon's justification was that she and her husband had paid for the ground, and that 'what was his was hers' (para 18).

In this action the company sought reduction of the disposition. The EGM was attended by only one shareholder, Mrs Sneddon. No notice of the meeting had been given to the other shareholder (Mr MacCallum), and the meeting was inquorate and the 'resolution' invalid. It followed, the company argued, that the disposition fell to be reduced. No plausible defence having been stated, the court granted summary decree.

It may be noted that a decree of reduction is, as such, of limited value unless it causes the disponee's name to be removed from the Land Register by rectification: see *Short's Tr v Keeper of the Registers of Scotland* 1996 SC (HL) 14. It is not clear whether Campbell Sneddon was a 'proprietor in possession' and, if so, on which of the grounds in s 9(3)(a) of the Land Registration (Scotland) Act 1979 the company hoped to be able to achieve rectification.

(38) McGraddie v McGraddie
[2012] CSIH 23, 2012 GWD 15-310

The pursuer and his wife had lived for many years in Albuquerque, New Mexico. When his wife became seriously ill, the pursuer determined to return to Glasgow and commissioned his son, the first defender, to buy a flat. Money was sent for that purpose. The flat was duly bought and the pursuer came home to live in it. The son had, however, taken title in his own name. A year or so later, the pursuer gave his son a second sum of money (£285,000). Within a few weeks this too had been used to buy a house, with title this time taken in the name of the son and his wife (the second defender). The litigation was a result of disagreement as to the basis on which the money was handed over. The pursuer's case was that his son was simply being appointed as agent, to buy the houses on the pursuer's behalf. Accordingly, the pursuer sought an order that the houses be conveyed to him. The defenders' position was more complicated but in its essentials amounted to saying that the first house was to be used for the benefit of the defenders' family, and that the second cheque was an outright gift.

Following a proof, the Lord Ordinary found for the pursuer: see [2009] CSOH 142, 2009 GWD 38-633 (*Conveyancing 2009* Case (60)), and [2010] CSOH 60, 2010 GWD 21-404 (*Conveyancing 2010* Case (48)). On appeal, the defenders conceded in respect of the first house (though without admitting any wrongdoing) but continued to argue that the money used to buy the second had been an outright gift.

Reversing the Lord Ordinary, an Extra Division of the Court of Session emphasised the weight that should be given to the trial judge's assessment of the evidence. An appeal should be allowed on the facts only where, as Lord Hamilton said in *Hamilton v Allied Domecq plc* 2006 SC 221 at para 83, the trial judge had 'plainly gone wrong'. In the present case, the Lord Ordinary had perhaps been too much influenced by the demeanour of the witnesses and had not paid sufficient attention to 'non-contentious and objective facts' surrounding the purchase of the second house (para 40). Because the appeal was concerned only with this house, it was possible for the evidence to be subject to 'a highly intensive scrutiny' (para 39). That scrutiny suggested that the non-contentious facts were far more consistent with the evidence of the defenders than that of the pursuer. The following facts in particular were consistent with the payment being a gift and not a commission to buy a house for the pursuer: (i) by the time the second house was being bought, the pursuer had been back in Glasgow for a year and had no need to commission his son to buy for him; (ii) he did not visit the house; (iii) the money was handed over seven weeks before settlement; (iv) the sum given was not the same as the sum expended on the house; (v) part of the money was used by the defenders for quite different purposes, such as buying cars; (vi) the pursuer made no effort to live in the house, or to challenge the defenders' occupation or regularise it by a lease.

(39) McIrvine v McIrvine
[2012] CSOH 23, 2012 GWD 9-171

Like the *McGraddie* case just discussed, this was a father/son dispute. The case involved a farm at Culdrain, Gartly, Aberdeenshire. Among other matters, it was concerned with an issue that seldom comes before the courts: slander of title. The petitioner was the son and the respondent was the father, their names being John D McIrvine and John A McIrvine respectively. The property was originally owned by McIrvine senior. In October 1988 he disponed it to his wife and to his son as trustees for the partnership of J D & D McIrvine. (In May 1989 McIrvine senior was sequestrated. No doubt that fact forms part of the overall story, but we are unable to say precisely what part.) In July 1989 Mrs McIrvine died. Her will set up a trust, in which her husband was to have an improper liferent (what is also called a beneficiary liferent or trust liferent) of the residue of her estate. Her estate was not confirmed to at this stage. Her death meant that the partnership no longer had more than one partner, and thus ended. What the partnership agreement said was to happen to the partnership assets upon dissolution is unclear. But the only person now with a real right in the farm was McIrvine junior, being the sole surviving trustee. Notwithstanding the 1988 transfer, McIrvine senior continued to operate the farm and to run it as if still owner. (The reasons for this are not clear.) Eventually, in 2005 or 2006, father and son fell out.

Three separate court actions ensued. (i) The son raised a sheriff court action against the father for count, reckoning and payment in respect of his dealings with the farm at Culdrain, and was successful, obtaining decree for £300,000: *McIrvine v McIrvine* 2012 GWD 32-638. (ii) The father confirmed to his late wife's estate and raised a sheriff court action of count reckoning and payment against his son for his dealings with her assets; the fate of this action is unknown to us. (iii) The son raised the present action, in the Outer House, against his father, seeking possession of the farm, interdict against interference with that possession, and interdict against 'slander of title'. It is this third action, in which the petitioner was successful, which is noted here. We quote the succinct statement of the Lord Brodie (para 10):

The present petition was presented by reason of the petitioner's wish to sell the Subjects and the receipt of an offer ... from the Forestry Commission which was acceptable to the petitioner. The petitioner avers that the respondent unlawfully interfered with the proposed sale to the Forestry Commission. On or about 28 July 2010 the respondent caused an offer to be made for the subjects at a price of £650,000 by Huntly Farming Ltd. The directors of that company are partners in the firm of R & R Urquhart LLP, Solicitors, who act as agents for the respondent. Although not disclosed at the time of the offer, R & R Urquhart subsequently admitted that the beneficial owner of Huntly Farming Ltd was the respondent. The petitioner instructed his agents to ignore the offer from Huntly Farming Ltd, it being his view that the respondent did not have funds to pay the offer price and that the offer was a sham. The petitioner accordingly instructed his agents to proceed with the sale to the Forestry Commission. It had been intended to settle that sale on 15 September 2010 with payment by the Forestry Commission of a purchase price of £647,000. However, the respondent caused R & R Urquhart to send to the solicitors acting for the Forestry Commission an e-mail dated 10 September 2010 in the following terms:

> We intimate that we are instructed by John A McIrvine (A) of Culdrain Farm, Gartly, Aberdeenshire. ... We are aware that Ledingham Chalmers are also representing him. We have preliminary reason to believe that A may have an interest in the ownership, which failing the tenancy, which failing a servitude right of pasturage, and if our initial belief, based on information meantime provided turns out to be correct, then A's son, John D McIrvine (D), who may purport to be the owner, may not be in a position to grant vacant possession. A has made representations to [an MSP] who we understand will be raising this matter with the Forestry Commission. May we please request that a moratorium period of say two months is allowed to resolve matters between A and D, prior to the Forestry Commission being dragged into a potential material family dispute with title consequences ... ?

The respondent produced a photocopy of a document that appeared to be a disposition of the property from the son back to the father. 'It was prepared by CMS Cameron McKenna (Scotland) LLP and printed on paper with the word "Draft" prominently displayed on each sheet. It was apparently sent to the respondent by CMS Cameron McKenna, which firm then acted for both the petitioner and the respondent, under cover of a letter dated 21 March 2005' (para 16). The document appeared to have been signed, ostensibly by McIrvine junior, but was unwitnesssed. It had not been recorded or registered. This latter point, apart from the other difficulties, was evidently fatal to the respondent. As Lord Brodie put it (para 17): 'The pretended disposition is irrelevant to the question of who owns the subjects. In terms of s 4 of the Abolition of Feudal Tenure etc (Scotland) Act 2000, ownership of land shall pass on registration or recording. The pretended disposition has neither been registered nor recorded.'

The respondent also founded on his first wife's will. He pled (para 21):

[I]n terms of Mrs Doris Catherine McIrvine's Trust Disposition and Settlement, the respondent was given an elementary [alimentary?] 'life rent use and enjoyment of the whole rest, residue and remainder of my said means and estate, whether heritable or moveable, real or personal'. The same property included Mrs McIrvine's rights in the partnership property which included Culdrain Farm and accordingly the respondent retains a liferent right to use and enjoy the said partnership property, insofar as it belonged to Mrs McIrvine.

The Lord Ordinary observed (para 21):

Mr Artis [for the petitioner], I thought charitably, described this passage as containing a *non sequitur*. I would have been less kind. In my view these averments display fundamental misconceptions as to the nature of both partnership and trust property. Where heritable estate is part of partnership property it is held by the partners in trust. ... The heritage belongs to the partnership. [T]he partners have a *jus crediti* or personal claim only. It was that personal claim that devolved on the late Mrs McIrvine's trustees and executors in terms of her Trust Disposition and Settlement. The trustees thereafter held that claim as part of the residue of the late Mrs McIrvine's estate, of which the respondent had a liferent. That liferent is a beneficiary liferent and not a proper liferent. The respondent's interest is that of beneficiary with a *jus crediti* in respect of what is held by the testamentary trustees. The respondent has no real right in respect of the Subjects.

This is a sound exposition of the law. Mrs McIrvine and her son owned the property jointly in trust, and so when she passed away the son was the only person with a real right. Whatever right Mr McIrvine senior may or may not have had to the farm, it was not a real right. (It might be added, by way of footnote, that partnerships can now take title in their own name, though in practice this seldom happens: Abolition of Feudal Tenure etc (Scotland) Act 2000 s 70. We might also add that the expression 'an interest in the ownership' (see above) is one that would puzzle a property law expert.)

The Lord Ordinary then dealt with the 'slander of title' issue (para 23):

To communicate directly with a potential purchaser's solicitors as [the defender's solicitors] did on the respondent's instructions is hardly commensurate with acting in good faith. At best for the respondent, [their solicitors'] expression of opinion has the look of being reckless and, as I have already indicated, it was clearly intended to harm the petitioner's prospects of selling the subjects. I regard that as sufficient to amount to slander of title and in the whole circumstances I would see the petitioner as being entitled to interdict of any repetition.

Finally, para 8 says that on 25 July 1995 the petitioners disponed the property to the respondent and his second wife. Were that so, the present action would make little sense. And para 6 says that no title has been registered since 1989, meaning that the alleged 1995 disposition is yet another puzzle in this puzzling case.

LAND REGISTRATION

(40) Trustees of the Elliot of Harwood Trust v Feakins
2012 GWD 10-194, Sh Ct

In dispute was whether a disposition of a landed estate by the pursuers to the defender did or did not convey a lodge. Although the deed plan was drawn at a miserly 1:25,000, the court was able to conclude, on a balance of probabilities, that the lodge was indeed included. Accordingly, the Register was accurate in showing the lodge as within the defender's title, and the pursuers' application for rectification failed. See **Commentary** p 157.

WARRANDICE

(41) Morris v Rae
[2012] UKSC 50, 2013 SLT 88

A warrandice claim presupposes 'eviction'. The latter (which has a special meaning in the law of warrandice) can be either judicial or extra-judicial. In this case the person suing in warrandice argued that there had been extra-judicial eviction in respect that a third party with an incontestable title had entered a claim to the property, which claim they had settled by acquiring the property. An Extra Division held, by a majority, that while the third party may have been entitled to become owner, it was not owner at the time it entered its claim. Hence there was no eviction and the action fell to be dismissed. See [2011] CSIH 30, 2011 SC 654, 2011 SLT 701, 2011 SCLR 428 (*Conveyancing 2011* Case (39)). The pursuer appealed to the Supreme Court. **Held**, allowing the appeal, that it would be sufficient title for eviction if the third party could be proved to have had an unqualified entitlement, exercisable immediately, to demand a transfer from the owner. See **Commentary** p 125.

RIGHT-TO-BUY LEGISLATION

(42) Pairc Crofters Ltd v Scottish Ministers
[2012] CSIH 96, 2013 GWD 1-42

Part 3 of the Land Reform (Scotland) Act 2003 confers on crofting communities the right to buy their land, subject to a variety of ifs and buts. The crofters of Pairc, in the Isle of Lewis, sought to do so. The consent of the Scottish Ministers, something that the 2003 Act requires, was granted. The landowner challenged the buy-out, on the grounds that (i) part 3 of the 2003 Act was incompatible with the ECHR and (ii) that the Crofting Community Right to Buy (Ballot) (Scotland) Regulations 2004, SSI 2004/227 were incompatible with the ECHR. Both challenges failed.

Information about the buy-out can be found at the crofters' website (www. pairctrust.co.uk). According to this website, and indeed other sources, the landlord company, Pairc Crofters Ltd, is controlled by Barry Lomas, an accountant in Leamington Spa. If that is correct the name of the company seems surprising. The decision may mark the beginning of the end of this contentious buy-out which has been in the news almost since the 2003 Act came on stream.

LEASES

(43) L Batley Pet Products Ltd v North Lanarkshire Council
[2012] CSIH 83, 2012 GWD 37-745

The pursuer was the mid-landlord and the defender was the occupational sub-tenant of a property in Cumbernauld. The sub-tenancy ended on 18 January 2009. In terms of a minute of agreement (which was a separate document from the sub-lease), the sub-tenant had been authorised to carry out certain alterations to the property, with an option to the mid-landlord to require restoration, exercisable before the ish. The mid-landlord sent a written notice calling for restoration, which reached the defender two days after the ish. But the mid-landlord had also (it was averred) made to the sub-tenant an oral demand for restoration, and had done so a few weeks before the ish. The court had to decide whether the minute of agreement required the notice to be in writing, or whether oral notice could suffice. In the Outer House it was held that oral notice was sufficient: [2011] CSOH 209, 2011 GWD 4-73 (*Conveyancing 2011* Case (62)). The sub-tenant reclaimed, successfully, the Inner House holding that oral notice was not sufficient.

(44) R M Prow (Motors) Ltd Directors Pension Fund Trustees v Argyll and Bute Council
[2012] CSOH 77, 2012 GWD 21-438

The pursuers granted the defender a 20-year lease over 64A John Street, Helensburgh. The lease had a rent review mechanism and on 19 July 2010 a surveyor wrote to the defender proposing a new, higher, rent. This letter contained numerous errors (including an error as to the identity of the landlords) and on 24 August 2010 the surveyor sent a second letter with the errors corrected. The tenant did not begin to pay the higher rent, nor did it serve a counter-notice objecting to the new rent. The landlords raised an action of declarator that the rent now payable was the higher rent.

The Lord Ordinary **held** that the numerous errors in the first letter rendered it invalid, but that the second letter was valid, and accordingly decree in favour of the pursuer was granted.

The tenant's attack on the second letter was that it was sent by a surveyor, whereas the lease said: 'Any written notice or intimation given by the Landlords to the Tenants ... shall be validly given if given by letter signed under the hand of an officer of the Landlords.' The Lord Ordinary held (in conformity with previous case law on similar clauses, such as *Blythswood Investments (Scotland) Ltd v Clydesdale Electrical Stores Ltd* 1995 SLT 150) that this provision was permissive and not mandatory.

The case contains valuable discussion of the argument, frequently deployed, that a notice is valid, notwithstanding errors, if a 'reasonable recipient' would understand its meaning. Lord Hodge's four propositions on this issue in *Batt Cables Plc v Spencer Business Parks Ltd* 2010 SLT 860 were approved. There is an extensive body of case law in England on this issue, beginning with *Mannai*

Investment Co Ltd v Eagle Star Life Assurance Co Ltd [1997] AC 749. Whether the position in Scots law is precisely the same as in England is perhaps not settled.

It may be added that the case illustrates the dangers that can attend the use of styles. Here the landlord was a trust, three of the trustees being natural persons and the fourth a company. What could an 'officer' mean in this context? Indeed, what does 'officer' mean in any context, except, perhaps, that of Her Majesty's Armed Forces? And what does 'signed *under the hand*' mean? As opposed to what? The foot? In other words, how, if at all, does it differ in meaning from 'signed'?

(45) Morris v Eason
[2012] CSOH 125, 2012 GWD 27-564

Partnerships often give rise to problems about heritable property. This is an example. In Dura Street, Dundee, there was a surgery called the Terra Nova Medical Centre. It was owned by MPIF Holdings Ltd, and held on a 21-year lease, granted in 2006 to four doctors, A, B, C and D. Whether, to be precise, the lease was granted to (i) the four doctors as such, or (ii) to the four doctors as trustees of their partnership, or (iii) to their partnership as such, is not wholly clear, but it seems that the first was the case. The lease allowed free assignability subject to one or two conditions, notably the continued use of the property as a surgery. Possibly the lease was registered in the Land Register, but if so that fact does not emerge. Nothing turned on the point, and although a lease for over 20 years cannot be a real right unless so registered (Land Registration (Scotland) Act 1979 s 2) a contract can be a valid lease without being a real right.

Not long after the lease was entered into, A, B and C retired, and the practice was carried on by D plus some new doctors, who were in a partnership called the Terra Nova Medical Group. A, B and C offered to assign the lease, but this offer was refused, for reasons that do not appear. The result was that A, B, C and D were the tenants but the current partnership was in business at the premises without any clear legal basis. The problem was not resolved by agreement, and the upshot was the present action. A, B and C sued the current partners and their partnership. D was included as a defender but did not enter appearance. The others did. The action sought declarator that the defenders had no right to occupy the property, and removing. Although the point is not quite clear, it seems that the action was raised by A, B and C as individuals (see above).

There were two aspects to the case, one substantive and the other procedural. The substantive one was whether the defenders had any right to occupy the property. In the absence of any assignation of the lease, and in the absence of any sub-lease (and sub-letting seems to have been forbidden by the terms of the lease), the defenders' position was weak. They suggested that there might have been some sort of implied 'licence', but had no pleadings to support that, and we would note that even if there had been some sort of licence, it had presumably come to an end by the very fact of the raising of the action (if not before). The defenders' pleas were dismissed as irrelevant.

The procedural defence – less hopeless than the substantive defence – was that the pursuers lacked title to sue. The basis for this argument was that the lease was held by four parties (A, B, C and D) but that only three of them were suing. Where property is, as here, held *pro indiviso*, all parties are supposed to join in any action of removing. Whilst this proposition is generally true, there can be exceptions. The Lord Ordinary (Woolman) quoted p 82 of Sir John Rankine's *Law of Leases in Scotland* (3rd edn, 1916): 'The defence would not be listened to if tendered by a mere squatter, occupying without semblance of right.' He concluded: 'As I hold that the defenders occupy without a right, Rankine supports the proposition that they are not entitled to query the pursuers' title to sue' (para 27.) The authorities in this area were carefully reviewed (though possibly there might have been some discussion of *Price v Watson* 1951 SC 359).

(46) Calmac Developments Ltd v Murdoch
2012 GWD 27-565, Sh Ct

A residential tenancy agreement (for property at 39 Calside, Dumfries) said: 'The Date of Entry will be 29th April 2011. The Let will run from that date until 28th October 2011 …'. The tenant did not flit at the ish, and the landlord raised an action of removing. The question for the court was whether the tenancy was a 'short assured tenancy'. If it was, then the tenant had no defence. The Housing (Scotland) Act 1988 s 32(1)(a) says that such a tenancy has to be 'for a term not less than six months'. The Act does not say how the six months should be calculated. The sheriff (George Jamieson) held (paras 27 and 28):

> I interpret the lease in stipulating the term ran from the date of entry on 29th April 2011, meant it ran from midnight on the 28th with the result the term of the lease was exactly six months and was correctly constituted as a short assured tenancy. Actual entry was for less than six months as the tenant entered on the afternoon of 29th April 2011: but the term was for six months and that is what matters for the purpose of section 32(1)(a) of the Act.

(47) Midlothian Innovation and Technology Trust v Ferguson
[2012] CSOH 189, 2013 GWD 1-3

The pursuer held a five-year lease of property at Pentlandfield Business Park in Roslin, Midlothian. The lease contained a purchase option, which the pursuer exercised. The lease was renounced. (Whether a disposition was granted is not clear.) But there then arose a dispute about liability for repairs, which was remitted to arbitration. This in turn led to a dispute about whether arbitration was possible given that the lease was now at an end. It was **held** by the Lord Ordinary (Woolman) that the arbiter had full power to decide the matters at issue between the parties.

(48) Mountwest 838 Ltd v Backmuir Trading Ltd
[2012] CSOH 131, 2012 GWD 28-571

Backmuir Trading Ltd owned a farm in Aberdeenshire. It entered into a contract with Mountwest 838 Ltd under which the latter acquired an option to acquire a long lease at the farm for a wind farm. One term of the contract was:

> 6.1 The Tenant shall provide to the Landlord a copy of any proposed application for planning permission (including for the avoidance of doubt an Environmental Statement or Environmental Impact Assessment) prior to submission of the same to the relevant Planning Authority. ...

> 7.1 The Landlord may determine this Agreement by written notice to the Tenant if ... the Tenant materially fails to perform or observe any of its obligations ... and such failure or event is incapable of remedy or it is capable of remedy and the Landlord have served on the Tenant written notice specifying the failure or event and requiring it to be remedied within a reasonable time (to be specified in the notice and taking into account the nature of the obligation in question) and the Tenant has failed to do so.

In June 2011 Mountwest made a planning application but did not copy it to Backmuir. Backmuir sent to Mountwest a notice:

> It has come to our attention that an Application for Planning Permission has been submitted to Aberdeenshire Council for the erection of two wind turbines. ... In terms of the Windfarm Agreement entered into between us at the time we purchased Mains of Cairnbrogie in April 2009, Mountwest is under certain obligations in terms of clause 6.1. Mountwest has failed to perform and observe any of its clause 6.1 obligations. We require you to remedy this failure if it is capable of being remedied. Insofar as clause 6.1 requires Mountwest to provide certain documentation, this documentation should be provided in accordance with the terms of clause 6.1 within a period of 21 days.

Mountwest responded, within that deadline, by supplying all the documentation that should have been supplied initially. But curiously, that did not end the matter. Backmuir, after receiving the complete documentation, decided that the breach had not been remediable in the first place, because the documentation should have been copied to Backmuir 'prior to submission' of the planning application, and that was something that could no longer happen. Mountwest did not accept the resulting rescission, and the question for the court was whether the rescission was valid. The action took the form of declarator and reduction.

The Lord Ordinary (Woolman) held that the breach was a remediable one, and had been remedied. It was true that the 'prior to' requirement could no longer be complied with, but Backmuir could simply have requested Mountwest to withdraw the application, and begin again. 'If Backmuir had wished to insist on Mountwest withdrawing its application and beginning the process again, that was a simple message to convey' (para 41). Accordingly the notice of rescission was invalid.

(49) Kirkham v Link Housing Group
[2012] CSIH 58, 2012 Hous LR 87

A tenant in social accommodation (12 Moorelands Place, Addiewell, West Lothian) sued her landlord for damages after she tripped over a raised edge of a paving slab on the path leading to her front door. She based her case partly in delict but also in contract, alleging that the landlord had been in breach of its repairing obligation. She failed at first instance (2010 SLT 321), and her reclaiming motion has now been dismissed.

Clause 5.3 of the tenancy agreement bound the landlord to attend to problems of which it was aware, but the landlord had been unaware of this problem. Clause 5.4 imposed a duty to inspect 'the common parts' but the path in question served only the pursuer's house and so did not fall under 'common parts'. Clause 5.8 imposed an overall repairing obligation on the landlord, including an obligation to keep all 'pathways' in repair. Obviously there were difficulties in making this clause cohere with the previous clauses. The view was taken that clause 5.8 should not be construed as trumping the more specific provisions of the earlier clauses.

(50) South Lanarkshire Council v McKenna
[2012] CSIH 78, 2013 SLT 22

There have been many attempts to invoke Article 8 of the ECHR (right to respect for private and family life) as a defence to actions of removing. Two English cases have reached the Supreme Court: *Manchester City Council v Pinnock* [2011] 2 AC 104 and *Hounslow London Borough Council v Powell* [2011] 2 AC 186, as a result of which the issues have been fairly well scrutinised. In the present case a local authority seeking to evict a tenant on the ground of anti-social behaviour was met by the plea that the tenant's human rights were being violated. The specific question was whether s 36 of the Housing (Scotland) Act 2001 was ECHR-compatible. The Inner House held that it was.

(51) Salvesen v Riddell
[2012] CSIH 26, 2012 SLT 633, 2012 SCLR 403, 2012 Hous LR 30

This case concerned the Agricultural Holdings (Scotland) Act 2003, and since we do not cover the law of agricultural tenancies, it falls outside our remit. It is however noteworthy because the Inner House declared s 72 of the 2003 Act invalid as being outwith the Scottish Parliament's legislative competence. For valuable discussion see Daniel J Carr, 'Not Law' (2012) 16 *Edinburgh Law Review* 410, and Malcolm M Combe, 'Human rights, limited competence and limited partnerships: Salvesen v Riddell' 2012 SLT (News) 193. It is understood that the decision has been appealed to the Supreme Court.

(52) Mountain's Trs v Mountain
[2012] CSIH 73, 2012 GWD 33-663

Sir Denis Mortimer Mountain's trust disposition and settlement had the following unusual provision:

> All land, forming part of Delfur Estate lying north of the Delfur Lodge woodland policies (which for the avoidance of doubt are excluded) but to include WOODHEAD

and MAINS OF CAIRNTY FARMS and the other land running to the north together with the whole sporting rights thereon to my said Son WILLIAM whom failing to his eldest or only Son but both expressly subject to my Son William and his Son agreeing to rent the agricultural land to my Son Edward in his own right or in partnership as my Son Edward shall determine at local market rental values as shall be determined in the first instance by my Trustees, so long as Edward wishes to be involved in the farming thereof, declaring that my trustees shall arrange an agricultural lease arrangement in favour of Edward that will extend for Edward's life only but not thereafter whom also failing to my son EDWARD whom also failing to his eldest or only Son. ...

In summary, the land was left to William, and Edward was to have a lifetime lease of it. But there was a difficulty. The legislation on agricultural tenancies has mandatory provisions about assignation, succession and so on, provisions that would be inconsistent with the terms of the lease as required by the testamentary trust. A draft lease was negotiated, which by its terms sought to oust the legislation. But there was uncertainty as to whether this would work, something of particular concern to the trustees because if it did not work – ie if the legislation were to trump the terms of the lease – then the trustees would have acted in breach of the trust.

Section 27 of the Court of Session Act 1988 says:

Where any parties interested, whether personally or in some fiduciary or official capacity, in the decision of a question of law are agreed upon the facts, and are in dispute only on the law applicable to those facts, it shall be competent for them ... to present to the Inner House a case ... setting out the facts upon which they are so agreed and the question of law arising from those facts; and the parties may ask the Court either for its opinion or for its judgment on that question of law.

Under this provision the trustees submitted a special case. It was heard by the First Division, the leading opinion being given by the new Lord President (Gill) who is noted for his expertise in the law of agricultural tenancies.

It was held, in the first place, that the proposed lease would be a valid lease for the purposes of the Leases Act 1449, ie that its effect would not be limited to a simple contractual effect as between the parties, but would have real effect. That having been established, the Lord President observed (at para 21) that there were

five issues; namely (1) Does the lease confer on the second party a 1991 Act tenancy? (2) if not, does it confer on the second party a SLDT or a LDT under the 2003 Act? (3) being a lease of agricultural land, is it valid if it does not qualify as a lease under either the 1991 Act or the 2003 Act? (4) if it is a valid lease that is outwith the scope of those Acts, can the tenant's interest be validly bequeathed by him; and (5) if not, is the tenant's interest capable of being transferred after his death to an eligible acquirer under the 1964 Act?

The third question was answered in the affirmative, and the others in the negative.

(53) Mirza v Salim
[2012] CSOH 37, 2012 SCLR 460

This was the third action in a protracted dispute between landlord and tenant. The first two have not been reported or appeared online, but some information about them is available from the current case.

The owner of land, Khalil Ahmed, agreed to lease it to Suriya Khan, but under exception of a certain part of the land (the reserved area). By mistake the lease as drafted and signed failed to exclude the reserved area, ie it included the whole area owned by the landlord. The length of the lease is unclear, but it appears to have been registered in the Land Register and so must have been for a term of over 20 years. It seems that the tenant did not take possession of the reserved area. Later the landlord transferred the whole property to the current pursuer, Mohammed Mirza, and the tenant transferred the tenancy to the current defender, Fozia Salim. Thereafter Mirza began developing the reserved area. At this stage Salim raised an action of interdict, on the ground that the reserved area was within the lease. Interim interdict was obtained. Before the case could proceed further, Mirza raised an action under s 8 of the Law Reform (Miscellaneous Provisions) (Scotland) Act 1985 to have the lease rectified so as to exclude the reserved area. This action (the second action in the dispute) was successful. (Rectification under the 1985 Act is possible as between singular successors of the original parties.) As a result the first action, the interdict action, failed.

Mirza now raised an action for damages for the loss said to have been caused by the interim interdict, which had been obtained, he pled, in bad faith. In seeking to make out his case, the pursuer sought disclosure of correspondence between the defender and her solicitors. The defender pled that the correspondence was privileged. The pursuer's application for disclosure was refused.

(54) Pentland-Clark v Maclehose
[2012] CSIH 29, 2012 GWD 18-372

James Clark, a Fife farmer, died in 1985. Litigation about his estate has been going on ever since. The dispute has more than once been in the media, including a story in the *Sunday Mail* on 1 April 2012. There have been numerous separate actions. Two earlier rounds (at least) have appeared in the law reports: *Clark v Clark's Exrs* 1989 SLT 665, and *Sarris v Clark* 1995 SLT 44.

Mr Clark married the present pursuer in 1958, the marriage ending in divorce in 1977. In 1982 he married again. He was survived by three children, all of them by his first wife. His will left his estate in four equal shares to the three children and his second wife. As for the first wife, she received a settlement at the time of the divorce including a right to an income which, it seems, was to continue notwithstanding his death. Thus she was a creditor in his estate. The executry had still not been finalised by 1999, at which time there was a petition for the estate to be placed under a judicial factory. The petition was granted. The judicial factory has likewise proved long-lived, for it is still in operation.

The original judicial factor died in 2006, and in 2007 the court appointed the first Mrs Clark as his replacement. In some of the actions she seems to have sued in a personal capacity but the present action is in her capacity as judicial factor. Latterly at least she has been a party litigant. The first defender in the current action is the second Mrs Clark (now, following re-marriage, known as Mrs Maclehose).

The focus of the dispute has been the manner in which the executry estate was administered. But to be more specific is difficult. The court comments (para 5) that the pursuer's averments

> do not serve to identify, with any reasonable degree of ease or clarity, the nature of the case against the defenders. … Rather the articles of condescendence serve to obscure the case in a morass of irrelevancy and repetition. The effect of this has been that, each time judges have been required to adjudicate on the issues, he, she or they have required to spend many hours, and sometimes days, poring over the pleadings and productions in an attempt to get to grips with just what the pursuer's complaint may be.

One central element concerned a lease granted by the late Mr Clark, just before he died, in favour of a partnership consisting of himself and his second wife, with the lease to pass to the survivor of them. The second Mrs Clark was eventually paid a substantial sum from the estate in order to give up this lease. The pursuer argued that this payment was inappropriate. 'The essence of the claim is … that there was some form of fraudulent scheme whereby the first defender's tenancy, as transmitted to her through the lease and contract of co-partnery, was regarded as a valid one by the executors whereas, it is contended, it was not so valid' (para 12). The reason why it was not valid, argued the pursuer, was that title to the farm was vested in a bank under an *ex facie* absolute disposition, and that the bank had not consented to the lease. Though the executors eventually repaid the bank all that it was due, that did not alter the fact, argued the pursuer, that at the relevant time the lease was not valid, and that accordingly the payment made to the first Mrs Clark was inappropriate.

We are not in a position to express any views about the general merits of the dispute. (For the pursuer's side of the story see www.doutrustlaw.com.) But the specific argument just mentioned was surely unsound, and rightly rejected by the court. This is not merely because it appears that the executors acted appropriately in regarding the lease as valid, because they had obtained opinions to that effect from no fewer than three noted members of the bar, later to become, respectively, Lords Hope, Gill and Dervaird. More fundamentally, even if the bank did have the right to reduce the lease, that fact was irrelevant. Whatever else a lease is, it is a contract and so binds the parties to it. Suppose that the bank had in fact reduced the lease, and sold the property free of it (which in fact did not happen, because the bank was repaid all that had been borrowed). Even then, after a reduction, the result would not have been that the contract was invalid. The landlord would have been in breach of the (valid) contract, and liable to damages. The amount of the damages would have been the value of the lease to the tenant. So whether the lease was valid in a question with the bank was neither here nor there.

Finally, we note that on the website mentioned above there is a passage saying that 'Martin Frost ... and Andrew McNamara ... have bought up the rights to the case', but if that is so then their role is not apparent at this stage of the dispute.

STANDARD SECURITIES

(55) Accord Mortgages Ltd v Edwards
2012 Hous LR 105, 2012 GWD 22-445, Sh Ct

The Conveyancing and Feudal Reform (Scotland) Act 1970, as amended, says that where a creditor seeks to enforce a standard security over residential property, certain special rules apply. In this case the creditor averred that the debtor had died, that her estate had been sequestrated, and that the property, though in itself residential property, was vacant. On that basis the creditor sought declarator '(i) that the defender is in default within the meaning of standard condition 9(1)(a) of sch 3 to the Act; (ii) that the subjects are not used to any extent for residential purposes within the meaning of s 20(2A) of the Act; and (iii) that the pursuers have the right to sell the subjects and to enter into possession and exercise all other rights and powers under the standard security, in terms of the Act'. It was **held** by the sheriff (P J Braid) that the relevant time for determining the residential status of property was at the time of enforcement and that accordingly this was not residential property for the purposes of the Act.

(56) Northern Rock (Asset Management) plc v Fowlie
2012 Hous LR 103, 2012 GWD 32-640, Sh Ct

As in the previous case, the creditor in a standard security over residential property raised an enforcement action, including a declaratory crave that the property was, at the time of enforcement, unoccupied and so not residential property for the purposes of the Conveyancing and Feudal Reform (Scotland) Act 1970. The previous case was cited to the court, and was approved by the sheriff (Philip Mann).

(57) Northern Rock (Asset Management) plc v Millar
2012 SLT (Sh Ct) 58, 2012 Hous LR 2

Under the Heritable Securities (Scotland) Act 1894 s 5B(2) and the Conveyancing and Feudal Reform (Scotland) Act 1970 ss 24 and 24A, a creditor seeking to enforce a standard security over residential property must effect certain 'pre-action requirements'. Details are given in the Applications by Creditors (Pre-Action Requirements) (Scotland) Order 2010, SSI 2010/317, para 2(4) of which says that 'the information required to be provided to the debtor ... must be provided as soon as reasonably practicable upon the debtor entering into default'. What does 'default' mean in this context? In our view the term is not used in any consistent sense in the legislation. The sheriff (A F Deutsch) concluded that 'default' in para 2(4) of the 2010 Order should be interpreted as meaning service of the calling-up notice. Hence the required information must be sent after the calling-up notice, but before the action is raised.

(58) Northern Rock (Asset Management) plc v Doyle
2012 Hous LR 94

This, like the previous case, was concerned with the interpretation of the Applications by Creditors (Pre-Action Requirements) (Scotland) Order 2010, SSI 2010/317, and was also heard by Sheriff A F Deutsch. The issues were similar, but the pursuer advanced lines of argument not explored in the earlier case. The sheriff adhered to his interpretation of the 2010 Order.

These cases illustrate the need for the standard security legislation to be reviewed, not least in respect to the enforcement provisions, which, whether reasonable or not in terms of their broad policy, are not clear enough in their wording, and often hard to interpret and apply. A review of the legislation by the Scottish Law Commission has been announced.

(59) Northern Rock (Asset Management) plc v Youngson
2012 Hous LR 100, 2012 GWD 33-662, Sh Ct

The Conveyancing and Feudal Reform (Scotland) Act 1970 s 24(5)(b), as amended, says that, in the case of residential property, enforcement of a standard security is permissible only if such enforcement would be 'reasonable'. In this action the question arose as to whether the creditor had to include an express averment as to reasonableness in the initial writ. **Held** (by Sheriff Philip Mann), albeit 'with some hesitation', that an averment of reasonableness was not necessary.

(60) Platform Funding Ltd v X
12 April 2012, Glasgow Sheriff Court

Information about this decision is available only on the website of the Govan Law Centre (http://govanlc.blogspot.co.uk/2012/04/decree-for-repossession-refused-in.html), but it appears to be a case of some significance, so we note it here. A bank sought to enforce a standard security. The debtor was not herself making any payments, but some payments were being made by the Department of Works and Pensions. It seems that the debtor had made an offer to pay off arrears at a rate that would take about six years to complete. The lender thought this too long and in any event the past history made it doubtful whether payments would be made. The sheriff accepted the English case of *Cheltenham and Gloucester Building Society v Norgan* [1996] 1 All ER 449 as persuasive authority, and **held** that six years was a reasonable period given that it was less than the remaining term of the loan (which was about nine years). Decree was refused.

(61) Bank of Scotland plc v Stevenson
2012 SLT (Sh Ct) 155, 2012 Hous LR 60

How are calling-up notices served? Section 19(6) of the Conveyancing and Feudal Reform (Scotland) Act 1970 says: '[T]he service of a calling-up notice may be made by delivery to the person on whom it is desired to be served or the notice may be sent by registered post or by the recorded delivery service to him at his last known address. ...' Is keyhole service by sheriff officer competent? In *Santander UK plc v Gallagher* 2011 SLT (Sh Ct) 203, 2011 Hous LR 26 (*Conveyancing 2011* Case (63)) it was held that such service is not competent. Similar facts arose in the present case, and the sheriff (G Jamieson) reached the opposite conclusion: service by sheriff officer *is* competent.

The judgment exhibits spectacular learning and makes irresistible reading. We hope our readers are familiar with all the statutes referred to, such as the Citation Act 1540, the Citation Act 1592, the Citation Act 1686, the Citation Act 1693, the Debtors (Scotland) Act 1832, the Citations (Scotland) Act 1846, the Citations (Scotland) Act 1849, the Citation Amendment (Scotland) Act 1882, the Sheriff Courts (Scotland) Act 1907, the Conveyancing and Feudal Reform (Scotland) Act 1970, the Consumer Credit Act 1974, the Interpretation Act 1978, the Debtors (Scotland) Act 1987, the Housing (Scotland) Act 1988, the Housing (Scotland) Act 2001, the Homelessness etc (Scotland) Act 2003, the Bankruptcy and Diligence etc (Scotland) Act 2007, the Public Services Reform (Scotland) Act 2010, and the Home Owner and Debtor Protection (Scotland) Act 2010.

The decision is certainly a commonsensical one, and the sheriff's analysis is persuasive at the technical level. Thus although there now exists a conflict of authority at the same level of the judicial hierarchy, we venture to suggest that the decision of Sheriff Jamieson should be regarded as settling the matter.

(62) 2004/2005 Eurocentral Hotel Syndicate Trustees v Hadrian SARL
[2012] CSOH 59, 2012 GWD 15-302

The pursuers owned the Dakota Hotel at Eurocentral in Motherwell. There was a standard security over the property for a loan of £13.5 million. The creditor issued a calling-up notice and marketed the property, entering into a provisional sale agreement. The pursuers raised an action seeking interdict and interim interdict against sale, the chief ground being that the property had not been marketed properly. This was a hearing on interim interdict. The Lord Ordinary (Hodge), having reviewed the evidence, **held** that the pursuers' case was weak and refused to grant interim interdict.

The case is notable for what the Lord Ordinary says about the competency of interdict against a sale by a heritable creditor. Two decisions, *Associated Displays Ltd v Turnbeam Ltd* 1988 SCLR 220 and *Gordaviran Ltd v Clydesdale Bank plc* 1994 SCLR 248, had been widely seen as holding that such interdict is not competent, though their soundness in law had been doubted by commentators (including ourselves). The Lord Ordinary held that interdict against sale by a heritable creditor is indeed competent (albeit that he refused such interdict on the facts of the case). He said (para 19):

> [T]he only question of incompetence in those cases was the wording of the interdicts sought. For good reasons the court may be slow to grant an interim interdict against a creditor from realising the security subjects without clear evidence of a breach of s 25 of the 1970 Act or some other legal wrong and may prefer to leave the debtor to claim damages. But that is not an issue of competency.

SEXUAL PROPERTY

(63) Thomson v Mooney
[2012] CSOH 177, 2012 GWD 39-769

The parties began to cohabit in 2005 and parted in 2007. Following their separation, the pursuer raised this action seeking payment of two sums namely (i) £35,000 and (ii) £68,434. As to the first, the parties had bought a house together at English Row, Calderbank, Airdrie. Title had been taken in joint names, and most of the price had been raised by a joint mortgage. But the whole deposit, £70,000, had, pled the pursuer, been paid by him alone. He now argued that the defender had been enriched to the extent of 50% of the amount, ie £35,000. As to the second head of claim, the pursuer said that he had made various payments to, or on behalf of, the defender's business, located in Uddingston, which went by the name of 'Bib and Tucker'. He now wanted those payments, said to total £68,434, reimbursed. Both claims were based in the law of unjustified enrichment.

The defender pled negative prescription in respect of the first claim, the house having been bought just over five years prior to the raising of the action. That five years is the relevant period for unjustified enrichment claims was accepted. But as with so many prescription arguments, the point at issue was when the prescriptive clock began to tick. The defender argued that the clock began to tick at the time of the purchase; the pursuer argued that it began only when they split up, the reason being that they had intended to marry, and that whilst the defender was *enriched* when the house was bought, she was only *unjustifiably* enriched when the plan of marriage was given up. This argument did not persuade the Lord Ordinary (Drummond Young), who accordingly **held** that the first claim had indeed prescribed. As to the second claim, proof before answer was allowed.

(64) Barbour v Marriott
2012 GWD 18-358, Sh Ct

The pursuer and the defender were long-term cohabitants. The pursuer disponed to the defender a property that he owned in Castle Douglas. The terms of this disposition are not known to us but it seems that it was gratuitous. What narrative clause it contained, if any, is also unknown. The defender also acquired another property in Castle Douglas, direct from a third-party seller. After the parties broke up, the pursuer claimed that the defender held both properties in trust for him. As to the second property, he claimed that he had bought it on missives and paid for it, but had directed his solicitors that the disposition should be to her rather than to him.

The pursuer asked the defender to dispone both properties to him, which she declined to do. In the present action he sought declarator of trust and an order requiring the defender to dispone both properties. He also sought interim interdict to prevent her selling the properties, and the present phase of the case was about the question of interim interdict. It seems that there was no documentary evidence to support the assertion that the defender held the properties in trust. The pursuer said that the reason for the arrangement was that he wished to ensure that, if he became insolvent, the properties would be protected from his creditors.

At first instance the sheriff held that interim interdict should not be granted because the pursuer's averments of a trust were doomed to failure due to lack of relevancy. 'Although trusts no longer require to be constituted by declarations in writing, a trust is not constituted by mere tacit understanding but requires a declaration of trust by the truster with sufficient substance to it to justify its description as a juridical act' (quoted in para 11 of the appeal case). The pursuer had failed to aver any such declaration. On appeal, the sheriff principal (B A Lockhart) reversed the sheriff's decision and granted interim interdict. He considered that at this stage, before a proper debate on relevancy had taken place, it was not possible to say that the pursuer's averments were doomed to fail in respect of relevancy. The case does not mention *Clark Taylor & Co Ltd v Quality Site Development (Edinburgh) Ltd* 1981 SC 111, an important authority about the constitution of trusts in Scots law, and which was key to the next case.

One aspect that seems not to have been considered, at least at this stage in the litigation, is a certain internal tension in the position taken by the pursuer. On the one hand, he wished, he pled, to vest title in his cohabitant so that if he became insolvent he could say to his creditors that the properties belonged to her absolutely. (Any concession of the existence of a trust would have been fatal to this argument, because creditors can attach the beneficiary's interest.) On the other hand, if he remained solvent but his cohabitant parted from him he wished to be able to say that the properties did *not* belong to her absolutely, but were held in trust for him. In other words, he seemed to have wished to have it both ways: to assert a trust or deny a trust as suited his convenience. In fact, one might go further. If his intention was that the properties should be immune to his creditors, as he himself averred, that seems to imply that he did *not* intend there to be any trust (because if there was a trust, his beneficial interest would be open to attachment by his creditors). The inference is difficult to avoid that he intended the defender to be the unqualified owner, merely trusting her (in the ordinary sense of the word) to administer the properties as he wished. It was mentioned above that the precise terms of the disposition are not given. But if it contained a 'love favour and affection' clause then the natural inference would be that this was a case of donation.

It was accepted in the case that a trust could be constituted without writing, and that is true. But it may be noted that s 1(2)(a)(iii) of the Requirements of Writing (Scotland) Act 1995 says that writing is necessary for 'a trust whereby a person declares himself to be sole trustee of his own property or any property which he may acquire' and it might perhaps be argued that this provision was applicable.

The sheriff principal's decision has been forcefully criticised by Ken Swinton ((2012) 80 *Scottish Law Gazette* 54):

> With respect to the Sheriff Principal ... there is simply no room for inference. Either there is a declaration of trust or there is not. ... While there may be a *prima facie* case in relation to unjust enrichment or potentially a remedy under the Family Law (Scotland) Act 2006 s 28, there is no room to infer the existence of a trust from the circumstances in the absence of some averment of there being a declaration of trust. ... The decision does not appear to cohere with the established principles of the Scots law of trusts.

The law about the constitution of trusts seems unsatisfactory in more than one way. Suppose that the pursuer had averred that the defender had agreed to transfer the two properties to him when he so requested. There would have immediately been the problem that an agreement to transfer heritable property must be in writing. No doubt that is why he averred a trust. But the paradox is that a trust is a more powerful arrangement than a mere agreement, for it affects third parties such as creditors. And yet our law says that the *greater* the effect the *less* is required to create that effect. The law is in a muddle.

Finally, there is evidently considerable tension between this case and the next, in which, though the facts were somewhat different, the Lord Ordinary took an approach nearer to that of the sheriff than to that of the sheriff principal.

(65) Johnston's Tr v Baird
[2012] CSOH 117, 2012 GWD 25-514

Like the previous case, this was a case in which it was argued that a trust existed as between cohabitants, not on the basis of express agreement, but on the basis of implication. Indeed, the case for an implied trust was stronger than in the previous case, because there was a written agreement. X and Y were cohabitants, X owning the house. They split up. X sold the house and paid half the proceeds to Y. Soon thereafter X was sequestrated, and his trustee in sequestration sued Y for the return of the money, on the basis that the payment had been a gratuitous alienation made by someone insolvent.

About 18 months after the property was originally bought, X and Y had entered into a formal cohabitation agreement:

1.1 The home is a property purchased in the sole name of the first party for convenience.

1.2 The parties agree that the home shall be owned by the parties in equal shares.

Clauses 6 and 7 are not quoted in the case but are summarised by the Lord Ordinary (Uist) thus (para 3):

> Clause 6 said that the agreement would terminate in the event of the death or marriage of either party or their separation. Clause 7.1 provided that, in the event of termination other than as a result of the death of either party, the home would be sold and the proceeds divided between the parties in the proportions provided in Clause 1.

Clause 8 provided:

> In the event of termination as a result of the death of either party, the following transitional provisions shall apply. In the event of this agreement being terminated as a result of the death of the first party, unless otherwise provided in a will, the second party shall have the right to remain living in the home for three calendar months from the date of such death and shall vacate the home upon the expiry of the third calendar month to enable the home to be dealt with by the first party's personal representatives as they shall see fit.

In his defence to the action, Y pled that this agreement created a trust, under which X owned the property, but owned 50% in trust for Y. Y also pled that the payment had been for adequate consideration. The case was continued in relation to the second defence, to allow a proof. But the first defence – that there was a trust – was dismissed. The first and most obvious point to note about the agreement is that it says nothing about 'trust'. It does say that the property is 'owned by the parties in equal shares'. That cannot be read literally because, as every law student knows, the only way that X could have made Y a 50% owner would have been by registered disposition. Might the 'ownership' provision be interpreted creatively as meaning that although X was sole owner, he held in trust for himself and Y?

The Lord Ordinary referred to *Clark Taylor & Co Ltd v Quality Site Development (Edinburgh) Ltd* 1981 SC 111, and continued (para 14):

> [O]n no conceivable view could it be said that the Cohabitation Agreement established a trust granted by the debtor in favour of the defender of a one half *pro indiviso* share in the home. The full requirements of the test for the establishment of a trust set out by Lord President Emslie in *Clark Taylor and Quality Site Development (Edinburgh) Ltd* are simply not met. It is notable that the submission for the defender made no reference to these requirements. In my opinion the Cohabitation Agreement, properly construed, created in the defender only personal rights enforceable against the debtor. The first requirement mentioned by Lord President Emslie, namely, that there must be in existence an asset, is clearly satisfied as the asset in this case was a one half *pro indiviso* share of the home. The second requirement, that there must be a dedication of the asset or right to defined trust purposes, is, in my opinion, not satisfied. Neither is the third requirement that there be a beneficiary with defined rights in the trust estate nor the fourth requirement, that there must be delivery of the trust deed or subject of the trust or a sufficient and satisfactory equivalent to delivery, so as to achieve irrevocably divestiture of the truster and investiture of the trustee in the trust estate. While it may be arguable that the signature of the

defender on the Cohabitation Agreement amounted to a satisfactory equivalent to delivery, I fail to see how irrevocable divestiture of the truster and investiture of the trustee in the trust estate could be said to have been achieved.

The pursuer also argued that clause 8, which contemplated X being able to deal with the property by testament, was inconsistent with a trust, but the Lord Ordinary did not base his decision on this argument.

Although not dealing with heritable property, another 2012 case, *Rangers Football Club plc, Ptr* [2012] CSOH 95, 2012 SLT 1156 is worth mentioning as also illustrating the reluctance of the Scottish courts to recognise implied trusts.

(66) Gow v Grant
[2012] UKSC 29, 2012 SLT 829

Though not a conveyancing case, this Supreme Court decision may be of some interest to conveyancers. Mr Grant and Mrs Gow owned their own properties and were both in employment. They met and began to cohabit. She moved in with him and sold her house. The money was spent partly in paying off her debts and partly on joint living expenses. After a time she gave up work. Later they separated and she sued him under s 28 of the Family Law (Scotland) Act 2006.

The sheriff awarded Mrs Gow £39,500 for the 'economic disadvantage' she had suffered because it had been her house that had been sold and because, if she had not sold it, its value would have increased. The defender appealed, and the Inner House reversed the decision. The pursuer in turn appealed to the Supreme Court, which allowed the appeal and reinstated the decision made at first instance.

We will not discuss the decision in detail, since the area belongs to family law, though we cannot resist quoting Fiona Sasan's interesting observation: 'I do wonder whether, as is entirely possible in the current climate, if Mr Grant's property value had dropped during the period of cohabitation and Mrs Gow had wisely preserved her sale proceeds in a savings account, Mr Grant would have been able to ask for an award from Mrs Gow on the basis of fairness!' ('Cohabitees and the principle of fairness' (2012) 57 *Journal of the Law Society of Scotland* Aug/5.)

SOLICITORS AND SURVEYORS

(67) Phimister v D M Hall LLP
[2012] CSOH 169, [2013] PNLR 6, 2012 GWD 35-720

Mr Phimister was interested in buying an old farmhouse with outbuildings and some ground at Puttingbrae, Drybridge, Buckie, Aberdeenshire. He had plans to develop it. He instructed a mortgage valuation from D M Hall LLP. After receiving the valuation (£230,000) he concluded missives and settled the bargain at £240,000. On taking possession he found that the site was not large enough for the development that he had had in mind. He sued the surveyor, on the basis that the mortgage valuation report had said: 'It is understood that the entire site extends to approximately 1.12 acres', a figure which had come from the seller's sales particulars. The pursuer argued that the defender should have noticed the discrepancy and have mentioned it in the report, and that the defender's failure to do so had caused him loss.

The action failed. The Lord Ordinary (Glennie) **held:** (i) 'The language used in the report ('it is understood that …') makes it clear that the surveyor's understanding of the area of the site comes not from his own measurement but from elsewhere. … If the pursuer believed that the report was confirming the size of the site – and I have no reason to doubt that he was telling the truth on this matter – he was mistaken in that belief, and obviously so. He had no reasonable basis for so believing' (para 20). (ii) In any event, the valuation (£230,000) had been a reasonable one and accordingly there had been no loss. The pursuer 'might not have been able to develop it [the property] as he wished but, on the evidence, he could have sold it on without loss, since that was its market value' (para 28).

The decision convinces. The pursuer could see with his own eyes what he was buying and it is hard to see how he could have relied, in relation to the boundaries of the property, on the terms of the valuation report. (It emerges at para 15 that 'the title deeds … gave the true area of the site', but did so in metric measure, and the pursuer 'did not know how to convert hectares to acres'. We abstain from comment.) Whether he considered a claim against the seller based on misrepresentation is not disclosed, though any such claim would also have been problematic.

(68) Credential Jersey Ltd v DLA Piper Scotland LLP
[2012] CSOH 96, 2012 GWD 23-458

The pursuer sought damages of about £4.6 million against the defender for alleged conveyancing negligence. At this stage of the litigation the facts are unclear, but seemingly the pursuer held a commercial property portfolio through a trust. It proposed to sell all or part of this portfolio, but the sale fell through because of an alleged title problem for which the defender was said to be responsible. There was a dispute between the parties as to whether the proposed sale was by the pursuer, in relation to its beneficial interest under the trust, or by the trust, or perhaps by both. There seems also to have been disagreement as to whether the defender had been instructed by the pursuer or by the trust or by both. The defender's attempt to have the action dismissed failed, and proof before answer was allowed.

(69) Cheshire Mortgage Corporation Ltd v Grandison
[2012] CSIH 66, [2013] PNLR 3, 2012 GWD 30-609

This decision (in which this case was taken together with the next case) affirmed the decision of the Lord Ordinary: [2011] CSOH 157, 2012 SLT 672, *Conveyancing*

2011 Case (69). In outline the facts were that a fraudster impersonated the owner of a house, and raised money by granting a standard security over it, forging the signature of the real owner. The lender later sued the law firm that had acted for the fraudster. See **Commentary** p 150.

(70) Blemain Finance Ltd v Balfour & Manson LLP
[2012] CSIH 66, [2013] PNLR 3, 2012 GWD 30-609

This decision (in which this case was taken together with the previous case) affirms the decision of the Lord Ordinary: [2011] CSOH 157, 2012 SLT 672, *Conveyancing 2011* Case (70). The facts were essentially the same as in the previous case. See **Commentary** p 150.

(71) Wyatt v Crate
[2012] CSOH 197

The pursuers instructed a sole practitioner, Mr Crate, to put in an offer to buy a house in West Kilbride, Ayrshire, the price being £160,000. This offer, dated 6 March 2007, received a qualified acceptance dated 23 March 2007. On 17 April Mr Crate sent a letter concluding the bargain. The transaction later settled. Thus far, thus ordinary. (A few days after conclusion of missives, Mr Crate died. To what extent this may have played a part in the story is unclear. Presumably the conveyancing transaction was taken over by another firm. In the present action the defenders were the executors.) The problem was that Mr Crate, or his staff, had failed to communicate in sufficient detail the terms of the qualified acceptance of 23 March. The pursuers said that if they had known in detail of its terms they would not have concluded missives, at least on those terms. (What precisely the letter of 23 March said is not disclosed. It may be that warranties of physical quality were excluded.) Before the present case the Law Society had investigated and had concluded that there had been inadequate professional service. It had ordered that the fee should be waived, and that compensation of £600 should be paid. But the pursuers were not satisfied. They sought damages of £38,747.27. This sum represented various repair works carried out on the property.

The Lord Ordinary (Boyd of Duncansby) dismissed the action. In the first place, the pursuers' written pleadings were insufficiently specific as to how the failure to explain to the pursuers the terms of the qualified acceptance resulted in the need for the repair works (para 43).

> [A]ll that the pursuers have provided is a schedule of expenditure with no attempt to relate these to any of the conditions or modifications thereto in the missives. The pursuers do not offer to prove that any of the items of expenditure in the schedule arose as a result of the deletion of a condition of the offer contained in the qualified acceptance of 23 March. In the absence of such averments there is nothing to demonstrate how any of these items of expenditure flow from the firm's alleged breach of duty.

Secondly, by the time that the pursuers proceeded to settle the transaction, they did know the terms of the qualified acceptance. '[I]t seems to me to be clear, if not self-evident, that where a principal decides to ratify a contract made without his authority but wishes to maintain his rights against the agent he must make his position clear at the time of ratification. If he does not then the presumption must be that he has exonerated the agent' (para 30).

Because the action was dismissed, the defence suggestion that what had happened was simply that the pursuers had bought a property for £160,000 that was in fact worth £160,000, and so had suffered no actual loss, was not explored.

BOUNDARIES, FENCES AND PRESCRIPTION

(72) Smith v Crombie
[2012] CSOH 52, 2012 GWD 16-331

The pursuer and the defenders owned neighbouring houses in Sixth Street, Newtongrange, Midlothian. When the pursuer, then aged 90, left for a holiday in Blackpool, the defenders – even as the car bearing the pursuer was being driven away – began to take down the boundary fence between the properties. A rear extension was then built which, if the fence marked the true boundary, encroached on the pursuer's property. In this action the pursuer sought the removal of the alleged encroachment.

Both houses, which had previously been rented, were feued in the mid-1980s. The properties were described by a verbal description and a plan. Neither was satisfactory. The former described each property as being bounded by the other; the plans were based on the OS map but, it was agreed by both parties, were inaccurate. Both properties were still held on Sasine titles.

Following a proof, the Lord Ordinary (Matthews) found (i) that the true boundary was a line drawn perpendicularly from the centre of the party wall, (ii) that the fence had been in the wrong place, having encroached into the defenders' property, (iii) that, making such use of the plan as its unintelligible nature allowed, the pursuer's title was not *habile* to allow him to acquire the encroached-on strip by prescription, and accordingly (iv) that the defenders' extension was built wholly on their own land and did not encroach on the pursuer's property. The defenders were assoilzied.

It is hard to comment on this decision without having seen the titles and heard the evidence. For the court to have ignored, by and large, the written titles and to have substituted a boundary line of its own choosing, the plans must have been virtually unusable. The finding on prescription is perhaps a little surprising. If the plans were difficult to interpret, then it must follow that they could be read in more than one way. And provided the pursuer's possession was consistent with a *possible* reading of the plans – even if that reading was not the best one or even especially plausible – then the title would indeed have been *habile* for the purposes of prescription.

(73) Corrie v Craig
2013 GWD 1-55, Sh Ct

The pursuer sought (i) payment of one half of the cost of erecting a dry-stane dyke on the common boundary with the defenders' farm and (ii) an order for an expert to draw up proposals for the repair or erection of a dyke on another section of the boundary and for apportionment of the cost. The application in respect of (i) was based on unjustified enrichment and in respect of (ii) on the March Dykes Act 1661. After a proof, both applications were refused. In relation to (i), while, it was held, an action lay in unjustified enrichment, the pursuer's claim was based on the cost to him of making the wall and not, as it ought to be on the gain to the defenders which resulted. In relation to (ii), an ordinary stock-proof fence was already in place and there was no basis for replacing it with an expensive dry-stane dyke. See **Commentary** p 155.

DILIGENCE

(74) Playfair Investments Ltd v McElvogue
[2012] CSOH 148, 2013 SLT 225

This was an important decision about the interaction between inhibitions and missives. See **Commentary** p 123.

COMMON GOOD

(75) Portobello Park Action Group Association v The City of Edinburgh Council
[2012] CSOH 38, 2012 SLT 944 rev [2012] CSIH 69, 2012 SLT 1137

This was a major decision on that obscure but far from insignificant subject, the law of common good. It was **held** that the City of Edinburgh Council had no power to appropriate part of a public park in the Portobello area of Edinburgh to build a new school. See **Commentary** p 172.

PART II

STATUTORY DEVELOPMENTS

STATUTORY DEVELOPMENTS

Scotland Act 2012 (c 11)

From a conveyancing point of view, the most important change in the new Scotland Act is the prospective disapplication to Scotland of stamp duty land tax (s 29), and the nomination of tax on transactions involving interests in land as a 'devolved tax' (s 28, adding a new part 4A chapter 3 to the Scotland Act 1998). It is now for the Scottish Parliament to provide a replacement for SDLT, and a Land and Building Transactions Tax (Scotland) Bill has been introduced by the Scottish Government. See **Commentary** p 177 and also Isobel d'Inverno, 'Taxes heading north' (2012) 57 *Journal of the Law Society of Scotland* Oct/16.

Bringing the law into line with practice, the Scottish Executive is now officially re-named the Scottish Government, and the Scotland Act 1998 is amended accordingly (s 12). Another change worth mentioning is that, in future, one of the Crown Estate Commissioners is to have special responsibility for Scotland, and 'must be a person who knows about conditions in Scotland as they relate to the functions of the Commissioners' (s 18, inserting a new para 1(3A) into sch 1 to the Crown Estate Act 1961).

Finance Act 2012 (c 14)

Minor amendments to Stamp Duty Land Tax are contained in ss 212–217. See **Commentary** p 178.

Land Registration etc (Scotland) Act 2012 (asp 5)

This important and substantial Act re-casts the law of land registration and replaces the Land Registration (Scotland) Act 1979. See **Commentary** p 105. A number of incidental provisions came into force on 11 July 2012 and a few more, as a result of the **Land Registration etc (Scotland) Act 2012 (Commencement No 1) Order 2012, SSI 2012/265**, on 1 November 2012. Otherwise the Act is not yet in force.

Agricultural Holdings (Amendment) (Scotland) Act 2012 (asp 6)

This short Act completes the minor amendments to the Agricultural Holdings (Scotland) Acts 1991 and 2003 which were begun by the Public Services Reform (Agricultural Holdings) (Scotland) Order 2011, SSI 2011/232 (for which see

Conveyancing 2011 p 57). The Act extends the definition of 'near relative' in sch 2 part III of the 1991 Act to allow grandchildren to succeed to tenancies (s 1). It also nullifies any term in a limited duration tenancy which provides for upwards-only or landlord-only rent reviews (s 2), although (s 4(2)) the change is prospective only. These changes are discussed by Colin Clark in an article published at p 57 of the *Journal of the Law Society* for June 2011. The Act came into force on 12 September 2012 (s 5(2)).

As, however, Alasdair G Fox notes in the September 2012 issue of the *Journal* (p 28):

> the process is not to end there. The Government has made it plain that it wishes to see a vibrant tenanted sector in Scotland and that it has high expectations of stakeholders and, in particular, landlords to deliver this. It has committed itself to a further review of the Agricultural Holdings (Scotland) Acts before the end of the current administration and will, if it considers it necessary, legislate to provide the framework before the next election.

As a first step, the Tenant Farming Forum ('TFF') appointed a group to review s 13 (rent variation) of the Agricultural Holdings (Scotland) Act 1991, giving it the unenviable task of trying to reconcile the views of landlords' interests (which prefer the existing process, based primarily on evidence of comparable lettings) with those of tenants' interests (which would assess rent on the basis of the productivity of the holding). Its report, issued on 28 November 2012 (www.tenantfarmingforum.org.uk/tff/pubs.aspx), recommended leaving s 13 in its present form while attempting to improve the operation of the existing rent review formula in light of the clarification provided in the Moonzie decision (ie *Morrison-Low v Paterson's Exrs* [2012] CSIH 10, 2012 SC 373). Other issues on the TFF's agenda include improvements, waygoing compensation, repairs and renewals, diversification, succession and assignation. As Alasdair Fox concludes, '[i]t is not difficult to think of many other matters which, coupled with those already enacted in 2011 and 2012, would make it more sensible to tear up the 1991 and 2003 Acts and start again, hopefully with something much less complicated, less prescriptive, more relevant to the second decade of the 21st century, and in a single Act'.

Long Leases (Scotland) Act 2012 (asp 9)

This Act provides for the automatic conversion of ultra-long leases into ownership on a date to be appointed, but with the possibility of opt-outs. A lease qualifies if it is registered, has a term of more than 175 years, and has an unexpired duration of more than 175 years (or, in the case of a dwelling house, 100 years) (s 1). See **Commentary** p 132. The Act is not yet in force.

Money Laundering (Amendment) Regulations 2012, SI 2012/2298

The 2012 Regulations make a series of amendments to the Money Laundering Regulations 2007, SI 2007/2157 (for which see *Conveyancing 2007* pp 48–49), with effect from 1 October 2012. There is nothing here that will make any difference to how money-laundering checks are handled on a day-to-day basis, although it may be noted that 'a person, when he prepares a home report' is exempt from the Money Laundering Regulations (2007 Regulations reg 4(1)(f), substituted by the 2012 Regulations reg 4).

More change is on the way. A *Report on the application of Directive 2005/60/EC on the prevention of the use of the financial system for the purpose of money laundering and terrorist financing*, COM(2012) 168 final, was adopted by the European Commission in April 2012. This contains an examination of the current, third anti-money laundering Directive and concludes that, although the existing framework appears to work well, some modifications are necessary to adapt to the evolving threats posed. A fourth anti-money laundering Directive is expected by the end of 2013, which will lead in turn to revised Money Laundering Regulations.

Meanwhile in a Chamber judgment by the European Court of Human Rights in the case of *Michaud v France* (application no 12323/11; www.echr.coe.int), it was held unanimously on 6 December 2012 that the (EU-derived) obligation on French lawyers to report their suspicions regarding possible money laundering activities by their clients does not violate the ECHR Article 8 right to respect for private life or interfere disproportionately with legal professional privilege.

Crofting Register

In this series we do not cover crofting law, but nevertheless mention major changes. The commencement of the Crofting Register, on St Andrew's Day 2012, is such a change. Established by part 2 of the Crofting Reform (Scotland) Act 2010, the Crofting Register will gradually supersede the existing Register of Crofts kept by the Crofting Commission. This will be the first map-based system of recording croft land and associated rights. As well as crofts, the Register also covers common grazings and land held runrig. There are currently around 18,000 crofts. The register is free to view online, and can be accessed direct on www.crofts.ros.gov.uk/register.

The Register is maintained electronically, and each croft has its own 'registration schedule' (the equivalent of a title sheet) with its own 'alpha-numeric identifier'. The first croft to be registered is to be C1, the second C2, and so on. The first common grazing or land held runrig to be registered is to be CG1, the second CG2, and so on. In addition to showing the boundaries of crofts, common grazings and land held runrig against the OS map, the Register also contains information on the tenant or owner-occupier crofter on the land as well as the landlord and/or landowner of the registered land.

Registration in the Crofting Register, whether for the first time or subsequently, depends on certain trigger events which, in the main, relate to actions requiring a regulatory application to the Crofting Commission for approval to change some aspect of the croft land, such as an application to assign or divide a croft (ss 4 and 5). However, during the first year of the Register the triggers do not apply and registration is voluntary. To encourage such voluntary registration, there is a modest discount of £20 on the registration fee of £90 for groups of ten or more crofters who submit community applications during this initial period: see the **Crofting Register (Fees) (Scotland) Order 2012, SSI 2012/295** amended by the **Crofting Register (Fees) (Scotland) Amendment Order 2012, SSI 2012/328**.

Applications for registration are made to the Crofting Commission (s 7(1)) and then passed on to the Keeper of the Registers of Scotland, who maintains the Register. In most cases an applicant for first registration must, on receipt of the certificate of registration, give public notice of the registration by placing an advertisement, for two consecutive weeks, in a local newspaper circulating in the area where the croft is situated, and affixing a conspicuous notice in the prescribed form to a part of the croft. The form of notice is prescribed by the **Crofting Register (Notice of First Registration) (Scotland) Order 2012 SSI 2012/296**.

As there is often limited documentary evidence supporting the extent of and interests in a croft, common grazings or land held runrig, s 14 of the Act allows first registrations to be challenged in the Scottish Land Court for an initial nine-month period.

Registration does not transfer ownership: on the contrary the transfer of ownership of the croft – or, where the croft is not owner-occupied, of the land on which the croft is situated – is itself a trigger event for registration. An owner-occupied croft is transferred by transfer of the land on which the croft is situated, which in turn requires registration in the Land or Sasine Register in the usual way. See the **Crofting Register (Transfer of Ownership) (Scotland) Regulations 2012, SSI 2012/297**, reg 2.

The provisions of the Crofting Reform (Scotland) Act 2010 are supplemented by the **Crofting Register (Scotland) Rules 2012, SSI 2012/294** as amended by the **Crofting Register (Scotland) Amendment Rules 2012, SSI 2012/327**.

Property Factors (Scotland) Act 2011

The Property Factors (Scotland) Act 2011 seeks to do three main things. In the first place it sets up a public register of property factors for the estimated 140–200 factors (including local authorities and housing associations) currently in business. Registration is essential for continuing in that business: it is an offence for an unregistered person to operate as a property factor. The main provisions are in the Act with some supplementary requirements in the **Property Factors (Registration) (Scotland) Regulations 2012, SSI 2012/181**.

Secondly, the Act provides for a Code of Conduct, to be prepared by the Scottish Ministers (s 13). This has now been done, following consultation: see the **Property Factors (Code of Conduct) (Scotland) Order 2012, SSI 2012/217**, and, for the Code itself, www.scotland.gov.uk/Publications/2012/07/6791/0.

Finally, there is a new system of dispute resolution by application to the homeowner housing panel (in effect the same body, but with a different name, as the private rented housing panel).The rules can be found in the **Homeowner Housing Panel (Applications and Decisions) (Scotland) Regulations 2012, SSI 2012/180**.

For further details about the Act, see *Conveyancing 2011* pp 109–16, and see also Grant Hunter, 'Factoring in good practice' (2012) 57 *Journal of the Law Society of Scotland* Nov/40. Useful links can be found at www.scotland. gov.uk/Topics/Built-Environment/Housing/privateowners/property factors/ 2011Act. For the most part the Act came into force on 1 October 2012 (s 33(2)), but the provisions on registration (with some exceptions) came into force earlier, on 1 July 2012: see the **Property Factors (Scotland) Act 2011 (Commencement No 2 and Transitional) Order 2012, SSI 2012/149**.

A minor amendment to the Act is made by the **Property Factors (Scotland) Act 2011 (Modification) Order 2012, SSI 2012/269**. This gives the Scottish Ministers discretion to keep off the Register certain private information relating to conviction of offences involving fraud or other dishonesty, violence or drugs, and certain other matters.

Energy Performance of Buildings (Scotland) Regulations

The Energy Performance of Buildings (Scotland) Regulations 2008, SSI 2008/309, transposed in part the Energy Performance of Buildings Directive (Directive 2002/91/EC): see *Conveyancing 2008* pp 47–48. Among other things, the Regulations introduced a requirement for buildings to have an energy performance certificate which must be made available to prospective buyers and tenants. Partly in response to a new directive, Directive 2010/31/EU on the energy performance of buildings, the 2008 Regulations were amended three times in 2012: see (i) the **Energy Performance of Buildings (Scotland) Amendment Regulations 2012, SSI 2012/190**, (ii) the **Energy Performance of Buildings (Scotland) Amendment (No 2) Regulations 2012, SSI 2012/208**, and (iii) the **Energy Performance of Buildings (Scotland) Amendment (No 3) Regulations 2012, SSI 2012/315**.

The amendments range from the trivial to the quite important. Of importance to conveyancers is the new reg 5A, inserted by SSI 2012/208 reg 6, which provides that as from 9 January 2013 'where a building or building unit is offered for sale or let, the owner of the building or building unit must ensure that any advertisement in commercial media offering the building or building unit for sale or let, as the case may be, states the energy performance indicator for that building or building unit'. An energy performance indicator is defined (reg 2(1), as now amended) as 'an indication of the energy efficiency or performance rating of a building or building unit calculated using the methodology approved in accordance with regulation 7 and expressed on a scale of A to G (with G representing the lowest rating)'. As one might expect, 'advertisement in commercial media' includes advertising in newspapers and on the internet (reg 5A(3)).

Changes are also made to the energy performance certificate. Already it contains recommendations for improving energy performance. Since 1 October 2012 this must be supplemented by a statement that more detailed information on the cost effectiveness of the recommendations is contained in a separate recommendations report (reg 6(1)(ca), inserted by SSI 2012/190 reg 5).

Registration of residential private landlords

Subject to some exceptions, private landlords must register with the local authority before they let a house. The rules are contained in part 8 of the Antisocial Behaviour etc (Scotland) Act 2004 supplemented by the Private Landlord Registration (Information and Fees) (Scotland) Regulations 2005, SSI 2005/558 and by part 1 of the Private Rented Housing (Scotland) Act 2011. For details see *Conveyancing 2004* pp 92–95 and *Conveyancing 2011* pp 53–54. Much of part 1 of the 2011 Act is not yet in force, but s 1 was commenced on 1 July 2012 by the **Private Rented Housing (Scotland) Act 2011 (Commencement No 3) Order 2012, SSI 2012/150**. Section 1 amends the list of factors, in s 85 of the 2004 Act, to which a local authority is to have regard in deciding whether the applicant is a 'fit and proper person to act as a landlord'. This now includes convictions for firearms and sexual offences, as well as matters related to property maintenance and control of antisocial behaviour. Consequential changes are made to the 2005 Regulations by the **Private Landlord Registration (Information and Fees) (Scotland) Amendment Regulations 2012, SSI 2012/151**.

Re-named conservation body

Conservation bodies are bodies which are able to create and hold conservation burdens under s 38 of the Title Conditions (Scotland) Act 2003. A conservation burden is a personal real burden which preserves or protects the natural or built environment for the benefit of the public. The first list of conservation bodies, prescribed by the Title Conditions (Scotland) Act 2003 (Conservation Bodies) Order 2003, SSI 2003/453, was amended by the Title Conditions (Scotland) Act 2003 (Conservation Bodies) Amendment Order 2004, SSI 2004/400, the Title Conditions (Scotland) Act 2003 (Conservation Bodies) Amendment Order 2006, SSI 2006/110, the Title Conditions (Scotland) Act 2003 (Conservation Bodies) Amendment (No 2) Order 2006, SSI 2006/130, the Title Conditions (Scotland) Act 2003 (Conservation Bodies) Amendment Order 2007, SSI 2007/533, and the Title Conditions (Scotland) Act 2003 (Conservation Bodies) Amendment Order 2008, SSI 2008/217. The **Title Conditions (Scotland) Act 2003 (Conservation Bodies) Amendment Order 2012, SSI 2012/30** does not add any new bodies but acknowledges the change of name of an existing body from 'The Trustees of the New Lanark Conservation Trust' to 'New Lanark Trust'. The complete list of conservation bodies is now:

All local authorities
Aberdeen City Heritage Trust
Alba Conservation Trust
Castles of Scotland Preservation Trust
Dundee Historic Environment Trust
Edinburgh World Heritage Trust
Glasgow Building Preservation Trust
Glasgow City Heritage Trust
Highlands Buildings Preservation Trust

Inverness City Heritage Trust
New Lanark Trust
Plantlife – The Wild-Plant Conservation Charity
Scottish Natural Heritage
Sir Henry Wade's Pilmuir Trust
Solway Heritage
St Vincent Crescent Preservation Trust
Stirling City Heritage Trust
Strathclyde Building Preservation Trust
Tayside Building Preservation Trust
The John Muir Trust
The National Trust for Scotland for Places of Historic Interest or Natural Beauty
The Royal Society for the Protection of Birds
The Scottish Wildlife Trust
The Trustees of the Landmark Trust
The Woodland Trust
United Kingdom Historic Building Preservation Trust

PART III
OTHERMATERIAL

OTHER MATERIAL

High Hedges (Scotland) Bill

The issue of high hedges has been a constant – one might even say a thorny – presence in or around the Scottish Parliament almost since the first moment of devolution. An initial proposal for legislation was lodged, by Scott Barrie MSP, as long ago as May 2002. Two further proposals, in 2003 and 2006, were equally unsuccessful. A pressure group, Scothedge (www.scothedge.colwat. com), was formed with a membership of more than 200, and campaigners were heartened by the passing of legislation on the topic in England and Wales (the Antisocial Behaviour Act 2003 part 8), the Isle of Man (Tree and High Hedges Act 2005) and, most recently, Northern Ireland (High Hedges Act (Northern Ireland) 2011). A public consultation by the Scottish Government in 2009, following on from a much earlier consultation in 2000, showed strong support for legislation. (See *Conveyancing 2009* pp 71–72.) The present Bill is the result. It is a member's Bill, introduced on 2 October 2012 by Mark McDonald MSP, but with Government support. The Bill has been making slow progress through the legislative procedure, Stage 1 being completed on 28 January 2013. But, given Government support, it will presumably reach the statute book in the course of 2013.

Hedges are, of course, usually blameless and to be welcomed. But, beyond a certain height, they can block a neighbour's light and views and, in some cases, be an instrument of war. In recent years the problem has been exacerbated by the planting of fast-growing species such as the Leyland cypress (*Cupressocyparis leylandii*) which can grow at a rate of a metre a year and can reach heights of 30 metres.

A 'high hedge' under the Bill (s 1(1)) is one which

(a) is formed wholly or mainly by a row of 2 or more evergreen or semi-evergreen trees or shrubs,

(b) rises to a height of more than 2 metres above ground level, and

(c) forms a barrier to light.

Single trees or shrubs are thus excluded even where they block out the light, presumably on the basis that the Bill should not move in the direction of introducing a general right to light. There is no requirement that the hedge should be on the boundary. There might be a question as to whether two adjacent tall trees situated elsewhere might not fall within the definition – and, if so, whether that is really what is intended.

The Bill confers protection only on owners or occupiers of a 'domestic property' (s 2(1)) and the chosen mechanism is public law rather than the private law typically associated with neighbourhood disputes (nuisance, encroachment, common interest, real burdens, and servitudes). A person aggrieved by a neighbour's hedge must first take 'all reasonable steps to resolve the matters in relation to the high hedge' (s 3(1)), which presumably refers to negotiation rather than clandestine destruction. The experience in England and Wales has been that the threat of taking matters further is usually sufficient to produce action on the part of the neighbour (*High Hedges (Scotland) Bill: Policy Memorandum* paras 35–37).

If negotiation fails, an application is made to the local authority (s 2), which intimates the application to the neighbour and allows 28 days for representations (s 6). The local authority must then decide 'whether the height of the high hedge adversely affects the enjoyment of the domestic property which an occupant of that property could reasonably expect to have' (s 6(5)). In reaching this decision the local authority must have regard to all the circumstances of the case, including the effect of the hedge on the amenity of the area and whether the hedge is of cultural or historical importance (s 6(7)). If it is persuaded by the application, the local authority issues a 'high hedge notice' (s 8), which binds the owner – as opposed to the occupier – of the neighbouring property. Successors are equally bound, which may suggest that a new provision will be needed in missives (s 9). There is a right of appeal, within 28 days, to the Scottish Ministers (s 12). If the notice is not complied with, the authority can arrange for the work to be carried out and the cost recovered from the owner (ss 22–25). Successors must also pay provided the local authority registers a 'notice of liability for expenses' in the Land or Sasine Register (ss 26 and 27), a device which is evidently modelled on the equivalent notices in the Title Conditions (Scotland) Act 2003 s 10A and the Tenements (Scotland) Act 2004 s 12. But presumably matters will rarely reach this point, and such notices are likely to be uncommon.

Land and Buildings Transaction Tax (Scotland) Bill

The Scotland Act 2012 devolves to the Scottish Parliament the right to levy taxes on transactions involving land. The plan is that on 1 April 2015 stamp duty land tax will be replaced by a new Scottish equivalent with the (hardly catchy but soon to be familiar), name of 'land and buildings transaction tax' (LBTT). A consultation paper, *Taking forward a Scottish Land and Buildings Transaction Tax* (www.scotland.gov.uk/Publications/2012/06/1301), was published by the Scottish Government on 7 June 2012 and an *Analysis of Responses* on 1 November 2012. A Bill to legislate for the tax, the Land and Buildings Transaction Tax (Scotland) Bill, was introduced to the Scottish Parliament on 29 November 2012. At 70 sections and 18 schedules (so far), the Bill is neither short nor simple. The new tax, as might be expected, bears a close resemblance to SDLT, but there are important differences, the most significant of which is the replacement of the 'slab' structure of the latter by a series of thresholds so that, rather like income tax, it is only the consideration *above* a particular threshold which attracts the higher rate. See **Commentary** p 177. A further Bill, likely to be called the Tax Management Bill, is set to be introduced in 2013 and will provide the nuts and bolts of tax administration for all devolved taxes including LBTT.

Draft Companies Act 2006 (Amendment of Part 25) Regulations

Cynics say that the motto of the old DTI and its successor, the DBIS, is 'on your marks, get set, stop!' The Companies Act 2006 (Amendment of Part 25) Regulations were supposed to have been in place in 2011, and then in 2012, and even now are, at the time of writing, only in draft form (see www.bis.gov.uk/ assets/biscore/business-law/docs/c/12-1025-companies-act-amendment-part-25-regulations-draft). But for many months the commencement date has been announced as being 6 April 2013, so perhaps something is now going to happen.

Part 25 of the Companies Act 2006 sets out the rules for the registration of company charges, such as standard securities granted by companies. In broad terms these provisions are much the same as the provisions in the Companies Act 1985 (part XII), but there are a number of changes, one of which is that the entire system can be altered by statutory instrument (s 894). This draft statutory instrument would repeal most of part 25, and replace it with new provisions, inserted by amendment into the 2006 Act. One organisational change worth noting is that in the past the English and the Scottish provisions have been separate; the proposed legislation would result in a single set of provisions. There are also draft Limited Liability Partnerships (Application of Companies Act 2006) (Amendment) Regulations which would apply the new regime to LLPs, also from 6 April 2013.

The new rules would not bring about major changes for conveyancing in Scotland. Standard securities would continue to need to be registered in the Companies Register, as well as in the Land or Sasine Register, on pain of nullity. The period, as under current law, would be 21 days from registration in the Land or Sasine Register. Petitions for late registration would continue to be possible.

Finally, it is worth noting that part 2 of the Bankruptcy and Diligence etc (Scotland) Act 2007 would set up a new system for registering floating charges, but it has yet to come into force.

Registers of Scotland

Mapping

In *A report on mapping in the Land Register,* published in December 2011 (www. ros.gov.uk/pdfs/mapping_in_the_land_register_in_scotland.pdf), Registers of Scotland sets out certain past policies and future plans in relation to mapping. There is, for example, a helpful account of the way in which the regular digital updates received from Ordnance Survey are used to refresh individual title plans but without, it is stressed, affecting the registered legal extent (para 10). When the Land Registration etc (Scotland) Act 2012 comes into force, this will be a statutory duty (s 11(7)). OS updates maps on a five-year cycle using methods (on-site surveys with Global Navigation Satellite System technology or aerial photography) that can potentially deliver absolute positional accuracy of around ±0.1 m. This compares with the ±0.4 m and ±1.1 m of the scales used in the Land Register for, respectively, urban areas (scale: 1:1,250) and rural areas (scale 1:2,500).

Mountain and moorland are surveyed by OS on a much smaller scale (1:10,000) which achieves an accuracy of only ±4.0 m. Problems occur where it is necessary to register, and therefore map, a building or other similar feature in an area mapped as mountain or moorland. RoS policy is to have the feature re-surveyed on a larger scale (para 30). The position will improve in the future as OS upgrades its mapping of these areas and uses a larger scale for pockets which are rural rather than mountain or moorland.

Where a plan drawn to a scale larger than the OS map accompanies an application for registration or rectification, the Keeper is generally reluctant to include it on the title sheet. This is because it may 'create an inaccuracy when considering an existing adjoining Land Register registered title involving a smaller-scale plan' (para 25). The report continues, not without a dash of drama (para 26):

> [T]he knock-on effect of accepting such plans and conveying real rights on registration would be enormous. The effect would be to create a confusing picture of legal title on the cadastral map allowing the creation of competing titles and gaps in title all over the country. The usurped titles that currently have real rights to land would lead to widespread litigation and indemnity claims against the Keeper. Such a solution would, in all likelihood, have significant resource implications for Registers of Scotland.

A persistent concern is discrepancies between legal and occupational boundaries. It is, says the report, for solicitors to ensure that any plan submitted accords with the former. Otherwise solicitors might be in breach of the new obligation, in s 111(3) of the 2012 Act, to 'take reasonable care to ensure that the Keeper does not inadvertently make the register inaccurate'. Those who breach this duty 'may become liable to the Keeper for the cost of corrective conveyancing, rectification, and compensation' (para 38).

Deed plan criteria

A new publication from Registers of Scotland, *Deed Plan Criteria: A guide for conveyancers and other legal professionals* (www.ros.gov.uk/pdfs/dpc.pdf), provides guidance on how plans should be drawn up, and gives helpful examples of best practice to be adopted when preparing such documents. The five key principles are (p 7):

(1) The scale of the Deed Plan must be appropriate to the scale of the Ordnance Survey Map.

(2) The scale and orientation must be displayed on the Deed Plan.

(3) The Deed Plan must contain sufficient surrounding detail to enable the position of the subjects to be fixed.

(4) The boundaries of the subjects must be clearly shown, preferably with measurements.

(5) References on the Deed Plan must be clearly identifiable

RoS warns that '[a]ny newly prepared plan that does not adhere to the guidelines in the DPC may not be accepted for registration purposes' (p 6). Part 4 gives examples of commonly submitted plans that do not meet the required criteria.

In the majority of applications to the Land Register digital data are not required. However, in applications that cover a large area of ground, or contain complex plotting on to the OS map, digital data are welcome, allowing the Keeper to combine digital plans within the systems used to support the Land Register (p 24).

Coverage

Land Register coverage rose from 21.18% of the land mass in June 2011 to 23.33% a year later, the largest annual increase for several years. Some 56.03% of all properties are now on the Register. For further details see Registers of Scotland's *Land Mass Coverage Report 2012* (www.ros.gov.uk/pdfs/landmasscoveragereport2012.pdf). Once it is in force, the Land Registration etc (Scotland) Act 2012 s 48 will increase the rate of coverage by closing off the Register of Sasines to dispositions, leases and, eventually, standard securities and other deeds, while s 29 will allow the Keeper to register unregistered land on her own initiative and even in the face of the owner's opposition.

Halving of rejection rates

A fee of £30 for the rejection of an application was introduced on 10 January 2011. In its first year of operation, RoS reports that rejection rates have fallen by 50% (see p 9 of the *Journal of the Law Society of Scotland* for February 2012). Most rejections are connected with the application form, the registration fee, or a combination of both.

Discounted prices for new-build houses

Since 1 September 2008 solicitors acting for purchasers of new-build houses have had to disclose any incentives offered by seller-developers which would otherwise mask the actual price paid by the client. (See *Conveyancing 2008* pp 66–67 and *Conveyancing 2011* p 72.) In a note which appeared in the *Journal of the Law Society of Scotland* in February 2012 (p 9), RoS expresses the view that the price given in the application form, and disposition, should be the actual price and not, for example, the headline price at which the house was advertised.

Northern Rock plc: change of name to Virgin Money plc

With effect from 12 October 2012 Northern Rock plc (company number 6952311) changed its name to Virgin Money plc. RoS advises as follows (www.ros.gov.uk/public/news/northernrock_to_virgin_name_change.html):

Land Register

Standard Securities executed before 12 October 2012

Any standard security granted in favour of Northern Rock plc executed before 12 October 2012 but submitted as part of an application for registration on or after that date may be accepted if the application form specifies Virgin Money plc as the applicant. The Certificate of Incorporation on Change of Name does not require to be produced with any application, but the Keeper would expect it to be listed on Form 4.

Discharges executed before 12 October 2012

Discharges executed on behalf of Northern Rock plc must be executed before 12 October 2012. They can be accepted for registration after that date.

Standard securities and discharges executed on or after 12 October 2012

On or after 12 October 2012, no standard security or discharge should be granted in favour of or by Northern Rock plc. Any such deeds submitted for registration will be rejected at intake.

General Register of Sasines

Standard securities executed before 12 October 2012

Any standard security granted in favour of Northern Rock plc before 12 October 2012 but presented for recording on or after that date may be accepted if the Sasine Application Form specifies Virgin Money plc as the applicant.

Discharges executed before the 12 October 2012

Discharges executed on behalf of Northern Rock plc must be executed before 12 October 2012. They can be accepted for recording after that date.

Standard securities and discharges executed on or after 12 October 2012

On or after 12 October 2012, no standard security or discharge should be granted in favour of or by Northern Rock plc. If any such deed is presented for recording, it will be rejected.

To this may be added that the original Northern Rock plc was itself split in 2009 into (i) the original company (company number 3273685), renamed as Northern Rock (Asset Management) plc and (ii) a new company (company number 6952311) which, confusingly, was given the name of the old, ie Northern Rock plc and is now (since 12 October 2012) called Virgin Money plc. (See further *Conveyancing 2009* pp 58–59.) Many but not all standard securities were assigned to the new company (ie to what is now Virgin Money). In obtaining a discharge it will be necessary to have care that it is granted by the correct creditor.

FOI and statutory notices

In some previous years we have noted cases in which the Scottish Information Commissioner, acting on the basis of the Freedom of Information (Scotland) Act 2002, has ordered local authorities to release details of statutory notices within their area to organisations such as Miller & Bryce. See *Conveyancing 2007* pp 62–64 and *Conveyancing 2008* pp 72–73. Decision 060/2012 is another such case. Miller & Bryce made 53 separate requests to Dundee City Council, each in respect of notices under a separate Act. See www.itspublicknowledge.info/applicationsanddecisions/Decisions/2012/20110082.asp. The Council's defence was the usual one, namely that disclosure would or would be likely to prejudice substantially the Council's commercial interests because the information could be used by competitors, such as Millar & Bryce, to provide property enquiry certificates (2002 Act s 33(1)(b)). The Commissioner, however, was not persuaded that disclosure would of itself create such substantial prejudice. Further, insofar as the requests dealt with environmental information, she found that the Council had not made out a defence under reg 10(5)(e) (commercial confidentiality) of the Environmental Information (Scotland) Regulations 2004, SSI 2004/520, and so must disclose under reg 5.

SPCs and alternative web portals

For a number of years now the internet has been chipping away at the competitive advantage which a local presence gives to Solicitors Property Centres. In a combative article in the September 2012 issue of the *Journal of the Law Society* (p 5), Malcolm Cannon, the CEO of the ESPC and chairperson of SPC Scotland, extols the virtues of SPCs and cautions against competitors offering alternative web portals. On average, a property on espc.com will be viewed over 500 times in the first week it goes online, and the website has more than 650,000 visits a month. By contrast, if the 'shiny packaging' is stripped away, the likes of Zoopla, Rightmove and s1homes

> offer a lot less than an SPC. They can be more expensive for the solicitor, push their own conveyancing lawyers, and some recommend and offer a service which cuts out the selling agent altogether. I do not believe that any solicitor estate agent wants a future dominated by these players, stealing their core business from under their nose.

The issues, however, are far from straightforward, as Sally Swinney notes in an online response:

> I would agree. However when you are continually losing clients to non-solicitor estate agents because you don't offer Rightmove or the other portals, you can only accept that for so long. It might be true that advertising on dozens of internet portals isn't the best way to advertise but the public don't always see it that way. More is good as far as they are concerned, in my experience. The biggest difference about these portals is they have national advertising campaigns which bring them much more to the public's knowledge than the SPCs. The more they advertise, the more the public will wish to advertise on them.
>
> ESPC is far more expensive than advertising on Rightmove; it is easier to download the properties onto Rightmove. Our clients simply were not prepared to pay for home report, marketing fee and then the ESPC fee when Rightmove and many of the other portals offer advertising for a much lower fee. In order for solicitors to use ESPC it has to compete with Rightmove and all of the other portals. Quite simply it and the

other SPCs do not. Until they do solicitors like us will have no alternative but to use these portals.

Property sales and consumer protection

On 13 September 2012 the Office of Fair Trading published a 66-page *Guidance on Property Sales*, OFT 1364 (www.oft.gov.uk/shared_oft/estate-agents/OFT1364. pdf), explaining the application to this sector of the Consumer Protection from Unfair Trading Regulations 2008, SI 2008/1277 (which transposed the Unfair Commercial Practices Directive, 2005/29/EC) and the Business Protection from Misleading Marketing Regulations 2008, SI 2008/1276 (which transposed the Misleading and Comparative Advertising Directive, 2006 /114/EC). These important Regulations, in force since May 2008, have largely superseded the Property Misdescriptions Act 1991, which is now to be repealed. They mark a shift from the detailed rules of the Act to a set of general principles of a kind which require the new *Guidance* to explicate. The *Guidance* is aimed at all property sales businesses, from estate agents and property developers to intermediate websites that facilitate contact between buyers and sellers. The rules on misleading omissions in the provision of information seem particularly important. The executive summary:

> The CPRs and BPRs ('the regulations') are in force and property sales businesses ('you') are expected to comply with them. The regulations have broad coverage and the way they impact on your business will depend on the particular services you offer. Key aspects of the legislation are set out below. If you treat your consumers, business customers and competitors fairly, then you are unlikely to breach the regulations. However, if you treat them unfairly, you may face criminal or civil enforcement action.
> The CPRs prohibit you from engaging in unfair commercial practices when you deal with consumers:
>
> - 'Consumers' are individuals who are acting for purposes outside their business. This goes further than just your actual or prospective clients or actual property buyers. For example, if you are acting for a seller, 'consumers' also includes potential buyers or even potential viewers of the property.
> - 'Commercial practices' covers the whole range of your business activities that may affect consumers, for example your practices when you advertise your services, offer pre-agreement advice to a client, describe property for sale, negotiate and make sales, and handle complaints about your conduct.
> - 'Unfairness' may arise from:
>   - giving false or misleading information to consumers ('misleading actions') or
>   - hiding or failing to provide material information to consumers ('misleading omissions'), or
>   - exerting undue pressure on consumers ('aggressive practices'), or
>   - not acting with the standard of care and skill that is in accordance with honest market practice and in good faith (failing to show professional diligence), or
>   - engaging in one of the 'banned practices'. Examples include displaying a trust mark (such as a logo) without authorisation and claiming falsely to be a member of a professional body or an approved redress scheme, when you are not.

Apart from the banned practices (which are banned outright), these breaches have a threshold: the commercial practice will be unfair if it affects or is likely to affect the transactional decision making of the average consumer.

- 'Transactional decision' is defined widely and is not simply a consumer's decision to use your services or not, or to buy a property or not. It could, for example, be a client's decision to accept an offer, or a buyer's decision to view a property, commission a survey or instruct a conveyancer.

- The 'average consumer' is someone who is reasonably well-informed, and reasonably observant and circumspect. For example, an average consumer would pay some attention to documentation given to them, but not necessarily to the small print unless key points in it are brought to their attention. An average consumer would check out publicly available facts for themselves where this is straightforward to do, although what checks they actually make will be influenced by the information that you have given them.

- The important question is whether your act or omission is likely to have an impact on the average consumer, not an actual consumer (who may be more or less well-informed, observant or circumspect than the average one).

The CPRs' prohibition on misleading actions is very similar to the prohibi-tion on making false or misleading statements provided by the Property Misdescriptions Act 1991. The CPRs' prohibition on misleading omissions places an additional duty on you: to provide the 'material information' that the average consumer needs, according to the context, to make an informed transactional decision.

- The average consumer who is thinking of signing a contract with you is likely to need to know such things as: what services you will provide, your fees and charges, your terms of business, and any tie-in period.

- The average consumer who is considering whether to view a property is likely to need to know, as a minimum: the asking price, location, number and size of rooms, and whether the property is freehold or leasehold.

- In the most straightforward sales, the material information that you should give to potential buyers may be quite basic (little more than the information described in the bullet above). However, depending on the circumstances of each sale, material facts could include the length of the lease, the level of charges payable under a lease, uncertainties known about title, major structural defects, lack of connection to mains services, etc.

- At the outset of the marketing process, you are not expected to research issues that are outside your line of business, for example, where your business is marketing property and the issues are ones that a surveyor or conveyancer would investigate. However, should you become aware of such information later on, you cannot ignore or suppress it. If the information is material, you will need to disclose it.

The BPRs prohibit you from engaging in misleading activities in your dealings with other businesses. Your advertising to attract new clients is covered as well as your advertising of property for sale. The BPRs also set out the conditions under which you are allowed to make comparisons with your competitors.

To satisfy your obligations under the CPRs and BPRs, you need to treat consumers, business customers and competitors fairly. It will help if you can show that you act diligently, in keeping with any professional standards and taking reasonable steps to avoid committing a breach. For example

- You take care in gathering and presenting the information that you will use to advertise your services and market property.

- You have systems and safeguards in place to ensure that your marketing information is accurate, balanced and does not leave out material facts.

- When you see or hear something that puts you on notice that there might be a problem, you take reasonable steps to establish the facts for yourself. For example, you ask questions, carry out your own checks and/or consult official sources, as necessary.

- You act promptly to correct or update your marketing and to pass on information whenever new information becomes available.

- Where you have exhausted the steps that you can reasonably be expected to take, you are open about any remaining gaps in your knowledge.

Missives chains

At one time the 'chains' that bedevil the sale of houses in England were almost unknown in Scotland. That is no longer so. In a study on *Home Buying and Selling* published in 2010 the Office of Fair Trading found, from an admittedly small sample, that 21% of sellers in Scotland said they were in a chain as compared to 46% in England (see para 8.26). The blame, according to Ian Ferguson and Paul Carnan, writing in the *Journal of the Law Society* in September 2012 (p 31), lies partly with slow lending decisions and partly with the recession-driven shift from buying first to selling first. They give the following example of a chain:

> A purchaser (P1) cannot conclude missives with the seller (S1) because P1 has no offer of loan. S1 cannot enter missives for purchase with S2 till his sale to P1 is concluded and S1's offer of loan issued, and so on up the chain.

In cases like this, not even standard missives can do much to help.

Home reports: ESPC consumer survey

In March 2012 the Edinburgh Solicitors Property Centre published the results of a survey of the views on home reports of 295 consumers who had bought, sold, or attempted to sell a property since December 2008, when home reports were first introduced (www.espc.com/news-events/news/home-reports-what-the-public-think). Most buyers found home reports helpful, though not essential. Sellers, as might be expected, were less enthusiastic, with 65% describing home reports as not helpful to them as sellers. One third of buyers finished up instructing a survey of their own.

Figures for house sales

Scottish property sales for July–September 2012 were at the lowest level for the time of year since official records began in 2003, according to Registers of Scotland (www.ros.gov.uk/public/news/quarterly_statistics.html). The total of 19,868 properties sold was 2.1% below the same period last year, and less than half that when the market was at its peak in 2007–08. The average price of a home in Scotland also dropped by 2.3%, to £159,310.

New FSA rules for mortgage lending

On 25 October 2012 the Financial Services Authority announced new rules for mortgage lending which are designed to 'hard-wire common sense into the mortgage market' and move away from the 'poor practices of the past' when affordability to borrowers was not sufficiently verified. The new rules come into force on 26 April 2014. They are summarised by the FSA as follows (www.fsa. gov.uk/library/communication/pr/2012/098.shtml):

- **All customers** – all customers will need to satisfy lenders that they can afford the mortgage, and provide evidence of their income. Most mortgage sales will require advice, particularly interactive sales (such as face-to-face or telephone sales). The new rules do not prevent higher loan-to-value lending, and interest-only will be allowed if the borrower can show that they have a credible repayment strategy.

- **First time buyers** – the new rules do not prevent higher loan to value mortgages being offered.

- **Existing borrowers that cannot meet the new affordability requirements** – lenders can 'switch off' the affordability and interest-only requirements for existing borrowers who want to get a new mortgage for the same amount or less. While any lending decision is a commercial one, lenders will also be able to use these arrangements to take on the customers of other lenders. Lenders will, with immediate effect, be prevented from treating these customers less favourably than other customers.

- **Older consumers** – the new rules do not apply any age limits or prevent lending to older consumers, including beyond retirement.

- **Self-employed** – the new rules give lenders flexibility to decide what type of evidence of income to accept from self-employed customers.

- **Entrepreneurs (ie business people borrowing against their homes)** – a flexible approach applies and these borrowers will be able to secure a mortgage on an execution-only basis providing they confirm they are happy to 'opt out' of the suitability tests. Lenders must see a credible business plan before providing a mortgage.

- **Right-to-buy** – customers who are exercising their right-to-buy will always be required to get mortgage advice.

- **Shared equity** – customers who are also getting a second charge shared equity loan to assist in their property purchase will need to be able to afford the payments on the shared equity loan as well as their mortgage.

- **Credit-impaired borrowers** – our rules do not prevent customers with an impaired credit history from getting a mortgage, as long as they can afford it. Where they are consolidating debt they must get advice.

- **High net worth customers** – a flexible approach applies and these borrowers will be able to secure a mortgage on an execution-only basis providing they confirm they are happy to 'opt out' of the suitability tests.

Full details can be found at www.fsa.gov.uk/library/policy/policy/2012/12-16. shtml.

Buildmark online

On 30 October 2012 the NHBC launched a new online system for the acceptance of Buildmark cover. According to the NHBC website (www.nhbc.co.uk), it works in this way. On registering a plot with the NHBC the builder-developer is sent a policy number and an activation code which is then passed on to the solicitor acting for the buyer. The solicitor accesses his or her secure account on the acceptance portal and, using the policy number and activation code, accesses the Buildmark details of the plot. On being notified as to completion, the NHBC validates the completion information and makes the insurance certificate available to download. Perceived benefits of the new system:

- Conveyancers can easily and quickly check that a home has the benefit of cover before conclusion of missives.
- Builders will no longer have to store and send out acceptance packs.
- Conveyancers can easily check and print Buildmark warranty information: insurance certificates, CML cover notes, policy endorsements, warranty status, and policy documents.
- All plot and site changes will be updated by NHBC without the need to return paperwork.
- In the event that there is a problem with cover (eg if cover is not available because a builder is no longer registered with NHBC), that information will be available to view immediately.

SDLT: apportionment of price

HM Revenue and Customs (HMRC) has warned recently that 'where HMRC find property sale arrangements that have been artificially structured to avoid paying the correct amount of SDLT, these will be actively challenged, through the courts where appropriate. If HMRC is successful in challenging an SDLT arrangement entered into with the sole intent of avoiding the amount of SDLT properly payable, purchasers could be liable to pay the whole of the SDLT plus interest and potentially a penalty'. See www.lawscot.org.uk/members/member-services/professional-practice/professional-practice-updates/2012/may-2012. Solicitors who knowingly provide information in support of an incorrect tax return are liable to a penalty of £3,000 per submission, and to having their papers inspected in relation to *any* client. Although the issue arises mainly when acting for a buyer, it can also arise when acting for a seller.

The background law is in the Finance Act 2003 sch 4 para 4(1) which requires any apportionment between heritage and moveables in the price paid for a property to be done 'on a just and reasonable basis'. As Deborah Lovell of the Law Society's Property Committee explains ((2012) 57 *Journal of the Law Society of Scotland* May/38), HMRC is likely to look very closely at those apportionments which have the effect of reducing the percentage band of SDLT payable or indeed those that bring the price attributable to the heritage within the nil rate threshold.

Orsman v Revenue and Customs Commissioners [2012] UKFTT 227 (TC) is a recent example from England. Miss Orsman paid £250,000 for a house and a large number of items left behind by the previous owner. The contract of sale specified a purchase price of £250,000 and a 'chattels price' of £8,000. Attached to the contract was a list of fixtures and fittings. As well as items which were plainly not part of the land, such as fridges and washing machines, this also included some fitted items. The Revenue decided to investigate the SDLT return. A period of argument and negotiation followed at the end of which the Revenue issued a notice amending the SDLT return and assessing the chargeable consideration at £250,000 plus an additional £800 in respect of a worktop attached to the wall of the garage and the fitted units beneath it. This increased the SDLT payable from £2,500 to £7,524. On appeal the First-Tier Tribunal Tax Chamber upheld the Revenue's decision, and expressed the view that some of the other fitted items should also be regarded as 'land'.

For Scotland this issue will substantially disappear when, on 1 April 2015, SDLT is replaced by land and buildings transaction tax (LBTT), which will levy higher rates of tax only in respect of that amount of the consideration which exceeds the relevant threshold.

Lenders' conveyancing panels

In general

The trend for lenders to cut their panels of law firms continued in 2012. As Peter Nicholson points out ('Between a rock and a hard place' (2012) 57 *Journal of the Law Society of Scotland* Feb/11), this is partly a response to pressure from the Financial Services Authority, which regards the open-panel system as a major contributor to mortgage fraud and negligence cases. The extensive form-filling which is often now required to join or stay on a panel can also be seen in this light. Be that as it may, the consequences are potentially serious both for borrowers and, especially, for solicitors. For the former, it cuts down choice. For the latter, the fact that the same firm usually acts, in residential transactions, for both lender and buyer (a topic discussed further below) means that a failure to be included on the panel of a particular lender will exclude the firm from acting in any purchase for which that lender is providing the money. As lenders often have regard to the volume of business in deciding who should remain on their panel, small firms are particularly at risk.

Individual lenders

Both the *RBS* and the *Clydesdale Bank* have maintained an extensive panel but the latter, in an ongoing spat with the Law Society of Scotland, will not allow borrowers to instruct a non-panel solicitor for the purchase. Instead, a panel solicitor (in practice the same one) must act in both the purchase and the loan. This is because, the Law Society having criticised (on good grounds) a plan to extend to Scotland the procedure for separate representation used in England and Wales, the Clydesdale says that it is unable to agree a suitable alternative procedure for Scotland. See (2012) 57 *Journal of the Law Society of Scotland* Dec/41.

A similar spat with *HSBC* was resolved relatively quickly: see (2012) 57 *Journal of the Law Society of Scotland* Feb/13 and April/32. But while HSBC will thus allow a non-panel solicitor to be used for the purchase (though not the loan), the borrower is then faced with an additional fee of £160 + VAT for the bank's legal costs in respect of the security. This is all the more serious because, in January 2012, HSBC announced that its Scottish panel was being cut to a mere four firms, although two more are believed likely to join them and HSBC advises that other firms which meet its criteria can apply for membership. HSBC, however, has only around 1% of the mortgage market in Scotland.

Nationwide is in the process of cutting its Scottish panel from 700 to 500, and those firms which are spared are having to provide extensive information about themselves as part of a 'revalidation exercise'. In addition, Nationwide is undertaking a 'dormancy' exercise which involves dropping all firms which have not carried out any new security work during the past year (but subject to a right of appeal). In future (again subject to a right of appeal), Nationwide will operate a minimum volume threshold by which firms will be suspended from the panel if they have carried out fewer than four transactions within the past year.

Lloyds Banking Group attempted a 'dormancy' exercise in 2010 but abandoned it in the face of strong opposition, not least from the Law Society and the Scottish Law Agents Society: see *Conveyancing 2010* pp 70–71. All firms on the panel are having to complete a lengthy form. In another change of policy, LBG has now agreed to release title deeds to any firm involved in a sale or remortgage whether or not a member of the panel.

Lender requests for solicitors' files

The April 2012 edition of the *Journal of the Law Society* contains the following note (at p 33):

> Senior counsel's opinion has been taken by the Society, through the Professional Practice Committee, on requests by lenders to see solicitors' files relating to loan transactions where the borrower has defaulted. This is most likely in order to look

for evidence of non-compliance with the lender's instructions, contained in the *CML Handbook* or otherwise, with a view to bringing a claim against the solicitor.

The resulting guidance can be found in Section E, Division B of the consolidated Rules and Guidance on the Society's website.

In brief, if the *CML Handbook* or *BSA Mortgage Instructions* do not apply, counsel's view is that no implied authority exists by which the borrower is held to grant the lender permission to receive, or even to see, the underlying legal material which belongs to the borrower and the contents of which are confidential to him. These consist of documents concerned with the conclusion of the contract of sale and the transfer of the property, though the lender should be informed about matters relating to the purchase which may affect its position.

The standard instructions, where they apply, cannot detract from the borrower's property rights and contain nothing that amounts to a contractual permission (still less obligation) that the solicitor disclose the whole file to the lender.

Where the borrower client has consented to release, however, the solicitor is obliged to allow the bank to see the whole contents of the file, apart from those documents that belong to the solicitor. Such waiver by the client of the right to confidentiality must be 'voluntary, informed and unequivocal'. The solicitor must carefully consider the terms of any arrangement said to embody or imply borrower consent, and also ensure that no material is disclosed which does not fall within the ambit of that consent.

Separate representation for lenders and borrowers

The current excitement about separate representation for lenders and borrowers can probably be traced back to an article by Ian C Ferguson, a Council member of the Scottish Law Agents Society, which appeared in the *Scottish Law Gazette* in 2011 (p 60). The article attacks (among other exceptions) the exception to the rules on conflict of interest (Consolidated Practice Rules r 2.1.4(f)) by which the same solicitor can, and usually does, act for both lender and buyer in a residential purchase. Since then, separate representation has replaced home reports as the topic of the moment. Following a motion from the Scottish Law Agents Society at the Law Society AGM in May 2012, a Separate Representation Working Party was set up under the chairmanship of Ross MacKay and is taking views from the profession and other interested parties.

This (apparently) sudden interest in separate representation appears to have two main causes. One is alarm about the way in which lenders' panels are shrinking (see above), with the result that those excluded from acting for a particular lender are also, by and large, excluded from acting in purchases which that lender is financing. The other is a recognition that the increasingly burdensome duties heaped on solicitors by lenders are making it harder to represent both lender and buyer without risk of a conflict of interest, or indeed of being sued.

So, should the exception be abolished, and joint representation of buyer and lender prohibited? The arguments on both sides are well known: the difficulty is how much weight each should be given, and that in turn is likely to depend on the particular interest – solicitor, consumer, lender – of the person who is consulted. In favour of change are the removal of conflict of interest and a reduction in the number of claims against the Master Policy arising from breach of loan instructions. Against it is the additional expense to the borrower, and the possible delay and disruption in the transaction especially if the two solicitors take different views.

Predictably, lenders are opposed to the change: see the views of the Council of Mortgage Lenders expressed at www.cml.org.uk/cml/publications/ newsandviews/117/438. So too, one assumes, are bodies representing the consumer interest. Within the solicitors' profession itself there is considerable diversity of opinion, as Peter Nicholson charts in an article in the *Journal of the Law Society* in February 2012 (p 11). Among other helpful contributions to the debate, mention should be made of articles by Ken Swinton ((2012) 80 *Scottish Law Gazette* 41) and by Stewart Brymer (http://bit.ly/OQ1k2a). If joint representation can be demonstrated as positively dangerous from a professional point of view, then banning it would be a sensible outcome. Otherwise there is much to be said for leaving matters to the market, with borrowers and solicitors, between them or separately, deciding how they want to proceed. After all, there is (usually) nothing to prevent separate representation if that is what is wanted.

Fraud

Examples of typical mortgage fraud were given in *Conveyancing 2011* p 75. Some more examples of fraud (not confined to mortgages), and how to detect it, follow (and see also p 142 below).

Identity fraud and property URNs

In the April 2012 issue of the *Journal of the Law Society*, Morna Grandison of the Law Society's Interventions Department advocates looking at unique reference numbers (URNs) when checking identity documents. Issued by Ordnance Survey as a unique identifier for every property in the country, URNs are increasingly appearing on government and utility company documentation. So if, say, a utility bill and a council tax bill for the same property address show different URN references, one of the documents may be a forgery. (On URNs more generally, see an article by Stewart Brymer published at (2012) 118 *Greens Property Law Bulletin* 6.)

Revolving deposit schemes

In the same article, Morna Grandison warns that:

> Revolving deposit schemes/rebate schemes are currently one of the main issues affecting the mortgage fraud landscape. These schemes involve an introducer, or company, who approaches a distressed seller, claiming to have access to a large number of potential buyers. The seller then agrees to sell the property to an individual who is known only to the introducer, for a price that may be in excess of the property's current valuation. In advance of the deal, the seller must agree that part of the sale

price, perhaps tens of thousands of pounds, will immediately be transferred to the introducer on settlement.

However, the seller, along with his or her solicitor, may be unaware that the fee paid to the introducer is being passed to the purchaser as a deposit for the property purchase, hence the revolving deposit. Often false or manipulated valuations are employed, which ultimately results in the purchaser having 100% lending on the property, without the lender's knowledge. Solicitors who encounter clients engaging in such schemes should immediately contact the Society's Professional Practice Department for advice. Even when acting for the seller in these cases, your firm could be involved in handling the proceeds of crime.

Distressed property sales

The Financial Services Authority (FSA) has issued a Consumer Alert in relation to the following scam (www.fsa.gov.uk/consumerinformation/product_news/mortgages/distressed-property-sales). A person in financial difficulties agrees to sell his house at a discount in exchange for an immediate sale. The discount is often around 20% and can be as much as 35% below the market value of the property. The offer may include a promise to complete the deal within as little as 48 hours, pay the sum in cash, help to avoid legal and estate agent fees, and guarantee the sale. The buyer then asks the seller to state that the property is being sold for the full market value, thus allowing the buyer to borrow the full amount he has agreed to pay for the property from a lender.

Miscellaneous warning signs

Writing in the *Journal of the Law Society* for May 2012 (p 35), James McCann, Chairman of the Legal Defence Union, lists the following as warning signs in the particular context of prevention of money-laundering:

- A single source stream of similar business eg from a debt distress website, or introduced by a local entrepreneur, fixer, or 'gombeen man'.
- Discounted or back-to-back transactions, or any transaction where there has been agreement on price other than finding a true market value through the familiar sequence of marketing, closing date, competitive offers leading to missives, etc. This can be described as 'the already engaged couple' syndrome, ie any situation where the transacting parties come to you with a done deal, with an apparently inappropriate advantage to one or other, or to the intermediary, that would not appear in an arm's-length contract.
- Unusual flexibility, such as sudden change or substitution of a borrower or buyer under missives, suggesting the individual is a stooge for the mastermind who is making the vast profit.
- Any instructions about funds which are not moving in the normal way – that means, when purchasing property, anything other than the traditional large loan from mortgage lender, and small deposit from buyer's own funds. Any suggestion that a substantial deposit is already paid, and will therefore not be coming through your hands, should be viewed most sceptically – even if shown in a state for settlement from a supposedly blue chip firm. If there is a batch of high-tariff buy and sells, are you supposed to believe that the intermediary buying

(say) 10 properties for £150,000 each net, funded by an expensive commercial loan limited to £1.5 million, has already, somehow, funded 10 x £70,000 payments to account against a top line price of £240,000 each, upon which borrowing will ensue?

- Think when paying out. … Any payment to a third party, outside the obvious and normal, should cause you to think. Consider putting in your terms of business that you will not pay to anyone other than the client. It is obvious from these cases that the selling solicitor's health and happiness is on the line too, not just the buyer's agent who has to think about CML conditions. Why would any *bona fide* house-seller want to give most or all of the free proceeds to someone else? How can you say you are looking after the selling clients where a huge chunk of their very scarce equity is going to a fixer who has done nothing for them?

- That 'clear' title. Think about the supposedly clear title, when selling. Why not in effect 'moneylaunder', ie check the history of what you are selling in the same way you would check the cash to buy? How did the client, perhaps quite young, come to own an unburdened property worth several hundred thousand pounds? Insist on checking out, and vouching, any story received. For example: client produces deeds with clear title and you sell. Searches show security discharged some time before. However, after you pay out it is revealed, on a plaintive enquiry from a lender, that a forged discharge went on to the record while the scamster continued to pay the monthly instalments. Or the sale of a title shown clear in the searches, but the day your cheque to the client for the sale proceeds is cashed, and while your purchasing colleague is still awaiting the SDLT form to register the deeds, another solicitor belatedly sticks a standard security on the register, for a loan originally drawn down to buy the property you have just sold. These things have happened.

Social housing: ending the right to buy?

Hitherto tenants holding a Scottish secure tenancy from a social landlord have usually had some form of right-to-buy (RTB) entitlement. This allowed them to purchase the property they were renting at a discount. The level of discount varied and depended primarily on the length of time they had rented property from a social landlord and the type of RTB entitlement they had. There are two forms of RTB entitlement: (i) 'preserved', for tenancies starting before 30 September 2002, and (ii) 'modernised', for tenancies starting on or after 30 September 2002. 'Preserved' RTB entitlements have more generous discounts than those under 'modernised' RTB terms. The main provisions are found in part III of the Housing (Scotland) Act 1987, and in particular in s 61.

Since its introduction RTB has resulted in the sale of about half a million properties. That means that more properties have been lost from social rented stock than have been built – a depletion of social housing stock which, the Government has concluded, is unsustainable in the face of continued high levels of demand. Accordingly, with effect from 2 March 2011, and subject to some exceptions, part 14 of the Housing (Scotland) Act 2010 brought the right to buy to an end for new tenants and also for existing tenants taking on the lease of a house not previously let. See *Conveyancing 2010* pp 51–52. The right to buy, however, remains for existing tenants, except in certain 'pressured areas' where it has been suspended. That may be set to change.

A consultation paper on *The Future of Right to Buy in Scotland*, published by the Scottish Government on 7 June 2012 (www.scotland.gov.uk/Publications/2012/06/7065), argues for further reform, on the following (over-lapping) grounds (para 3.5):

- We cannot justify the discounts of up to 70% for tenants with a preserved right to buy. If we keep the right to buy, we aim to move all tenants on to the more reasonable 'modernised' discount. We estimate that around 49% of tenants of local authorities have a preserved right, which works out at around 149,000 households. For tenants of registered social landlords, it is estimated to be 58,000 (22%).
- It is unfair that some tenants benefit from much larger discounts than others.
- The law in this area is too complicated and it is difficult to understand for landlords and tenants.
- The right to buy is outdated and may have no place in today's Scotland with our focus on increasing the availability of affordable housing for those who need it most.

The underlying reason, of course, is the imbalance of supply and demand in the social housing stock. Getting on for 400,000 people are on the waiting lists for social housing, and housing is also needed for some 50,000 homeless people. 'We recognise', says the Government, 'that many people want to own their own homes but we do not believe that this should be at the expense of homes in the social rented sector' (para 3.4).

The proposal is either to restrict the discounts for those holding on 'preserved' tenancies or, more radically, to abolish RTB entirely. The consultation closed on 30 August 2012. The paper makes clear (para 3.10) that there would be a lead-in time for any change, thus allowing tenants to buy their homes under the current entitlements. This is presumably for ECHR reasons.

An *Analysis of Responses to the Future of Right to Buy in Scotland Consultation* was published on 16 November 2012. Most (87%) of those providing a view considered that there should be further restrictions on the right-to-buy legis-lation. Of those who provided a view, the vast majority (83%) favoured ending RTB altogether. Should RTB end, 73% of respondents who commented favoured a notice period of two years or less.

A Strategy for the Scottish Private Rented Sector

The total number of dwellings in Scotland in March 2010 was estimated at 2,483,000, including 273,000 that were privately rented. As the table below shows, in the period since 1999, the private rented sector has more than doubled its share of the total housing stock, rising from 5% to 11%. At the same time, social housing (local authority and housing association combined) as a proportion of tenure has declined, from 32% to 23%.

Percentage breakdown of Scottish housing stock

	1999	2001	2003	2005	2007	2009	2010
Owner occupied	61	64	65	66	66	66	65
Social rented	32	28	26	25	23	22	23
Private rented	5	6	6	8	9	10	11
Other	2	2	2	2	2	2	2

Wishing to 'set out a vision and strategic aims that will grow and improve the quality of the private rented sector in Scotland over the next decade', the Scottish Government published in April 2012 a *Consultation on a Strategy for the Private Rented Sector* (www.scotland.gov.uk/Publications/2012/04/5779) (from para 1.12 of which the table above was taken). This builds on the work of the Scottish Private Rented Sector Strategy Group, chaired by Professor Douglas Robertson of Stirling University, which is made up of representatives from Shelter Scotland, the Scottish Association of Landlords, Scottish Land & Estates, the Chartered Institute of Housing, the City of Edinburgh Council, COSLA, and the Association of Local Authority Chief Housing Officers. The 'vision' proposed by the Group is: 'A thriving and professional private rented sector that offers good quality homes and high management standards; inspires consumer confidence; and encourages growth and investment to further develop and improve the sector.' And in order to achieve this vision, the consultation paper proposes three 'strategic aims' for the decade ahead (para 1.9):

1. For **growth and investment**: to increase overall housing supply, and for more investment to develop and improve the existing sector;
2. For **better quality**: of property management, condition and energy efficiency; to be enabled by smarter, more targeted regulation; and
3. For **more informed** choices: to support and encourage consumer driven improvement of the sector.

In addition, the paper identifies a number of 'strategic challenges', while recognising 'inherent tensions and trade-offs' required between some of them. The strategic challenges are (para 1.10):

1. How to bring in more investment to increase the supply of housing and to improve quality, against a backdrop of challenging and uncertain economic times.
2. How to create a regulatory framework which is effective and proportionate, sets standards to ensure quality but is affordable and does not constrain growth.
3. How to tackle the minority of landlords who act unlawfully and have a disproportionate impact on the reputation of the sector overall.
4. How to take account of and support the needs of vulnerable tenants.
5. How to ensure that the sector meets the new and growing demand for rented housing, and provides an affordable housing option.
6. How to respond to the need for better energy efficiency and property condition.
7. How to empower tenants as consumers to drive improvement in the sector.

An analysis of responses received to this paper is available at www.scotland. gov.uk/Publications/2012/10/5873/0.

Housing Statistics 2012

The headline news from *Housing Statistics for Scotland 2012: Key Trends Summary 2011–12* (www.scotland.gov.uk/Publications/2012/08/2103) is as follows:

- **New housing supply**: new housing supply (new build, refurbishment and conversions) decreased by 2% between 2010–11 and 2011–12, from 17,267 to 16,882 units. This was driven by a decrease in private completions. The number of new housing association homes completed also fell but the number of local authority new build completions increased from 614 to 1,085.
- **New house building**: In 2011–12, there were 15,900 completions in Scotland, a decrease of 3% on 16,379 in 2010–11. However starts increased by 4% from 13,543 in 2010–11 to 14,098 in 2011–12.
- **Affordable Housing**: In 2011–12 there were 6,882 units completed which were funded by the Affordable Housing Supply Programme (AHSP, formerly known as Affordable Housing Investment Programme) – this figure is 5% down on the previous year.
- **Public sector housing stock**: At 31 March 2012, there were 319,384 local authority dwellings in Scotland, a decrease of 494 from the previous year.
- **Sales of local authority dwellings**: Sales of local authority dwellings fell by 17% in 2011–12, from 1,474 to 1,124. This continues the declining trend in sales observed over recent years, following the introduction of the modernised Right to Buy, which came into effect on 30 September 2002.
- **Public sector vacant stock**: At 31 March 2012, local authorities reported 7,847 units of vacant stock, of which 36% consisted of normal letting stock. This represents 1% of all normal letting stock, and is up slightly from the previous year.
- **Lettings**: During 2011–12 there were 27,263 permanent lettings of local authority dwellings, an increase of 6% on the previous year, where the figure was revised to 25,668. Lets to homeless households represented 42% of all lets made by local authorities in 2011–12.
- **Evictions**: Eviction actions against local authority tenants resulted in 1,057 evictions or abandoned dwellings in 2011–12 (608 evictions, 449 abandoned dwellings). This is largely unchanged from the previous year.
- **Housing Lists**: Applications held on local authority lists decreased by 4% to 187,935 in 2012.
- **Houses in multiple occupation**: In 2011–12, 9,352 applications were received in respect of the mandatory licensing scheme for houses in multiple occupation. At 31 March 2012 there were 13,356 licences in force, representing a decrease of 2% over the previous year.

The report contains further statistical data on each of these topics.

Sustainable Housing Strategy for Scotland

On 25 June 2012 the Scottish Government published *Homes that don't cost the earth: a consultation on Scotland's Sustainable Housing Strategy* (www.scotland.gov.uk/

Publications/2012/06/8390). This built on five main themes which emerged from a Greener Homes Summit held in November 2011. These were:

- A national retrofit programme to tackle fuel poverty, make sure we reach the climate change milestones set for housing and enable Scottish households and businesses to get the full benefit from energy company and other investment.
- Standards – to consider the role that regulation could play, alongside incentives, in driving uptake of energy efficiency measures.
- Financial market transformation to create long-term change in perception among surveyors, lenders and consumers of the real value of low carbon, energy efficient homes.
- New build market transformation to maximise the potential of the innovative design and construction techniques being developed by Scottish companies to create greener homes and neighbourhoods, which will in turn create export and other economic opportunities.
- Skills and training to capitalise on opportunities to make Scotland a market-leader in providing and exporting low-carbon housing solutions.

Consultation closed on 28 September 2012 and consultees' responses are available at www.scotland.gov.uk/Publications/2012/10/4512/0.

Reform of law on formation of contract

The Scottish Law Commission has followed up its recent discussion paper on *Interpretation of Contract* (Scot Law Com DP No 147, 2011) with a further paper on *Formation of Contract* (Scot Law Com DP No 154, 2012). The two headline proposals are to abolish the postal rule for acceptances – so that an offer will be accepted only when the acceptance reaches the offeror – and to make clear the legal effectiveness of execution in counterpart. The Commission also asks whether there should be a comprehensive restatement by statute of the rules on formation. The consultation closed on 29 June 2012.

Land Reform Review

In July 2012 the Scottish Government announced the setting up of an independent Land Reform Review (www.scotland.gov.uk/About/Review/land-reform). A three-member Land Reform Review Group, chaired by Dr Alison Elliot, is supported by a team of outside advisers, only one of whom is a lawyer. The Review was announced in this way:

> The Scottish Government is committed to generating innovative and radical proposals on land reform that will contribute to the success of Scotland for future generations.
>
> The relationship between the land and the people of Scotland is fundamental to the wellbeing, economic success, environmental sustainability and social justice of the country. The structure of land ownership is a defining factor in that relationship: it can facilitate and promote development, but it can also hinder it. In recent years, various approaches to land reform, not least the expansion of community ownership,

have contributed positively to a more successful Scotland by assisting in the reduction of barriers to sustainable development, by strengthening communities and by giving them a greater stake in their future. The various strands of land reform that exist in Scotland provide a firm foundation for further developments.

The Government has therefore established a Land Reform Review Group. The Group will identify how land reform will:

- Enable more people in rural and urban Scotland to have a stake in the ownership, governance, management and use of land, which will lead to a greater diversity of land ownership, and ownership types, in Scotland;

- Assist with the acquisition and management of land (and also land assets) by communities, to make stronger, more resilient, and independent communities which have an even greater stake in their development;

- Generate, support, promote, and deliver new relationships between land, people, economy and environment in Scotland.

In making these inquiries, the Group will bear in mind:

- the sustainability of its proposals for reform, including their economic impact;
- the importance of good stewardship and governance of land;
- the relationship between urban and rural concerns and opportunities;
- the relationship between local and national interests.

Some idea of how these extremely general terms of reference might be interpreted is given in the call for evidence issued by the Group, and in particular in the following statement:

Our work will not be limited to consideration of existing legislation. Already our attention has been drawn to a variety of potential reforms that would, for example:

- Expand community ownership of land, housing and other assets in both town and country and in all parts of Scotland;

- Diversify and broaden ownership of land in Scotland, where more land is owned by fewer people than anywhere else in Europe;

- Encourage (or oblige legislatively) owners of land to give local communities a greater say in how land is managed and used;

- Make it easier and cheaper for Forestry Commission land and other land in public ownership to be transferred to others;

- Improve the supply and lower the price of land for affordable and other housing in both town and country;

- Help create new pathways, for younger people especially, into farming and crofting;

- Enhance the position of tenant farmers by giving them a right (similar to the right enjoyed by crofting tenants since 1976) to buy their farms;

- Replace Council Tax and Business Rates with a tax on land values;

- Change the way in which fresh water resources are owned and managed in order to secure wider community benefit from these resources;

- Change the law of succession as it affects ownership of land.

The Group emphasises, however, that these examples are listed 'to indicate the potential scope of our enquiries (and to encourage submissions under these and other headings) rather than as pointers to our thinking'.

Another task for the Group is to review the working of the Land Reform (Scotland) Act 2003 and, to that end, the Scottish Government has published an *Overview of Evidence on Land Reform in Scotland* (www.scotland.gov.uk/ Publications/2012/07/3328) which summarises the results of a number of existing studies. The findings are of considerable interest. There is said to be no appetite for reform of the rules on access rights contained in *part 1* of the Act (but see below in relation to core paths). Visits to the outdoors have remained stable since 2006 and there has been a decrease in access problems being experienced. The introduction of core paths has been popular, although lack of funds has sometimes been a problem for local authorities. The community right to buy, in *part 2* of the Act, has had only limited success. A total of 142 applications from communities led to 95 acceptances, 33 opportunities to buy (when the landowner put the property on the market), and only 11 actual purchases. The areas purchased have been generally rather small – of the 11, four were of less than two hectares and only three were over 402 hectares – and have tended to involve specific facilities or buildings. One obvious barrier – that land can only be bought if the owner chooses to sell – does not apply to the crofting community right to buy in *part 3* of the Act. Yet not a single purchase has taken place under this part, and only two crofting community bodies, both in Lewis, have made applications. (One of these applications has become mired in litigation: see *Pairc Crofters Ltd v Scottish Ministers* [2012] CSIH 96, 2013 GWD 1-42 (Case (42) above).) Research suggests that the procedure is viewed as complex and resource-intensive and, possibly, as unworkable in practice. Other problems are insufficient awareness and promotion of the provisions, lack of funding support and advice, and the perceived lack of fit between the right to buy and other recent reforms of crofting legislation and policy.

The closing date for responses to the Land Reform Review Group was 11 January 2013. The Group expects to make a first report in May 2013. A draft final report will be completed in December 2013 and a revised final report in April 2014.

Older readers may feel they have been here before. Many of the issues mentioned above were canvassed in the wide-ranging review by the Land Reform Policy Group set up in the late 1990s and chaired by Lord Sewel, then a government minister. The main legislative outcome was the Land Reform (Scotland) Act 2003. It will be interesting to see the respects in which the new Review feels able to go beyond what was recommended a decade or so ago.

Suspension of access rights over core paths

Section 11 of the Land Reform (Scotland) Act 2003 allows local authorities to suspend statutory access rights over land, typically to allow the holding of some sort of event such as a car rally or an outdoor concert. If the suspension is for six or more days the approval of the Scottish Ministers is needed. The consequence of a s 11 order is that access rights cannot be exercised over the land in question for the period in question: see s 6(1)(j). As the legislation currently stands, this suspension of rights cannot apply to core paths because s 7(1) provides that: 'Section 6 above does not prevent or restrict the exercise of access rights over any land which is a core path'. A 'core path' is one which has been identified by the local authority under s 17 as one of a system of paths 'sufficient for the purpose of giving the public reasonable access throughout their area'.

This exclusion of core paths from s 11 orders has come to seem too inflexible. In a consultation document published in October 2011 (*Land Reform (Scotland) Act 2003: Consultation on Draft Order to Permit Temporary Closures of Core Paths*) the Scottish Government argues that it may 'occasionally' be desirable to close a core path (p 2):

> For example, the Forestry Commission Scotland have a condition attached to the use of the forest estate for motor sport that requires a section 11 closure for the management of public safety. They do not want to take any risk that members of the public will seek to exercise their rights along a core path through an event area. In addition a managed closure in an orderly basis with proper advance notification can also assist those seeking to plan access to an area which is closed for a specific time bound period.

The proposal is to substitute a new version of s 7(1) which would suspend access where a s 11 order has been made in respect of a core path. However, where the order lasts for six or more days, the Scottish Ministers would have to be satisfied either that suitable alternative arrangements for access will be in place or that no such arrangements are necessary. The closing date for responses was 11 January 2012.

Thirty-seven responses were received, all but two generally favourable. They are analysed at www.scotland.gov.uk/Publications/2012/09/6958/1. The Scottish Government is now planning to consult on a revised draft Modification Order accompanied by draft guidance issued under section 27 of the 2003 Act.

Consultation on proposed Community Empowerment and Renewal Bill

The Scottish Government published *A consultation on the proposed Community Empowerment and Renewal Bill* (www.scotland.gov.uk/Publications/2012/06/7786/0) on 7 June 2012. As the name of the proposed Bill suggests, the theme is 'community empowerment'. As the paper explains (Introduction paras 11-12):

> Some communities become more empowered through owning assets, controlling budgets, or generating their own income to re-invest. In some cases, communities may want to take action to tackle anti-social problems in the community, to meet demand for new or different services or to protect a valued resource. Others will want to have an enhanced role in shaping the services delivered on their behalf by others.
>
> We have separated our ideas for this Bill into three sections. Each contains a range of ideas, from new statutory rights and duties to smaller amendments to existing

legislation, that could act as a catalyst for a wide range of community enterprise, community development and public service improvement:

- **Strengthening Participation**: Services should be built around and with people and communities – paying attention to their needs, aspirations, capacities and skills. Having the right procedures, practices and organisations in place will help deliver effective community engagement. Consistent and high standards of engagement can be achieved through ensuring appropriate methods are used by those designing and delivering services to inform, monitor, evaluate and report on engagement.

- **Unlocking Enterprising Community Development**: Communities owning assets, and being able to bring unused and underused assets in their areas back into use, can in the right circumstances be a catalyst for unlocking community empowerment, enterprise and increasing social capital.

- **Renewing our Communities**: Vacant or unused property can blight areas, create barriers to economic development, and lead to increased social costs for local authorities. Property owners can help by taking responsibility for the effect their properties have on communities. Local authorities should have the appropriate powers to step in and take action where necessary and communities can play an important role by taking action and influencing how such property is dealt with in their areas.

One idea that is floated in the paper is to introduce a community right to buy similar to the one which exists for rural communities under part 2 of the Land Reform (Scotland) Act 2003 Another is to allow communities to take on unused public-sector assets such as former schools and health centres, and to become more involved in making decisions on local budgets. Public sector authorities may be required to publish a register of their assets and asset management plans. The consultation also seeks views on giving communities the right to ask local authorities to repair dangerous buildings, and giving authorities better powers to recover the costs of repairs to these buildings. Local authorities might also be empowered to enforce the sale or lease of empty homes, where the property is causing problems for neighbours or is in poor condition, or where there is high demand for housing in the area.

The consultation closed on 29 August 2012 and drew over 400 responses. A draft Bill is expected to be published in the spring of 2013, with introduction to Parliament before the end of the year. Progress can be followed at www.scotland. gov.uk/Topics/People/engage/cer.

Land Use Strategy for Scotland

Last year the Scottish Government set out the 'Vision', 'Three Objectives' and 'Ten Principles' for 'Sustainable Land Use' which comprise its 'Land Use Strategy for Scotland'. Details of all three can be found in *Conveyancing 2011* 75–76. The public's curiosity as to how things have been going in the first year of the Strategy was satisfied by the publication, on 27 June 2012, of *Getting the best from our land. A land use strategy for Scotland. Progress Statement 2012* (www.scotland.gov.uk/ Publications/2012/06/4649).

Solar panels

Solar panels can raise a variety of issues if the property is sold – issues about title to the panels themselves, about the contracts involved and about the feed-in tariff. On the website of GreenEnergyNet (www.greenenergynet.com/) there is a useful article, written in large part by MacRoberts LLP and Brodies LLP, that explores these issues: www.greenenergynet.com/businesses/articles/independent-guide-selling-your-house-solar-pv. It may be that, in future, standard-form offers will include provisions about solar panels.

Books

W M Gordon, *Supplement to Volume 1 of Scottish Land Law* (W Green 2012; ISBN 9780414018679)

David Johnston, *Prescription and Limitation*, 2nd edn (W Green 2012; ISBN 9780414018389)

Hector MacQueen and Lord Eassie (eds), *Gloag & Henderson: The Law of Scotland*, 13th edn (W Green, 2012; ISBN 9780414018181)

Kirsty Malcolm, Fiona Kendall and Dorothy Kellas, *Cohabitation*, 2nd edn (W Green 2011; ISBN 9780414018266)

H Mostert and M J de Waal (eds), *Essays in Honour of C G van der Merwe* (LexisNexis 2012; ISBN 9780409052015) (contains chapters on Scots property law by David Carey Miller, Roderick Paisley and Lu Xu)

Kenneth G C Reid and George L Gretton, *Conveyancing 2011* (Avizandum Publishing Ltd 2011; ISBN 9781904968528)

Peter Robson, *Residential Tenancies: Private and Social Renting in Scotland*, 3rd edn (W Green 2012; ISBN 9780414018174)

Eilidh Scobbie, *Currie on Confirmation of Executors*, 9th edn (W Green 2011; ISBN 9780414014619)

Andrew Todd and Robbie Wishart, *The Lands Tribunal for Scotland: Law and Practice* (W Green 2012; ISBN 9780414018891)

No Ordinary Court: 100 Years of the Scottish Land Court (Avizandum Publishing Ltd 2012; ISBN 9781904968511)

Articles

James Aitken, 'Business rates update' (2012) 117 *Greens Property Law Bulletin* 5

Derek Allan, 'Who do you think they are?' (2012) 57 *Journal of the Law Society of Scotland* Dec/14 (considering *Cheshire Mortgage Corporation Ltd v Grandison, Blemain Finance Ltd v Balfour & Manson LLP* [2012] CSIH 66, 2012 GWD 30-609)

Jennifer Ballantyne and John King, 'Wind farms: a challenge to registration' (2012) 57 *Journal of the Law Society of Scotland* May/10

Joy Barnard, '*RBS v Wilson*: light in the tunnel?' (2012) 57 *Journal of the Law Society of Scotland* May/22

David Bartos, 'Old wine in new bottles: common good in the 21st century' 2012 SLT (News) 233 (considering *Portobello Park Action Group Association v City of Edinburgh Council* [2012] CSIH 69, 2012 SLT 1137)

Douglas Bain and Catherine Bury, '*Hunter v Tindale*: tenement disrepair?' 2012 *Juridical Review* 215 (considering *Hunter v Tindale* 2012 SLT (Sh Ct) 2)

Andrew Bothwell, 'What constitutes "reasonable endeavours"?', http://bit.ly/QZ5Yde (considering *EDI Central Ltd v National Car Parks Ltd* [2012] CSIH 6, 2012 SLT 421)

Stewart Brymer, 'Digital signatures: the myth and reality' (2012) 117 *Greens Property Law Bulletin* 1

Stewart Brymer, 'Separate representation for borrower and lender', http://bit.ly/OQ1k2a

Stewart Brymer, 'Unique property reference numbers' (2012) 118 *Greens Property Law Bulletin* 6

Stewart Brymer, 'What do clients want from the conveyancing process?' (2012) 116 *Greens Property Law Bulletin* 4

Catherine Bury and Douglas Bain, 'Mere squatters?', http://bit.ly/YpgUGw (considering *Morris v Eason* [2012] CSOH 125, 2012 GWD 27-564)

Catherine Bury and Douglas Bain, '*Nelson v Kinnaird: vigilantibus et non dormientibus jura subveniunt* down on the farm' (2012) 80 *Scottish Law Gazette* 16 (considering *Nelson v Kinnaird* 11 October 2011, Perth Sheriff Court)

Daniel J Carr, 'Not Law' (2012) 16 *Edinburgh Law Review* 410 (considering *Salvesen v Riddell* [2012] CSIH 26, 2012 SLT 633)

R Craig Connal, 'Sale of heritable property and refusal to pay – continued' 2012 SLT (News) 53 (considering *AMA (New Town) Ltd v McKenna* 2011 SLT (Sh Ct) 73)

Malcolm M Combe, 'Access rights – a letter from America' (2012) 16 *Edinburgh Law Review* 110

Malcolm M Combe, 'Human rights, limited competence and limited partnerships: *Salvesen v Riddell*' 2012 SLT (News) 193 (considering *Salvesen v Riddell* [2012] CSIH 26, 2012 SLT 633)

Malcolm M Combe, 'Rural lessons for urban conveyancing' (2012) 57 *Journal of the Law Society of Scotland* Aug/32 (considering the community right to buy and its possible extension to urban areas)

Aileen Devanny, 'The work of the Private Rented Housing Panel' (2012) 116 *Greens Property Law Bulletin* 1

D J Cusine, 'A note on repugnancy' 2012 SLT (News) 221

Andy Duncan, 'The Tenements (Scotland) Act 2004 – everybody needs good neighbours' (2012) 118 *Greens Property Law Bulletin* 3

Andy Duncan, '*Mactaggart* burdens – there's going to be a murder' (2012) 119 *Greens Property Law Bulletin* 3

Andy Duncan and James Aitken, 'Taxing lease transactions: round pegs in square holes' (2012) 120 *Scottish Law Gazette* 3

Jacqueline Fordyce, 'The plight of the landlocked proprietor' 2012 SLT (News) 243 (considering *Innellan Golf Club v Mansfield* 12 July 2012, Dunoon Sheriff Court)

Greg Gordon, 'Immunity wearing off: *Jones v Kaney* in the Supreme Court' (2012) 16 *Edinburgh Law Review* 238 (considering *Jones v Kaney* [2011] UKSC 13, [2011] 2 WLR 823)

Graeme M Henderson, 'Developments in agricultural holdings law – increased rights = increased rents?' 2012 SLT (News) 133

Grant Hunter, 'Factoring in good practice' (2012) 57 *Journal of the Law Society of Scotland* Nov/40 (considering the Property Factors (Scotland) Act 2011)

Phil Hunter and Euan Mellor, 'Leases: where next?' (2012) 57 *Journal of the Law Society of Scotland* July/32 (speculating as to whether FRI leases, already far shorter than the traditional 25 years, will survive the 'green agenda')

Isobel d'Inverno, 'Taxes heading north' (2012) 57 *Journal of the Law Society of Scotland* Oct/16

Gordon Junor, 'Division and sale: disposal *inter se*', http://bit.ly/LvwYQc

Gordon Junor, 'Never mind the reasons' (2012) 57 *Journal of the Law Society of Scotland* June/33 (considering *Persimmon Homes Ltd v Bellway Homes Ltd* [2012] CSOH 60, 2012 GWD 15-304)

Gordon Junor, '*Portobello Park Action Group Association v City of Edinburgh Council*' [2012] CSIH 69, 2012 SLT 1137)

Frances Lyall, 'Non-established church property in Scotland: the Sleat appeal' (2012) 16 *Edinburgh Law Review* 258 (considering *Moderator of the General Assembly of the Free Church of Scotland v Interim Moderator of the Congregation of Strath Free Church of Scotland (Continuing) (No 3)* [2011] CSIH 52, 2012 SC 79)

Fiona MacDonald, 'Land Registration etc (Scotland) Act 2012' (2012) 121 *Greens Property Law Bulletin* 7 (discussing advance notices)

Kenneth Mackay, 'Court of Session 2: Land Court 0' (2012) 119 *Greens Property Law Bulletin* 5 (considering *Morrison-Low v Paterson's Exrs* [2012] CSIH 10 and *Salvesen v Riddell* [2012] CSIH 26)

Kenneth Mackay and James Rust, 'Expanding the country file' (2012) 57 *Journal of the Law Society of Scotland* June/22 (considering diversification of use in rural properties)

Nick Mackay, 'Power points and positive rights' (2012) 57 *Journal of the Law Society of Scotland* Oct/32 (considering the treatment of wind protection zones in leases for wind turbines)

Angus McAllister, 'The landlord's common law repairing obligation' 2012 *Juridical Review* 263

W W McBryde and G L Gretton, 'Sale of heritable property and failure to pay' 2012 SLT (News) 17 (considering *AMA (New Town) Ltd v McKenna* 2011 SLT (Sh Ct) 73)

James McCann, 'How to avoid that Guarantee Fund interview, and worse ...' (2012) 57 *Journal of the Law Society of Scotland* May/34 (considering prevention of money laundering, and associated record-keeping)

Geoffrey D Mitchell, 'When threats are enough' (2012) 57 *Journal of the Law Society of Scotland* Dec/32 (considering *Morris v Rae* [2012] UKSC 50, 2013 SLT 88)

Peter Nicholson, 'Between a rock and a hard place' (2012) 57 *Journal of the Law Society of Scotland* Feb/11 (considering lenders' panels and separate representation for lenders)

Peter Nicholson, 'Register reborn' (2012) 57 *Journal of the Law Society of Scotland* Jan/10 (discussing the Land Registration etc (Scotland) Bill with Sheenagh Adams and Gavin Henderson)

Christopher Rae, 'Commercial to residential conversions: beware the full picture' (2012) 119 *Greens Property Law Bulletin* 1

Christopher Rae, 'Interim schedules of dilapidations: the key differences between Scotland and England' (2012) 121 *Greens Property Law Bulletin* 3

Robert Rennie, 'The 20 year rule and the McLetchie amendment' (2012) 16 *Edinburgh Law Review* 114 (considering the exemptions to the 20-year rule for residential leases introduced by the Private Rented Housing (Scotland) Act 2011 ss 36 and 37)

Robert Rennie, 'The lodge with three names: *Lubbock v Feakins*' (2012) 16 *Edinburgh Law Review* 438 (considering *Trustees of the Elliott of Harwood Trust v Feakins* 2012 GWD 10-194)

Robert Rennie, Stewart Brymer and Donald Reid, 'The end of immunity for expert witnesses?' (2012) 80 *Scottish Law Gazette* 37 (considering *Jones v Kaney* [2011] UKSC 13)

Lynn Richmond, 'Reasonableness and the Roads (Scotland) Act 1984' 2012 SLT (News) 249 (considering *Sinclair v Fife Council* 24 August 2012, Kirkcaldy Sheriff Court)

Eilidh I M Ross, 'A time to take stock – crofting law in 2012' (2012) 120 *Greens Property Law Bulletin* 5

Fiona Sasan, 'Cohabitees and the principle of fairness' (2012) 57 *Journal of the Law Society of Scotland* July/15 (discussing *Gow v Grant* [2012] UKSC 29, 2012 SLT 829)

Addi Shamash, 'Fully secure? Protecting lenders when only part of a debt has been repaid'(2012) 117 *Greens Property Law Bulletin* 4

Addi Shamash, 'The weakest link: reviewing titles connected to insolvent companies' (2012) 116 *Greens Property Law Bulletin* 3

Christine Stuart, 'Property Factors (Scotland) Act 2011' (2012) 120 *Greens Property Law Bulletin* 1

Ken Swinton, 'Advance notice: the death knell for letters of obligation' (2012) 80 *Scottish Law Gazette* 11

Ken Swinton, 'An argument for separate representation: *Pocock's Tr v Skene Investments*' (2012) 80 *Scottish Law Gazette* 58

Ken Swinton, 'Dual representation in conveyancing transactions – time for a change' (2012) 80 *Scottish Law Gazette* 41

PART IV
COMMENTARY

COMMENTARY

LAND REGISTRATION ETC (SCOTLAND) ACT 2012

The most significant event in property law that took place in 2012 happened on 10 July when the Royal Assent was given to the Land Registration etc (Scotland) Act 2012. Nevertheless the treatment we give here of that Act is not a comprehensive one, for two reasons. One is that there is expected to be a substantial delay before the Act comes into force. No one yet knows the date, but the second half of 2014 would be a plausible guess, and it is possible that it could even be 2015.[1] In the second place, the Act raises so many issues that it would not be possible to do it full justice within the confines of an annual review. Accordingly, what follows is simply an overview, with glances at the more significant changes.

Overview

During the 1990s it became clear to everyone that the Land Registration (Scotland) Act 1979 suffered from serious problems, and eventually Registers of Scotland suggested to the Scottish Law Commission that a review of the Act should be carried out. The Commission carried out a detailed study, with extensive assistance provided by Registers of Scotland. The project was headed up, sequentially, by the present writers. Three discussion papers, followed by a final report, were published and are all available online:[2]

- Discussion Paper on *Land Registration: Void and Voidable Titles* (Scot Law Com DP No 125, 2004).
- Discussion Paper on *Land Registration: Registration, Rectification and Indemnity* (Scot Law Com DP No 128, 2005).
- Discussion Paper on *Land Registration: Miscellaneous Issues* (Scot Law Com DP No 130, 2005).
- Report on *Land Registration* (Scot Law Com No 222, 2010).

Much can be learned about the new legislation from a study of these papers.

---

1 But the Scottish Government has the power to bring different provisions into force at different times, and it might be that the provisions about electronic documents come into force earlier than the remainder, possibly even before the end of 2013.
2 At www.scotlawcom.gov.uk.

The 2010 report included a draft Bill. In 2011 the Scottish Government introduced to the Scottish Parliament the Land Registration etc (Scotland) Bill, based on the SLC draft but with a substantial number of changes, mostly minor. The Bill enjoyed cross-party support and was passed with only a modest number of amendments. The Law Society of Scotland supported the Bill, the main qualification being that it was unhappy with the criminal provision, discussed below.

The 2012 Act repeals most of the 1979 Act. But that is less dramatic than it sounds. The new legislation represents evolution, not revolution. The modern system of land registration, with title sheets, proper mapping and guaranteed titles will continue. Many of the changes could be described as under-the-bonnet changes. Probably the most important innovation, from the point of view of the conveyancer, is the system of 'advance notices', which should make the existing system of letters of obligation a thing of the past.

The 1979 Act is characterised by extreme brevity. It is the shortest land registration statute in the world. Whilst brevity is a merit in legislation, there can be too much of a good thing, and the 1979 Act is too brief. Much of the current land registration system is based on RoS practice rather than on legislation. Hence it is a system without proper foundations. For the most part, the system as created over the years by RoS has been a good one. A substantial part of the 2012 Act is taken up with pumping concrete into the foundations, ie giving to the existing system a proper legislative basis. Of course, for the most part this makes no difference to daily conveyancing practice.

Completion of the Land Register

Scotland is like an uncompleted jigsaw. At the most recent estimate, 23.33% of Scotland is in the Land Register.[1] The figure calculated by individual title units is higher, at around 56%, because smaller properties tend to change hands more quickly than larger properties. Although the percentages increase year by year, completing the jigsaw would, under current law, take centuries. That is because properties switch into the Land Register only on sale, and some properties can go unsold for generations, because they are owned by the same juristic person (eg local authorities, some companies and so on) on a long-term basis, or because, though owned by private persons, they are transferred inter-generationally by inheritance or donation, or held through trusts. Indeed, there are a few properties that have yet to make their first appearance in the Register of Sasines, which was established in 1617, even though under the legislation applicable to that register all transactions, not just sale, require recording. Unless something is done, in 400 years from now Scotland will still be an uncompleted jigsaw.

The current situation is inconvenient for clients and for conveyancers, who have to be familiar with two different systems. It is also unsatisfactory to the public at large. This last point merits a few words. Conveyancers tend to think

1 *Land Mass Coverage Report 2012*, available at www.ros.gov.uk/pdfs/landmasscoveragereport2012.pdf.

of property registration as something that is there to assist the conveyancing process, and that is indeed true. But it is not the whole truth. The Land Register provides information in a way that the Register of Sasines does not. The Land Register provides a zoomable, clickable, map of Scotland showing title boundaries. Anyone, not just conveyancers, can use it and understand it – and 'anyone' includes central government, local government, law enforcement agencies, and so on. 'Completion of the Land Register', the Bill's *Policy Memorandum* declared, 'is considered to be the most important policy aim of the Bill.'[1] The benefits of land registration can be fully realised only if the pace of registration increases. That is what the politicians want, and that is, in their eyes, the legislation's greatest merit. Politicians want to know who owns Scotland, and it is only a completed Land Register that will provide a full answer.

The 2012 Act has several measures aimed at speeding up first registrations and achieving 100% coverage within decades. We will mention three. First, any disposition of unregistered property triggers first registration, not just dispositions on sale.[2] So, for example, dispositions by way of gift, and dispositions by executors or trustees to beneficiaries, are covered. Secondly, in due course standard securities and other deeds will also trigger first registration.[3] Thirdly, the Keeper acquires the power to register unregistered properties, without needing the owner's consent.[4] The exercise of this power changes nobody's rights: it is essentially a question of migrating data from the Sasine to the Land Register.

Advance notices and letters of obligation[5]

In England, there is a system called 'search with priority' whereby an entry can be made at the Land Registry that will protect a buyer, provided that the transfer itself is registered within a certain defined period thereafter. Under current law there is no such possibility in Scotland.[6] Because of that, there is the system of letters of obligation which, understandably, is unpopular both with conveyancers and with their professional insurers, who have been considering whether cover should continue to be provided. And it is a system that does not serve clients well, because although at the end of the day a buyer is protected,[7] 'the end of the day' can be a long time, and sorting out the mess that arises when a letter of obligation has to be enforced may take months or even years.

---

1 *Land Registration etc (Scotland) Bill: Policy Memorandum* para 14.
2 Land Registration etc (Scotland) Act 2012 ss 48(1)(a), 50(1).
3 LR(S)A 2012 s 48(2)–(4).
4 LR(S)A 2012 s 29.
5 For discussion appearing in 2012, see Fiona MacDonald, 'Land Registration etc (Scotland) Act 2012' (2012) 121 *Greens Property Law Bulletin* 7, and Ken Swinton, 'Advance notice: death knell for letters of obligation' (2012) 80 *Scottish Law Gazette* 11.
6 The contrast with England is even more striking given that to a large extent a buyer will be protected anyway because of equity. Put another way, there is a double difference between England and Scotland, one being that equity generally protects an English buyer even before registration, and the second being that any gaps in that protection can be plugged by 'search with priority'.
7 Though there is sometimes scope for disputing liability on a letter of obligation.

The 2012 Act, in introducing advance notices,[1] does not abolish letters of obligation. They remain available for use. But it seems unlikely that they will be used once advance notices become available. Where they exist in other countries, the equivalent of advance notices are in standard use.[2] When the Act comes into force, the abandonment of letters of obligation and the introduction of advance notices may prove to be the greatest single change that conveyancers will experience.

How does the new system work? The seller or, more likely in practice, the buyer with the seller's consent, applies to the Keeper for an advance notice which, if granted, is registered in the Land or Sasine Register.[3] Although it could be done in paper form, in practice most applications will, no doubt, be electronic. The system will be available for first registrations as well as for dealings. The notice creates a 'protected period' of 35 days.[4] Provided that the 'protected deed' is registered within that time, the buyer has nothing to fear from adverse entries in that period, either in the Land Register or in the Register of Inhibitions. The existence of an advance notice does not prevent other entries being made, but such entries take effect subject to the advance notice.[5] Of course, if the deed is registered after the expiry of the 35 days then there is no protection, and the advance notice will have been of no help. But this should not cause problems, for if there is a delay in settlement, a new notice can be registered. If an owner grants two advance notices to different parties, the earlier trumps the later. Advance notices will show up in a search.[6]

The precise form of the application for an advance notice cannot yet be given, but it is likely to set out four things: the property, the granter, the grantee and the deed type.[7] If the property does not exist as a separate unit in the Land Register, as with a split-off transaction or first registration, then the application will have to have a proper plan, but otherwise the property is simply identified by title number. 'Deed type' will in practice usually mean a disposition, but advance notices are competent for any registrable deed. If X is selling to Y and Y is granting a standard security to Z, the X/Y advance notice will normally suffice. There will normally be no point in having a separate and additional advance notice for the Y/Z deed.

Electronic deeds and missives

Currently, only deeds within the ARTL system can be in electronic form, so that even where ARTL is being used – which is not often – many types of deed are excluded. Under the 2012 Act all conveyancing documents can be electronic,

---

1 LR(S)A 2012 pt 4.
2 The Scottish Law Commission made a particular study of the English and the German systems.
3 LR(S)A 2012 s 57. For Land Register titles the notice appears only on the application record. The registration fee cannot yet be known, but is likely to be under £10.
4 LR(S)A 2012 s 58.
5 LR(S)A 2012 s 59.
6 Assuming that the search is within 35 days. Advance notices die after that period.
7 Mirroring the contents of the notice itself: s 56.

including missives and non-registrable leases.[1] Any deed can be submitted for registration in the Land Register in electronic form, even if not within the ARTL system, and the same is true for the Register of Sasines in those cases where that register is still relevant. Electronic deeds are also capable of registration in the Books of Council and Session. There is, however, no compulsion to move to electronic documents: paper documents remain competent. The provisions in the Act about e-documents are framework provisions, in the sense that the technical details will be determined by statutory instrument. And there are practical issues still to be settled as to how and by whom the relevant electronic signatures will be issued.

There have been complaints about the practical working of ARTL. The 2012 Act does not address that issue, which is an issue not so much for law reform as for the IT experts.

Duty of care: civil and criminal

Under current law it is probably the position that conveyancers owe a duty to the Keeper to take reasonable care. But there is no specific judicial authority on the point. The Act says expressly that there is such a duty.[2] This provision, which is about civil law, has not been controversial. What has been controversial is a provision that imposes criminal liability in certain cases.[3] The Law Society opposed the provision, but without success.[4] In England, the Land Registration Act 2002[5] also has a criminal provision, but the new Scottish provision is in somewhat different terms and seems to go further than the English provision.

Speeding up the registration process

Registration can take too long: many months, and sometimes even years. As a response to this problem, the Act allows maximum periods to be set by the Scottish Ministers – 'periods' in the plural because different periods can be set for different types of case.[6] For example, for dealings with whole the maximum could be shorter than for transfers of part. The Act should also contribute in other ways to speeding up the process. For instance, the system of requisitions disappears: if an application does not have the necessary information or documentation, it will simply be rejected.

Inaccuracies

Inaccuracies cannot be wholly avoided: we live in an imperfect world. But as and when inaccuracies occur there needs to be a reasonable way of dealing with

---

1 LR(S)A 2012 pt 10. One consequence is that the Requirements of Writing (Scotland) Act 1995 is much amended.
2 LR(S)A 2012 s 111.
3 LR(S)A 2012 s 112. This provision was not in the Scottish Law Commission's draft Bill.
4 See Ross MacKay, 'Registering our concerns' (2012) 57 *Journal of the Law Society of Scotland* Feb/28.
5 LR(S)A 2012 s 123.
6 LR(S)A 2012 s 35.

them, and it is an objection to the current law that it fails to do that. Section 9 of the 1979 Act says that in many cases the register *must remain inaccurate*. Anyone who has tried explaining that to a non-lawyer will have found the task difficult. Under the 2012 Act, inaccuracies are rectifiable in all cases,[1] although the scope of inaccuracy is substantially reduced by the protection for good faith acquirers, discussed below.

The Keeper's Midas touch

The Keeper's 'Midas touch' (as it was called by the Scottish Law Commission) is the rule in the 1979 Act whereby if X is registered in the Land Register as having a right (ownership, security etc), and if that registration had no valid basis (eg the disposition was void), then X is nonetheless holder of the right in question, subject to the possibility of subsequent rectification.[2] For example, W dispones land to X, but the disposition includes a border area that W does not own. The disposition is void to that extent. But if the Keeper registers X as owner of the whole area, then X is owner of the whole area, unless and until rectification happens. This is so even if the Keeper excludes indemnity. This 'Midas touch' brings with it no benefits, either theoretical or practical, and merely makes problems harder to sort out when they do happen. (It is true that people need to be able to rely on what they see in the register, but that requirement can be delivered without using the Midas touch.) The 2012 Act abolishes it.[3] The abolition does not, however, mean that the guarantee of title is prejudiced or that good faith grantees cannot rely on what the Land Register says.

The guarantee of title

An important feature of the system introduced by the 1979 Act is that titles are (usually) guaranteed. This can take two forms: where a grantee's title is defective, the Keeper will either compensate the grantee,[4] or protect the grantee's title from challenge (compensating, instead, the other party whose rights are thereby infringed).[5] So the grantee receives either the 'money' or the 'mud',[6] more usually the latter; and a good faith acquirer in possession will almost always receive the 'mud', ie keep the property.[7] This mixture of two forms of guarantee is replicated in the 2012 Act,[8] but with a shift in the balance so that the grantee is more likely

---

1 LR(S)A 2012 s 80. The inaccuracy must, however, be 'manifest'.
2 Land Registration (Scotland) Act 1979 s 3(1).
3 This appears from the general scheme of the Act and is also stated, for avoidance of doubt, at s 49(4).
4 LR(S)A 1979 s 12.
5 LR(S)A 1979 s 9(3)(a).
6 To use the attractive shorthand found in T W Mapp, *Torrens' Elusive Title: Basic Legal Principles of an Efficient Torrens' System* (1978) para 4.24.
7 For the protection against rectification given to proprietors in possession see LR(S)A 1979 s 9(3)(a).
8 One change, largely terminological, is that under the 2012 Act the Keeper grants (at least in the normal case) a 'warranty' of title, which is conceptually rather like warrandice. If the grantee loses title by rectification, the Keeper must then pay up under that warranty. This replaces the language of 'indemnity'. See LR(S)A 2012 pt 7.

than before to be bought off with compensation. As before, however, the Register can always be relied upon, so that an acquirer taking in good faith from the person registered as owner receives a good title even if that person (though on the Register) was not owner at all.[1]

Uncompleted titles

The Act introduces two minor changes to the way uncompleted titles are dealt with. The first change is a simplification; the second is a (minor) complication. First, under current law, a disposition by an uninfeft proprietor that induces a first registration must contain a clause of deduction of title. Under the Act, the requirement for such a clause is abolished.[2] Secondly, under current law, once a title is in the Land Register notices of title are unnecessary. Under the Act, notices of title are restored.[3] Of course, even under current law the title and the midcouples have to be checked, so all that changes is, in effect, that a brief statement has to be signed to confirm that such checking has indeed taken place.

Shared plots

Imagine a development of 20 houses, with a common area including parking, a play park etc in which the owner of each house has a one-twentieth share. Under current practice the common area is included in each of the 20 title sheets. Under the 2012 Act, a common area can, at the Keeper's option, have its own title sheet, called a 'shared plot title sheet'.[4] The proprietorship section of such a title sheet would, instead of naming anyone, list the co-owning properties – the 'sharing plots' – and the title sheet of each sharing plot would, in its property section, refer to the shared plot title sheet. Dealings with a sharing plot (dispositions, standard securities etc) would automatically affect the shared plot, without the latter's title sheet having to be altered in any way.

The new system is simply a different way of presenting the same information. It is thought that it should prove a more transparent method. But as already mentioned, it is for the Keeper to decide whether to adopt this method, on a case-by-case basis.

A non domino dispositions

How the Keeper should handle *a non domino* dispositions has been a matter of debate over the years, and was one of the few areas where the Bill stirred controversy. The 1979 Act has no clear provision on the subject. That is put right

---

1 The land must, however, have been possessed for a year either by the granter, or by the granter and grantee in sequence: see LR(S)A 2012 s 86. Under the 1979 Act the acquirer becomes owner (due to the Midas touch in s 3(1)(a)) but the Register is considered inaccurate and vulnerable to rectification, especially if the acquirer does not take possession. Under the 2012 Act the acquirer becomes owner (due to s 86) and the Register is considered accurate and so can never be rectified.
2 LR(S)A 2012 s 101.
3 LR(S)A 2012 sch 5 para 9, amending various provisions of the Conveyancing (Scotland) Act 1924.
4 LR(S)A 2012 ss 17–20.

by the 2012 Act, although the provisions are significantly different from those originally recommended by the Scottish Law Commission. In outline, if the disponer has been in *de facto* possession of property for at least a year, and if the disponee pre-notifies anyone who appears to have better right to the property, the Keeper must then register the disponee, as a 'prescriptive claimant', and positive prescription can then run.[1]

Land certificates no more

Land certificates no longer have the significance they once had because their production to the Keeper is no longer required. The Act abolishes them. But of course people may still want an official extract of a title sheet, which comes to much the same thing as a land certificate, and the Act makes provision for such extracts, which may be either in paper or electronic form.[2] It is also possible to obtain formal extracts of registered deeds, something that cannot always be done under current law.

The cadastral map

The 1979 Act contemplated each title sheet with its own plan, so that the completed Register would consist of more than two million separate plans. The reality, however, is that there is only one plan, an electronic megaplan of the whole of Scotland showing registered properties and their boundaries. The plan attached to a land certificate is just a gobbet of data sucked from that megaplan, and squirted on to the land certificate. That map does not exist as a paper map, of course, but it exists nonetheless. The 2012 Act recognises the reality, and gives it a name: the cadastral map.[3] At present that is an unfamiliar term to most Scots lawyers, but it is an international term, and so should make the system easier to understand at the international level.

Souvenir plots

We mention souvenir plots only because they have to some extent been in the news during 2012, including an article by the Keeper.[4] Under current law, title to a souvenir plot cannot be registered.[5] It follows, to state the obvious, that someone who pays money for a souvenir plot does not acquire ownership of it.[6] Yet sellers of souvenir plots generally claim on their websites that buyers will acquire ownership. The 2012 Act adheres to the policy of the 1979 Act, making only minor technical revisions.[7]

---

1 LR(S)A 2012 ss 43 ff.
2 LR(S)A 2012 ss 104, 105.
3 LR(S)A 2012 ss 11–13.
4 'Caution the souvenir hunters' (2012) 57 *Journal of the Law Society of Scotland* Apr/10.
5 LR(S)A 1979 s 4(2)(b).
6 This would be the case even if sellers offered a disposition, which commonly they do not.
7 LR(S)A 2012 s 22(1)(b).

REAL BURDENS

Title to enforce: feudal burdens

Feudal burdens without feudal superiors

Feudal superiors may have gone, but real burdens of feudal origin remain. And today, getting on for ten years after feudal abolition, the question of who is able to enforce these burdens remains one of the central mysteries of conveyancing.

Sometimes the answer is to be found in the deed creating the burden – the 'constitutive deed' in the language adopted by the Title Conditions (Scotland) Act 2003.[1] In a deed of conditions for a housing estate, for example, there might be a clause conferring universal enforcement rights by means of what was once known, perhaps not very accurately, as a *ius quaesitum tertio*. But where the constitutive deed is silent, as it often is, enforcement rights must stand or fall in accordance with five provisions found in part 4 of the Title Conditions Act.[2] Each provides quite separately for enforcement rights, and more than one may apply, thus duplicating the effect of the other or others.

Of the five provisions, two – concerning facility burdens and service burdens – apply only to burdens with particular content[3] while a third – s 54 – is restricted to sheltered housing. It is the remaining two, being general in character, which are in practice much the most important. The first – s 52 – more or less re-states the common-law rules for implying enforcement rights. As such it is complex but workable, at least with care. The other, however – s 53 – breaks new ground, and has proved both hard to interpret and troublesome to apply. The decision in the new case of *Russel Properties (Europe) Ltd v Dundas Heritable Ltd*[4] – almost the first to consider s 53 – is therefore to be welcomed.

The case concerned the Westwood Neighbourhood Centre, a mixed development of flats, offices and shops in East Kilbride. The pursuer, a company owning many of the non-residential units in the Centre as well as two car parks, objected to the defender's proposal to lease part of its pub premises to Tesco for a 'Tesco Express' convenience store. Part of the anxiety was that some of the pursuer's tenants might quit their premises in the face of the competition.[5]

All owners in the Centre derived their titles, ultimately, from the East Kilbride Development Corporation. There does not seem to have been a deed of conditions, and burdens were imposed in a series of feu dispositions for individual units or groups of units. The defender's feu disposition[6] contained the following provision:[7]

---

1 Title Conditions (Scotland) Act 2003 s 4(1).
2 The same applies to non-feudal burdens created prior to 28 November 2004 but with the preservation, until 28 November 2014, of an additional common-law rule of enforcement, the rule in *J A Mactaggart & Co v Harrower* (1906) 8 F 1101. See TC(S)A 2003 ss 49(2), 50.
3 TC(S)A 2003 s 56.
4 [2012] CSOH 175, 2012 GWD 38-749.
5 Paragraph 23.
6 At least according to its land certificate.
7 Paragraph 9.

> Subject to the provisions of these presents the feu and the buildings and others erected thereon, or any part thereof, shall not be occupied or used for any trade, business or purpose other than that of a licensed public house and/or public restaurant and purposes ancillary thereto … without the written consent of the Superiors.

As the Tesco store was neither a licensed public house nor a public restaurant, it was clear that the use proposed under the lease to be granted by the defender was in breach of the burden. But did anyone have a title to enforce? The title of the feudal superiors, East Kilbride Development Corporation, had disappeared, with the feudal system itself, on 28 November 2004. And there was apparently nothing in the feu disposition to confer enforcement rights on co-feuars such as the pursuer. Insofar as the pursuer had title to enforce, therefore, it could only rest on either s 52 or s 53 of the Title Conditions Act.

Sections 52 and 53

Section 52 was plainly inapplicable: the reservation of a right in the superior to give consent took care of that.[1] This is because, under the former law, which s 52 largely replicates, a superior reserving a right to vary is supposed to have intended that he alone should be able to enforce the burdens.

That left s 53, a provision which had no counterpart in the old law and a main purpose of which was to give to neighbours the enforcement rights which were formerly held by superiors. Section 53(1) provides that

> Where real burdens are imposed under a common scheme, the deed by which they are imposed on any unit comprised within a group of related properties being a deed registered before the appointed day, then all units comprised within that group and subject to the common scheme (whether or not by virtue of a deed registered before the appointed day) shall be benefited properties in relation to the real burdens.

Out of this awkward wording it is possible to derive three requirements and a result.[2] The requirements are (i) that real burdens must have been imposed on a group of properties under a 'common scheme',[3] (ii) that the properties must be 'related' to one another, and (iii) that one at least of the constitutive deeds must have been registered before the appointed day. And the result, if the requirements are all satisfied, is mutual enforcement rights within the group of burdened properties, so that each property is at the same time both a burdened and a benefited property, and the burdens are thus 'community burdens'.[4]

There was no difficulty in respect of requirement (iii). If, therefore, the pursuer could show both (i) that the burden which it sought to enforce was part

---

1 TC(S)A 2003 s 52(2). For this point the court refers to the now displaced common law (and in particular to *Turner v Hamilton* (1890) 17 R 494) rather than to s 52(2): see para 10.

2 Section 53 is one of the provisions of the Title Conditions Act to be reviewed by the Justice Committee of the Scottish Parliament in the opening months of 2013: see www.scottish.parliament. uk/parliamentarybusiness/CurrentCommittees/59247.aspx.

3 This requirement is also found in s 52.

4 For the meaning of 'community burdens', see TC(S)A 2003 s 25.

of a 'common scheme' of burdens affecting both the defender's property and at least one of those belonging to the pursuer, and (ii) that these properties were 'related', then s 53 would be engaged, with the result that the pursuer would have title to enforce the burdens against the defender.

A 'common scheme'?

The idea of 'common scheme' is taken over from the former law, where implied enforcement rights would normally arise only in 'common scheme' cases. No definition is offered by the 2003 Act, but it is generally accepted that burdens are imposed under a 'common scheme' where (a) the burdens for each property are either the same or in some sense equivalent and (b) at least in the normal case, the burdens were imposed by the same person. Both requirements are captured in a passage from the Scottish Law Commission's Report on *Real Burdens* which was relied on by the court:[1]

> The idea of a common scheme ... is familiar from the rules on implied enforcement rights. Usually, but not always, the burdens will originate from a common author. While burdens in a common scheme are often identical, this is not a formal requirement. For example, in a mixed development of residential and commercial units, the burdens on the former will not be identical to those on the latter. Or within a tenement, different flats may be made responsible for the maintenance of different parts, or, if responsible for the same parts, the extent of liability may be different. But if burdens are not identical, there must at least be a sense of equivalence. An example comes from the deed litigated in *Cooperative Wholesale Society v Ushers Brewery*.[2] Here three units, feued by a common author, were used as a supermarket, a pub, and a betting office. ... While not identical, these prohibitions were clearly intended as equivalents, designed for the prosperity of the development as a whole.

In the present case all the burdens affecting the Westwood Neighbourhood Centre derived from a common author (the East Kilbride Development Corporation). On the other hand, the burdens on each property were far from identical. The question was whether they were sufficiently equivalent to qualify as a common scheme.

The use restriction in the defender's title, which the pursuer sought to enforce, was matched by a use restriction in the pursuer's title to the effect that:[3]

> The whole of the said shop and office premises and others shall be used for purposes falling within Classes 1, 2, 3, 4 and 15 of the Schedule to the Town and Country Planning (Use Classes) (Scotland) Order 1989[4] or for such other purpose (including a public library and doctor's surgery) as is appropriate to a neighbourhood shopping

---

1 Paragraph 17 of the opinion. See Scottish Law Commission, Report on *Real Burdens* (Scot Law Com No 181, 2000) para 7.13.
2 1975 SLT (Lands Tr) 9.
3 Paragraph 12.
4 It may be noted in passing that the reference to a statutory provision without repeating its terms in full is fatal to the validity of this provision as a real burden, for the full terms of a burden must be contained within the four corners of the deed. See TC(S)A 2003 s 4(2)(a) and *Aberdeen Varieties Ltd v James F Donald (Aberdeen Cinemas) Ltd* 1939 SC 788.

centre only and not for any other purpose without the written consent of the Superiors which consent shall not be unreasonably withheld or delayed.

The two restrictions are of course different, but it seems not implausible to regard them as 'equivalents, designed for the prosperity of the development as a whole' in the same way as in the Scottish Law Commission's example drawn from *Cooperative Wholesale Society v Ushers Brewery*. As the Lord Ordinary[1] said, East Kilbride Development Corporation 'appears to have conceived Westwood Neighbourhood Centre with a mix of properties within it'.[2] The Lord Ordinary's conclusion, nonetheless, was that there was no common scheme.

In reaching this conclusion the Lord Ordinary focused, less on the pursuer's main title, just discussed, to the non-residential properties, than on its title to the two car parks. Here the use restriction was rather different in character from the other titles. All building was prohibited, and a maintenance obligation was imposed which was declared enforceable by the other proprietors in the development as well as by the general public.[3] These differences, said the Lord Ordinary, were too large to indicate 'an underlying sense of equivalence'.[4]

It is no criticism of the Lord Ordinary to say that a different view might also have been possible.[5] But taking the Lord Ordinary's view as correct, it was not necessarily fatal to the pursuer's case. In order to succeed, the pursuer required to show only that *one* of its properties was part of the same common scheme as the defender's property. If the burdens on the car parks were not part of that scheme, then so be it: it did not disqualify the burdens on others of the pursuer's properties. And those burdens, as we have seen, could much more easily be regarded as equivalent to those affecting the defender.

There was also a further reason for the Lord Ordinary's decision. After quoting a passage from the *Cooperative* case which referred both to the 'matching obligations' on the different properties and to the enforcement rights expressed in the constitutive deeds, the Lord Ordinary continued:[6]

> In my view, the present case is clearly distinguishable. The required mutuality is absent. No reciprocal rights of enforcement are conferred.

Although the wording is perhaps a little unclear, it is thought that the final sentence is intended as a consequence of the sentence which precedes it (no mutuality, no enforcement rights) and not as a reference to the absence, in *Russel Properties*, of express enforcement rights (for, after all, if such rights had been conferred there would be no need of s 53). The mention of 'the required mutuality'

---

1 Lord Woolman.
2 Paragraph 16.
3 Paragraph 13. This last part was a dead letter: real burdens cannot be enforced by the general public.
4 Paragraph 20.
5 It should be noted that the decision was in respect of an (opposed) application for interim interdict, and that it may not have been possible to give full consideration to the arguments or the authorities. Although both views are tenable, our inclination is to say that, on the information available to us, there was indeed a common scheme.
6 Paragraph 21.

seems to refer back to para 18 of the Lord Ordinary's opinion where Lord Watson is quoted as saying, in *Hislop v MacRitchie's Trs*,[1] that there had to be a 'similarity of conditions or mutuality of interest'. Importantly, the 'or' in this quotation is a mistranscription for 'and'. The Lord Ordinary may perhaps not have appreciated that, for Lord Watson, similarity of conditions and mutuality of interest were not the same thing but, rather, were different and cumulative requirements; and, as is clear from the context in which the quotation appears, the latter refers to the mutual interest to enforce of co-feuars. Interest to enforce, it need hardly be said, is a quite distinct issue from whether there is a common scheme and hence title to enforce, and it would be out of place in a discussion of s 53.[2]

None of this is to say that the decision of the court is wrong. It may indeed be that there was no common scheme. But a final view cannot be reached without reviewing the totality of burdens imposed on each property, and indeed doing so by reference to the full text of the original deeds as opposed to the bleeding chunks carved out for the purposes of the title sheets. In a mixed development it is only to be expected that the use restrictions on different types of property will be different; to determine whether there is a common scheme overall it is necessary to have regard to the similarities and differences in the *other* burdens[3] imposed on the properties by East Kilbride Development Corporation.[4]

'Related properties'?

Having decided that there was no common scheme, the court was absolved from giving much attention to the question of whether the second requirement of s 53 was met – that the properties of the two parties should be 'related'. Unlike 'common scheme', the concept of 'relatedness' is a new one, introduced for the first time by the Title Conditions Act. Without offering a complete definition, s 53 gives a certain amount of guidance:[5]

> Whether properties are related properties for the purposes of subsection (1) above is to be inferred from all the circumstances; and without prejudice to the generality of this subsection, circumstances giving rise to such an inference might include –
>
> (a) the convenience of managing the properties together because they share –
>   (i) some common feature; or
>   (ii) an obligation for common maintenance of some facility;
> (b) there being shared ownership of common property;
> (c) their being subject to the common scheme by virtue of the same deed of conditions; or
> (d) the properties each being a flat in the same tenement.

---

1 (1881) 8 R (HL) 95 at 102.
2 As the Lord Ordinary indeed acknowledges at para 24. Even if the pursuer had been able to establish title, it may – like many another pursuer – have struggled to achieve the threshold of interest set out in TC(S)A 2003 s 8. For interest to enforce see below.
3 That there were other burdens is plain from the numbering (third, fifth, seven) of the burdens quoted in the opinion.
4 R Rennie (ed), *The Promised Land: Property Law Reform* (2008) para 3-25.
5 TC(S)A 2003 s 53(2).

In the event, none of the factors listed above was argued to apply and the Lord Ordinary concluded, having 'regard to the whole circumstances', that the properties had not been shown to be 'related'.[1] It may well be that those 'whole circumstances' – whatever they were[2] – were decisive and beyond argument. We would simply mention that a particular aim of s 53 was to ensure the survival of real burdens in developments. As the Deputy First Minister, Jim Wallace MSP, explained in introducing the provision, by amendment, to the Scottish Parliament:[3]

> The purpose of new section 48A[4] is to ensure that amenity burdens in all housing estates or tenements should be mutually enforceable by the owners of houses in the estate or of flats in a tenement. … [H]ouses on a typical housing estate would be related properties.

It might be thought that what was true of houses might also be true of the mixed units in a development such as the Westwood Neighbourhood Centre.

So who can enforce?

If the pursuer could not enforce the burdens, who can? The answer appears to be: no one. Section 53 having been found to be inapplicable, the neighbours are unable to succeed to the enforcement rights of their former superior. Tesco is free to open its convenience store. And the owners of the other units in the Westwood Neighbourhood Centre can ignore their title conditions and do as they wish.

Interest to enforce

Section 52

By contrast to the case just discussed, the burdens considered by the Lands Tribunal in *Whitelaw v Acheson*[5] seem to have raised issues of enforcement under s 52 of the Title Conditions (Scotland) 2003 and not under s 53. We say 'seem to have' because it was accepted without discussion that enforcement rights arose.[6] And no doubt this view was justified because the fact pattern was a classic one for the application of s 52. By a single feu charter granted in 1883 two plots of land were feued subject to a set of burdens. Later the plots came to be in separate ownership. There was thus a 'common scheme' of real burdens affecting the two plots, emanating from the same source. And because the feu charter was a deed common to the titles of both plots, the owner of each had the notice of the

---

1 Paragraph 22.
2 They are not listed in the Lord Ordinary's opinion.
3 Scottish Parliament, *Official Report*, Justice 1 Committee, 10 Dec 2002, cols 4371–72. The statement seems to have been made with *Pepper v Hart* [1993] AC 593 in mind.
4 Ie what is now s 53.
5 29 February and 28 September 2012, Lands Tribunal. The Tribunal comprised Lord McGhie and I M Darling FRICS. In the footnotes which follow the two decisions are distinguished as, respectively, '*Whitelaw* (1)' and '*Whitelaw* (2)'.
6 In the absence of enforcement rights, there is no entitlement to oppose an application for variation or discharge: see TC(S)A 2003 s 95(a).

common scheme which is the other main requirement of s 52. Unless, therefore, there was something in the feu charter to exclude co-feuars' rights – the classic example being a power of waiver in the superior[1] – s 52 would apply to the effect that the proprietor of each plot had title to enforce against the other.

Unhappy valley

The main significance of *Whitelaw*, however, lies not in title to enforce but in interest. First, however, it is necessary to say something about the facts, and about the decision reached by the Lands Tribunal. In the mid-1880s a house had been built on each of the plots comprising the 1883 feu, the plots today being numbers 199 and 201 Colinton Road, Edinburgh. The houses were close to the line of shops and business premises in Colinton Road known as 'Happy Valley', and they backed on to the Craiglockhart Tennis and Sports Centre. The Tribunal described number 201, perhaps a little unkindly, as 'a lovely family home but one with the significant adverse features of being on a busy main road on one side and looking out to a rather ugly sports centre and car park on the other'.[2]

Both houses were used for residential purposes but the application to the Tribunal, which was in respect of number 201, was to vary the burdens to the extent necessary to allow a change of use to a 'therapy and wellbeing centre'.[3] Planning permission had already been granted, but restricted to the hours of 10.00–20.00 on weekdays and 10.00–16.00 at weekends. The application was opposed by the owners of number 199.

Where an application is opposed, it can only be granted by the Lands Tribunal where it is 'reasonable' to do so having regard to the factors set out in s 100 of the 2003 Act.[4] Customarily, the Tribunal begins with factor (f) (the purpose of the condition), but often, as is now beginning to be acknowledged, that purpose is too general or unclear to be of much assistance. In the present case it was evidently concerned with protecting general amenity rather than amenity of any specific type and so did not advance matters.[5] Next the Tribunal considers factor (a) (change in circumstances), but here again, while these were dramatic enough, open countryside having turned into a fully developed housing area, they were seen as 'broadly neutral in the sense that they do not necessarily detract from the benefit of the conditions'.[6]

The nub of this case, however – as of most Tribunal applications – was the balance between factor (b) (the extent to which the condition confers benefit on

---

1 As in *Russel Properties (Europe) Ltd v Dundas Heritable Ltd* [2012] CSOH 175, 2012 GWD 38-749, discussed above.

2 *Whitelaw* (1) para 56. The context was whether the applicant's proposed change of use would lead to a reduction in the value of the respondents' house. The Tribunal held that it would not.

3 There was also a separate issue involving a rear extension: for details, see p 18 above.

4 Title Conditions (Scotland) Act 2003 s 98. See further G L Gretton and K G C Reid, *Conveyancing* (4th edn, 2011) paras 16-07–16-12; A Todd and R Wishart, *The Lands Tribunal for Scotland: Law and Practice* (2012) ch 6.

5 *Whitelaw* (1) para 23.

6 *Whitelaw* (1) para 28.

the benefited property) and factor (c) (the extent to which the condition impedes enjoyment of the burdened property). How significant was the real burden to each of the parties? And how serious would it be for the respondent if the change of use were allowed to go ahead? That in turn depended on what, precisely, the applicant had in mind. The variation sought was for use as a 'therapy and wellbeing centre'. However, the applicant:[1]

> made it plain that she saw no real limit to the scope of the therapeutic treatment she might provide. Her immediate plans included provision of reflexology, yoga classes, Tai Chi and dance therapy. She also foresaw treatment by way of aromatherapy, massage, Reiki and bi-aura. The latter are said to be types of 'energy work'.

For the respondents, however, what mattered most was what went on *outside* the house, and in particular the effect of increased movements of cars and pedestrians on the driveway.[2] The visual impact, at least, would be minimal, because people coming and going could not usually be seen from the respondents' house, although 'it would be possible to position a chair in the bay window so as to afford a view of the front part of the drive'.[3] But, as the Tribunal noted, there might be impact of a different kind:[4]

> There are potential uses of the subjects which would fall within the wide umbrella of 'therapy' which might give rise to different issues. Any form of therapy which involved groups might well give rise to a risk of such groups entering or leaving the subjects and, particularly when leaving, standing laughing or talking in the garden before dispersing. That could, potentially have quite a different impact on the benefited subjects compared with the simple movement of individuals, however frequent. Plainly treatment involving any kind of drug therapy might attract clients who could be seen as undesirable visitors. Other types of therapy might also be aimed at, or attract, similarly undesirable visitors. The applicant contemplated massage as an appropriate form of therapy. As we discuss further below it is not easy, in terms of title conditions, to distinguish between proper massage and massage facilities which are simply a cover for other forms of sexual therapy.

In the event, therefore, that the variation were allowed, it might need to be subject to restrictions.

If, however, the impact of varying the burden seemed acceptable, much the same might be said of the impact of *not* varying it. The burden impeded the use of the applicant's property, certainly; but the property could still be used for the purpose for which it was built and for which there was a lot of demand, ie as a house. Thus, the Tribunal concluded, 'although the present building restriction is a restriction on the applicant's enjoyment of the property as it would prevent her from developing to the full extent allowed by her planning permission, we do not regard it as unduly burdensome'.[5]

---

1 *Whitelaw* (1) para 62.
2 *Whitelaw* (1) para 33.
3 *Whitelaw* (1) para 15.
4 *Whitelaw* (1) para 36.
5 *Whitelaw* (1) para 45.

On balance, and it was evidently a fine one, the Tribunal was willing to support variation but subject to restrictions as to the type of therapy that could be practised. It was in formulating these restrictions that the issue of interest to enforce became of importance.

Interest: in general

By s 8(3)(a)[1] of the Title Conditions Act a person has interest to enforce a real burden if and only if:

> in the circumstances of any case, failure to comply with the real burden is resulting in, or will result in, material detriment to the value or enjoyment of the person's ownership of, or right in, the benefited property.

The first decision on s 8, *Barker v Lewis*,[2] found there was no interest to stop a close neighbour from using her property as a bed-and-breakfast business, thus suggesting a threshold which was unreasonably high. Matters, however, were improved somewhat by *Kettlewell v Turning Point Scotland*,[3] a decision of 2011, where neighbours in a housing estate were found to have interest to prevent use of one of the houses as care accommodation for adults with learning difficulties. The Tribunal in *Whitelaw* has now added to this shrinking tendency by suggesting that by 'material detriment' Parliament was simply pointing to a contrast with terms such as 'immaterial, insignificant, trivial'; on this view, with which we agree, only the trivial will be too little.[4] It is, however, early days yet, and until further case law tackles this issue it is prudent to assume a hurdle which might sometimes be tricky to surmount.

Interest and variation

On the merits of the application the Tribunal was inclined to vary the burdens to allow counselling as well as other one-to-one activities such as reflexology, Reiki and aromatherapy; group activities, however, such as dance, would not be permitted. The question was then: what words to use to express what was allowed and what was not? As a way of easing the problems of definition the Tribunal considered the use of a provision which allowed nothing more than counselling, on the basis that there would then in practice be no interest to prevent other one-to-one therapies which were of a related nature.[5] The

---

1 Special provision is made in Title Conditions (Scotland) Act 2003 s 8(3)(b) for affirmative burdens to defray a cost.
2 2008 SLT (Sh Ct) 17; see *Conveyancing 2008* pp 92–95.
3 2011 SLT (Sh Ct) 143; see *Conveyancing 2011* pp 87–90. In *Whitelaw* (2) para 13 the Tribunal took issue with the sheriff's reference to a burden having been 'departed from' when all he really meant was that, in the particular circumstances of the case, there was no interest to enforce it. Only the Tribunal has the power to 'depart from' burdens, through its jurisdiction to vary or discharge.
4 *Whitelaw* (2) para 12.
5 *Whitelaw* (1) para 70. In the end, the Tribunal went for making a list, allowing 'use of the subjects for psychotherapy by way of counselling, including group counselling, and by way of one-to-one forms of therapeutic treatment including (without prejudice to the generality) head hand and face massage and the technique known as "Reiki" but excluding body massage'.

underlying reasoning, however, can be questioned. Just because an owner is allowed to do X does not remove any interest to prevent him doing Y, even if X and Y are related activities. After all, there is nothing in most titles to prevent the carrying out of most activities, some of which might be highly unwelcome to neighbours; yet if a particular activity is prohibited, it is generally no answer, in resisting interest to enforce, to say that some other, equally loathsome, activity is not. No doubt it is true that if the value of one's property is already degraded by an activity *actually carried on*[1] in the property of a neighbour, it might not be materially degraded by another but unpermitted activity; more rarely, the same might also be true in respect of materiality of detriment. But there is no simple or automatic relationship between (i) what is permitted and (ii) interest to enforce in respect of what is not, and it may be that any sort of relationship will prove to be unusual.

A different but related argument, made for the respondents, was the following:[2]

> If a tribunal has reached the conclusion that removal of existing conditions would only be reasonable if certain conditions were put in their place, it is necessary to be satisfied that these conditions would be enforceable. If there was a perceptible risk that they might come to be unenforceable because another court or tribunal might take the view that the respondents had not shown sufficient interest to enforce within the meaning of sec 8(3)(a), it would follow that the conditions which had been seen to be necessary to justify removal of the existing title conditions were ineffective.

On this issue the Tribunal reserved its views.[3] But the argument strikes us as a good one: there should be no comfort – indeed there would be no point – in imposing replacement conditions if it is evident that they are unenforceable through lack of interest. Often, of course, it will be impossible to be sure about this, because interest is breach-specific. But if the conditions are sufficiently narrow that they can be breached in only one way, a view on the subject can be formed with reasonable confidence.

Interest and factor (b)

Of the factors which s 100 of the Title Conditions (Scotland) Act 2003 directs the Tribunal to weigh, probably the most important is factor (b): 'the extent to which the condition confers benefit on the benefited property'. Self-evidently, a condition which cannot be enforced confers no benefit. Hence, an inquiry as to interest to enforce may sometimes be unavoidable. Indeed if the threshold for interest is properly to be regarded as a high one, this could in some cases, the Tribunal warned, 'add significantly to the complexity of the balancing exercise required in exercise of our jurisdiction'.[4] To date, however,

---

1 As opposed to merely permitted under the titles.
2 *Whitelaw* (2) para 10.
3 *Whitelaw* (2) para 11. This was because of the late stage at which the argument was introduced.
4 *Whitelaw* (2) para 12.

the Tribunal has given scant attention to interest. Whether this will now change remains to be seen.

Interest to enforce and interest to oppose

Finally, mention should be made of a preliminary question which arose in *Whitelaw* as to the interest of the respondents to oppose the application. Under the Act, the right to make representations depends on having 'title to enforce the title condition',[1] by which is meant being owner[2] of a benefited property. And from this title flows the necessary interest to oppose the application. That, the Tribunal emphasised, is very different from interest in the sense of interest to enforce:[3]

> Although we heard some discussion of the question of interest to enforce the existing conditions, we are satisfied that we should proceed on the basis that the respondents have undisputed title and, as proprietors of the adjacent residential subjects, have a proper interest to oppose any change to the existing conditions. We are not persuaded that their interest falls to be measured by reference to the degree of interest necessary to enforce a condition in respect of any alleged breach in terms of section 8(3). That would require assessment of the particular facts and circumstances bearing on the breach. The question of materiality cannot arise except in such a context. We consider that it begs the question to consider the interest of the respondents only in terms of the proposed change. They plainly have an interest to maintain the existing condition.

INHIBITIONS AND MISSIVES

It is well established, as far as the common law is concerned, that if a seller is inhibited after conclusion of missives, it does not prevent the deal going ahead. Thus if Donald concludes missives to sell to Beryl on 1 May, with settlement to be on 1 June, and Ian inhibits Donald with effect from 15 May, the transaction can still settle, and the title that Beryl obtains is not open to challenge on the basis of the inhibition. It is equally well established that the Keeper, being aware of the law, will not exclude indemnity when registering Beryl, provided that the Keeper can be satisfied about the missives. The reason is that inhibition affects only 'future voluntary' transactions, and the authorities all say that a transaction that the inhibitee has *already* contractually undertaken to perform is not 'voluntary' in the relevant sense, because the inhibitee no longer has a choice whether to perform it. In this respect inhibition is different from other types of diligence, which trump third party personal rights.

This well-established law, however, was thrown into doubt by the Bankruptcy and Diligence etc (Scotland) Act 2007. That Act has extensive provisions about the law of inhibition, one of which, s 160, says:

---

1 Title Conditions (Scotland) Act 2003 s 95(a).
2 Or tenant or proper liferenter: see TC(S)A 2003 s 8(2)(a).
3 *Whitelaw* (1) para 4.

An inhibited debtor breaches the inhibition when the debtor delivers a deed –

(a) conveying; or

(b) otherwise granting a right in,

property over which the inhibition has effect to a person other than the inhibiting creditor.

This, read literally, seems to mean that pre-inhibition missives do *not* protect a disposition, so that in the example above Beryl's title *would* be challengeable on the basis of the inhibition. The Keeper has interpreted s 160 thus, or at least has taken the view that it was a reasonably possible interpretation, and has been excluding indemnity accordingly. The issue has now come before the courts, in *Playfair Investments Ltd v McElvogue*.[1]

The full underlying circumstances of the case are not clear, but a family dispute was involved. The pursuer was under the control of Michael Karus and the first defender was his sister; the dispute centred on two family companies, Cordelt Ltd and Mako Ltd, both of which owned heritable property. In the course of the dispute, Playfair Investments Ltd inhibited both companies on the dependence, the inhibitions taking effect in August 2011. But before August 2011 both companies had entered into deals relating to their heritable property, deals which had not yet been carried through by the time of the inhibitions.

There were two properties in question:[2] (i) a shop at 30–32 Canonmills, Edinburgh, owned by Mako Ltd, and (ii) a bar ('Bar Salsa') at 3 Cowgatehead, Edinburgh, owned by Cordelt Ltd. In relation to (i), Mako Ltd had concluded missives with JJB (Scotland) Ltd in August 2010 to lease the shop to the latter, with an option to buy. In May 2011 JJB (Scotland) Ltd served a notice on Mako Ltd exercising the option. In relation to (ii), Cordelt Ltd had concluded missives in May 2011 to sell Bar Salsa to Bruce Taverns Ltd.

The present phase of the dispute involved an application for recall of the inhibitions in relation to these two properties on the ground that, already before the inhibitions, the companies in question were contractually bound. The Lord Ordinary (Hodge) had no hesitation in concluding that s 160 had not changed the law about 'future voluntary acts', so that, to revert to the example given above, Beryl's title would not be open to challenge on the basis of the inhibition. He referred to the Scottish Law Commission project on which this part of the 2007 Act was based,[3] from which it appeared that there was no intention to change the law in this respect:[4]

I conclude that an inhibition does not strike at a transaction which the inhibited person is bound to carry out as a result of a pre-inhibition obligation. The reforms

1 [2012] CSOH 148, 2013 SLT 225.

2 It seems that there were other properties as well, but only two were involved in the case at this particular point.

3 Discussion Paper on *Diligence against Land* (Scot Law Com DP No 107, 1998); Report on *Diligence* (Scot Law Com No 183, 2001).

4 Paragraphs 23 and 24.

of the 2007 Act did not create a statutory code which excluded that common law characteristic of the diligence.

The decision will be welcomed by conveyancers, and should mean that the Keeper will no longer exclude indemnity in cases of this sort.[1] Of course, it is a question of the circumstances of each case as to whether the disposition is in fact protected by the missives, and no doubt the burden falls on the applicant to satisfy the Keeper. As will be seen, in the present case the Lord Ordinary was in fact *not* satisfied on this point.

Though the Lord Ordinary held that s 160 of the 2007 Act had not altered the 'future voluntary act' rule of the common law, he nevertheless declined to recall the inhibitions. There were several reasons for this,[2] but the most important was that he was not persuaded, on the evidence that was before him, that the proposed dispositions would in fact be 'voluntary acts' in the relevant sense. There had been considerable delay in both transactions and it was not clear that if the deals went ahead they would be purely and simply implementing the pre-inhibition obligations.

Another issue considered by the Lord Ordinary was whether a disposition is protected where it proceeds on pre-inhibition missives under which the inhibitee had the option to withdraw from the contract. He said:[3]

> I do not think that there is a general rule that a seller, who is entitled to rescind a contract of sale because of a purchaser's delay in payment of the price but who chooses or overlooks to do so, breaches an inhibition if he thereafter implements the extant contract.

Finally, whilst the point is not wholly clear, it seems that the application was for the *complete* recall of the inhibitions. If so, that would not have been appropriate. The 'future voluntary act' rule simply means that a particular transaction is protected from the inhibition. The inhibition remains effective in other respects. For example, suppose that the Donald/Beryl missives fall through, and Donald later resells to Bertie. The Donald/Bertie sale would not be protected from the inhibition. Accordingly, if Beryl had sought recall, the appropriate recall would have been limited in its terms to that particular transaction.[4]

WARRANDICE AND EXTRA-JUDICIAL EVICTION

Bad news for the purchaser

What is the position of a purchaser when, on first registration, the Keeper finds the title to be wanting? That was the unfortunate situation in *Morris*

---

1 But at the time of writing the Keeper seems not to have changed her policy. We are grateful to Lionel Most and Donald Reid for this information.
2 Paragraph 34.
3 Paragraph 30. We would agree: see G L Gretton, *Law of Inhibition and Adjudication* (2nd edn, 1996) p 99.
4 Gretton, *Law of Inhibition and Adjudication* p 60.

v Rae.[1] Back in August 2004 Ransom Developments Ltd had concluded missives for the purchase of 152 Dalmellington Drive, Ayr, at a price of £140,000. A disposition was granted on 23 August and an application made for first registration. On 8 June 2005 the Keeper wrote to Ransom's solicitors with bad news. No title existed to a significant part of the subjects disponed.[2] It appears that a plan attached to an earlier deed omitted the part in question. Evidently the plan was difficult to decipher, and Ransom's agents had not noticed anything untoward.[3] On closer inspection, however, the defect was beyond dispute.

By this time Ransom was engaged in building operations.[4] Sorting the title out was thus a matter of urgent necessity. Although what happened next is not disclosed in the court's opinions, it seems that Ransom opened negotiations with the person who appeared to be owner, a company called James Craig Ltd, and that the negotiations initially failed to prosper.[5] At any rate, on 18 November 2005, some five months after the Keeper's bombshell, solicitors representing Craig wrote asserting Craig's title and threatening to enforce it against Ransom. This, however, seems to have been no more than a bargaining position because, within a few months, the parties had reached agreement. Ransom was to pay £70,000; in exchange Craig would grant a disposition in respect of the missing area. Settlement of this transaction took place on 9 March 2006.

Ransom now looked to recover the £70,000 from Mrs Rae, the original seller and chose to do so under the warrandice clause of the disposition.[6] Warrandice is commonly thought of as a guarantee of good title, and in broad terms so it is. But no claim arises unless the disponee has been 'evicted': by itself the provision of a bad title is not a breach of warrandice. The meaning of eviction has been the subject of much previous litigation and, at its edges, remains rather unclear.[7] But in essence eviction requires two things. First, a person with better title to the property must actively assert that title; and secondly, either that title must be judicially declared ('judicial eviction') or, as Viscount Stair put it, the title must rest on a ground so 'unquestionable' that litigation would be a pointless formality ('extra-judicial eviction').[8] In *Morris v Rae*, Craig had not pressed its claim to the point of a court action, but so far as Ransom was concerned there

---

1 [2011] CSIH 30, 2011 SC 654, 2011 SLT 701, 2011 SCLR 428 *rev* [2012] UKSC 50, 2013 SLT 88.
2 It is not clear whether the application was rejected or whether the Keeper was willing to accept it but on the basis of exclusion of indemnity. The latter may have been the case: see [2012] UKSC 50 para 5 per Lord Hope. Unless otherwise stated, all references which follow are to the Supreme Court decision.
3 Paragraph 9.
4 Paragraph 4.
5 We infer this from the fact that James Craig Ltd, who could not have known of the Keeper's letter, made a claim for the property on 18 November 2005.
6 The action was actually raised by an assignee, Robert Morris.
7 K G C Reid, *The Law of Property in Scotland* (1996) para 707.
8 Stair, *Institutions* 2.3.46. This passage from Stair is quoted in the opinions of both Lord Hope (para 15) and Lord Reed (para 41). Those who have been troubled by the auto-corrective tendencies of Word will be pleased to note that in the quotation as given by Lord Hope (but not Lord Reed) 'declarator of distress' has been transformed into 'declaratory of distress'. As Lord Reed emphasised (para 46), finding fault with a *dictum* of Lord Eassie in *Holms v Ashford Estates Ltd* [2009] CSIH 28, 2009 SLT 389 at para 45, the test is entirely objective.

seemed no reason to doubt that such an action could not sensibly have been resisted.

Some more bad news

At this point, however, there was more bad news. Mrs Rae defended the warrandice action and in doing so averred that, far from the missing area belonging to Craig, it was actually the property of a Mr John Stevenson Lynch.[1] Investigation showed the averments to be true. While Craig had certainly owned the area at one time, Craig had disponed it to Mr Lynch as long ago as 1991. Ransom, it seemed, had paid Craig for nothing, and the second disposition was as worthless as the first.

Ransom's advisers worked quickly to put things right. Mr Lynch was contacted and agreed to grant a disposition to Ransom without further payment. His ownership, it seemed, was no more than an accident, a piece of careless conveyancing.[2] He had not intended to become owner, he had not known that it had happened, and, now that it was pointed out to him, he was evidently happy to do whatever was necessary to sort the position out. In the normal course of events that would have meant reconveying the area to Craig, but as Craig had sold to Ransom, it was to Ransom that Mr Lynch now conveyed. The disposition was granted on 30 July 2006 and registered by the Keeper without exclusion of indemnity.[3] Meanwhile the warrandice claim continued.

Extra-judicial eviction?

But for this second mix-up with titles, it could hardly have been disputed that eviction had taken place. On the version of the facts initially believed both by Ransom and by Craig, the position was entirely straightforward. Mrs Rae had disponed to Ransom land which belonged to Craig. Craig had asserted its title, by the letter of 18 November 2005. Ransom, having no defence to Craig's claim, had bought Craig off. It is true that there had been no litigation but, equally, on this view of the facts, no defence was available to Ransom. Although, therefore, there had been no judicial eviction of Ransom by Craig, there had certainly been extra-judicial eviction.

The re-written facts changed the position completely. Eviction requires active assertion of an unquestionably good title. But in *Morris v Rae* the active asserter (Craig) had no title, and the person who had a title (Mr Lynch) had not engaged in active assertion. It is true that Craig had the *means* to acquire such a title, as subsequent events were to prove. If not yet owner, Craig had a personal right to become owner. But the fact remained that Craig was not owner, and indeed never became owner as the title passed directly from Mr Lynch to Ransom.

---

1 This second bombshell was dropped in or around May 2006: see para 37.
2 According at least to the pursuer's averments.
3 As to whether this disposition was valid, see below.

For a majority of the Extra Division, this turn of events was an insuperable obstacle to a claim in warrandice. Craig was not owner when, on 18 November 2005, it asserted its title against Ransom; and in the absence of ownership Craig was not in a position to evict. In a judgment given in 2011 the Division dismissed the action.[1] The pursuer appealed to the Supreme Court.

In reaching its view, the Extra Division had relied on the decision of the First Division in *Clark v Lindale Homes*[2] including two passages[3] which referred to eviction by 'the competing title-holder' or 'the party with the competing title'.[4] But as the Supreme Court now pointed out, these passages had to be read in context and were in any event *obiter dicta*.[5] *Clark* had not been about the quality of the challenger's title; nor indeed was any other previous case. And no help, on that specific point, could be found in the institutional writers, in Mungo Brown's venerable *Treatise on the Law of Sale* (1821), or even in Robert Pothier's *Traité du Contrat de Vente* (1762), which had been influential in the treatment of warrandice by Brown and, later, by George Joseph Bell.[6] The question was thus an open one.[7]

The objection made to Craig's title was that he had a personal right and not a real right.[8] Yet a real right, the Supreme Court said, was not an indispensable basis for eviction. If Ransom's title had been voidable rather than void, eviction would have been procured by a reduction at the instance of a party whose right to reduce was necessarily only personal.[9] And while reduction was a special case, or at least a different case from that presently under consideration,[10] it showed that it was wrong to view matters too rigidly. As the authorities indicated, the essential requirement was that the challenger was 'in a position to make good his challenge'[11] by means of an 'unquestionable' title.[12] The threat, if it did not proceed to concluded litigation, must be shown to be 'capable of being made effective'.[13] But the precise way in which that might be done must be worked out 'according to the circumstances of each case',[14] and it was perfectly sufficient if, as in the present case, the challenger was 'in a position to compel the party in whom the real right is vested to transfer the title to him'.[15] Even if that was wrong, and a personal right was insufficient title, then, as Lord Reed

---

1   [2011] CSIH 30, 2011 SC 654, 2011 SLT 701, 2011 SCLR 428. See *Conveyancing 2011* pp 146–50.
2   1994 SC 210.
3   Respectively at 224 per Lord Morison and 220 per Lord President Hope.
4   2011 SC 654 at paras 9 and 10 per Lord Clarke.
5   [2012] UKSC 50 at para 24 per Lord Hope and para 39 per Lord Reed.
6   See Bell, *Principles* §§ 121–26.
7   Paragraph 3 per Lord Hope.
8   See para 18 per Lord Hope, para 39 per Lord Reed.
9   Paragraph 23 per Lord Hope, para 48 per Lord Reed.
10 Paragraph 49 per Lord Reed.
11 Paragraph 24 per Lord Hope.
12 Paragraph 45 per Lord Reed.
13 Paragraph 27 per Lord Hope.
14 Paragraph 24 per Lord Hope.
15 Paragraph 27 per Lord Hope. See also para 56 per Lord Reed ('an unqualified entitle-ment, exercisable immediately, to demand the transfer of the title currently vested in another person').

noted, an absence of title at the outset of the warrandice action might perhaps be cured by its acquisition as the litigation progressed.[1]

Underpinning, indeed determining, these technical arguments were questions of policy. The justification for extra-judicial eviction was, Lord Reed thought, 'essentially practical', reflecting 'the undesirability of pointless delay and expense, and pointless litigation, where eviction is ultimately inevitable'.[2] For the purchaser to defend an indefensible title 'would be a waste of time and money'.[3] A title, however, is no less indefensible just because the challenger has yet to take the necessary steps to complete his own title.[4] '[N]o useful purpose will be served by requiring the purchaser to resist the threat' until those steps have been taken. '[T]he only practical result of such a requirement would be pointless delay in the resolution of the purchaser's difficulties.'[5]

The Supreme Court allowed the appeal and remitted the case to the Outer House for the hearing of a proof before answer.

Third time unlucky?

There matters rest. Victory, at this point, is with the pursuer. But a proof has yet to take place and it cannot be assumed that the pursuer will succeed in proving his averments. There is, as Lord Hope noted, 'a substantial dispute as to the true state of the facts'.[6] Indeed there may be more bad news on the way. According to the defender's amended averments, it was wrong to suppose that Mr Lynch – the third, and most recent, person to be attributed with ownership[7] – was in fact the owner. On the contrary, he had disponed all the property acquired from Craig to himself and two co-trustees in 2002.[8] If that is true, then not only will the latest disposition obtained by Ransom be as ineffective as its two predecessors,[9] but the connection between Craig and the missing area may be too tenuous to qualify as a title for eviction

Evaluation

The idea that eviction need not always be judicial can be traced back as far as Stair's statement that 'warrandice will take effect where there is an

---

1 Paragraphs 52–55 relying in particular on *Westville Shipping Co Ltd v Abram Steamship Co Ltd* 1923 SC (HL) 68. In the present case, of course, no action was raised by Craig against Ransom.
2 Paragraph 51. See also para 26 per Lord Hope.
3 Paragraph 47.
4 Paragraph 26 per Lord Hope. In such cases 'the party who made the threat was ... in as good a position to make good the threat as he would have been if the real right had already been vested in him'.
5 Paragraph 51.
6 Paragraph 10 per Lord Hope.
7 The others being, first, Mrs Rae (the defender) and then James Craig Ltd.
8 Paragraph 10; see also para 59 per Lord Walker, a judge self-confessedly 'still largely unfamiliar with the intricacies of Scottish conveyancing'. With his retirement in March 2013, after more than a decade in the top court, he will have no opportunity to increase his knowledge.
9 Even so, as the disposition has been registered in the Land Register (indeed without exclusion of indemnity), Ransom will be the owner at least for now, although its title will be inaccurate and potentially vulnerable to rectification.

unquestionable ground of distress, though the fiar transacted voluntarily to prevent the distress'.[1] Yet, old as it is, this idea has lain virtually undeveloped until modern times. It was not until *Watson v Swift & Co's Judicial Factor*,[2] decided in 1986, that a person was held to be evicted by settling a court action to which there was no stateable defence. *Morris v Rae* has now extended the doctrine in two further respects. First, there can be eviction even though no action was raised at all; it is enough that the challenger makes a claim to which there is no defence. Secondly, the title of the challenger need not be complete provided he has the certain and immediate means of completing it.[3]

Both extensions are to be welcomed although only the second was much in doubt. They are fully consistent with the purpose of requiring eviction, which is to confine warrandice claims to titles which are bad in fact as well as in law – to titles, in other words, where the purchaser is subject to an active and ultimately successful challenge by a third party. So long, therefore, as a challenge is made, and is sure of success, there is no sense in insisting on litigation or on any particular form of title in the challenger. In the face of an irresistible challenge, the purchaser should be allowed to cut his losses, and in so doing to cut the amount which the seller must now pay out in warrandice.

A number of further points may be made. First, there is a difference between (i) facts which excuse eviction and (ii) facts which amount to (extra-judicial) eviction. A competing deed granted by the seller is a well-established example of the first. Settling a claim, as in *Morris v Rae*, is an example of the second.[4] From this it follows that in the first case (but not the second), a challenge by the competitor is not needed: the mere grant of the competing deed is enough. This distinction, however, is masked by language, with the second case sometimes being described as no more than a *threat* of eviction rather than as eviction itself. The potential for misunderstanding is captured in Lord Hope's opening statement that '[t]here can be eviction … if eviction is threatened'.[5]

Secondly, the case was decided in the Division, and argued on appeal, on the basis that the crucial time – the time when Craig must be shown to have had a right to the property – was when the threat was made. But even if this is correct, it seems a mistake to confine this time to a single day, the day (18 November 2005) when Craig's letter was sent. There was little clear-cut in the facts of *Morris v Rae*. Craig and Ransom were in negotiation for months. Letters were sent; threats were issued; offers were made. Matters became more complicated still

---

1 Stair, *Institutions* 2.3.46.
2 1986 SLT 217.
3 Paragraph 47 per Lord Reed (where 'for example he has an unqualified right to demand an immediate conveyance of it').
4 On this point the views of one of us have changed: compare K G C Reid, 'Warrandice in the sale of land', in D J Cusine (ed), *A Scots Conveyancing Miscellany: Essays in Honours of Professor J M Halliday* (1987) 152, 158 with K G C Reid, *The Law of Property in Scotland* (1996) para 707. In *Morris* at para 22 Lord Hope relies on the analysis given in the earlier of these publications. See also Bell, *Principles* § 895.
5 Paragraph 1. See also paras 18 and 45.

when the problem with Craig's title emerged. The challenge to Ransom was a process rather than a single event, and that process did not come to an end until, in March 2006, the parties finally came to terms.

More fundamentally, the focus on the time of the *threat* may itself be a mistake. Where a warrandice claim depends on eviction, and where the eviction is non-judicial – by voluntary surrender or accommodation[1] – what matters is that the surrender is made to the right person and for a good reason. And, logically, the time for determining these matters is the time of the surrender, ie of the eviction itself. Admittedly, the position may be different in the case of judicial eviction, for there the pursuer must have title to sue. But where the eviction is extra-judicial, it is the eviction itself which seems important and not the threat or claim on which the eviction proceeds. Indeed that seems to have been the view of Lord Hope (although the issue is not discussed as such) because he concludes his opinion by holding that 'the pursuer will be entitled to the remedy he seeks if he can prove that, *when RDL [Ransom] yielded to the threat,* JCL [Craig] would have been immediately able to secure title to the disputed part'.[2] As it happens, on the facts of *Morris v Rae* it made no difference whether Craig's title was evaluated in November 2005 or in March 2006, for it was unchanged between these dates. But it might easily have been otherwise. If the title defect had been spotted in time, so that Ransom paid in exchange for a disposition which was valid,[3] the surrender to Craig would have been on the basis of an irreproachable title and the doubts and disputes about whether eviction had taken place might never have arisen.

A third point concerns Craig's title. The absence of a real right was excused by the alleged existence of a personal right. The nature of that personal right, however, was not examined nor indeed, so far as the opinions are concerned, disclosed. Although the pursuer described Mr Lynch's title as 'voidable',[4] the corresponding remedy accorded to Craig was said to extend beyond reduction to rectification or alternatively the right to a corrective reconveyance.[5] Rectification indicates a reliance on s 8 of the Law Reform (Miscellaneous Provisions) (Scotland) Act 1985 and the doctrine of error in expression.[6] A reconveyance might suggest a claim in unjustified enrichment. The former, however, as Lord Walker pointed out, is discretionary,[7] the latter subject to various defences. In

---

1 According to R J Pothier, *Treatise on the Contract of Sale* (transl L S Cushing, 1839) §§ 83 and 95, eviction is 'abandonment' of the property to the challenger, whether voluntarily or as a result of a court decree. In similar vein, M P Brown, *A Treatise on the Law of Sale* (1822), writes of eviction occurring 'when a party is deprived of a subject by the sentence of a judge' (§ 330) or 'where the vendee has delivered up the subject to the party claiming it, without a law-suit' (§ 353). Reaching an accommodation with the challenger (eg to acquire the property) is the equivalent of abandonment or delivering up.

2 Paragraph 32. But compare para 2 where Lord Hope mentions indiscriminately the date of the threat and the date of surrender. It is possible that Lord Hope was not using 'yielding to the threat' in the technical sense of eviction.

3 This is on the assumption, challenged by the defender's averments (as mentioned above), that Mr Lynch was owner of the missing area.

4 Paragraph 48.

5 Paragraph 57.

6 The pursuer's averments on this point are quoted in 2011 SC 654 para 6.

7 Paragraph 59.

view of the court's requirement that Craig have 'an unqualified title, exercisable immediately, to demand a transfer of the title vested in Mr Lynch',[1] it is surprising that the nature of that title was left unexplored.

Avoiding warrandice

Whatever else *Morris v Rae* might do, it exposes once again the limitations of warrandice. No remedy lies without eviction; and there is no eviction unless the person with the better title chooses to assert that title. Thus suppose, for a moment, that the negotiations with Craig had proceeded in the same harmonious fashion as the later negotiations with Mr Lynch. There would then have been no letter of 18 November 2005, and in the absence of such a letter – of a direct assertion of title – there would, it seems, have been no eviction. The moral is plain. The negotiating tactic must be to rile the third party. Only when he has been driven to make a claim can the disponee relax and come to terms, for only then has there been eviction. If this is Scots law, it is hard to be proud of it.

There is, however, another way. Missives standardly bind the seller to produce a good and marketable title, together with such documents and evidence as the Keeper may require in order to issue a land certificate without exclusion of indemnity. If such a clause was in the missives in *Morris v Rae*, Mrs Rae was plainly in breach of it. And, unlike with warrandice in the disposition, there is no requirement of eviction: if the title is bad, the seller is immediately liable. Of course, there may sometimes be reasons – as perhaps there were in *Morris v Rae* itself – which prevent a claim under missives. For example, the description of the subjects may be too vague to establish that the missing area was included. Or the missives may have expired after the customary period of two years – although it is normal, and sound practice, for the clause on good and marketable title to be made exempt from such expiry.[2] Or again, and especially in commercial missives, the arrangement may be that the buyer must satisfy himself as to title. In short, the option of pursuing a claim under missives may be excluded. But where it is available, it should always be chosen over a claim under warrandice.

LONG LEASES (SCOTLAND) ACT 2012

Outline

The Long Leases (Scotland) Act 2012 has been some time in the making – indeed, its history goes back to the second half of the 1990s, as part of the process that led to the abolition of feudal tenure. Ultra-long leases, such as leases for 999

---

1 Paragraph 57 per Lord Reed. Lord Hope imposed the additional requirement 'that no proceedings would have been required to secure that result' (para 32), by which seems to be meant that it must have been clear in advance that Mr Lynch would co-operate. It is not explained why the prospect of litigation, even if bound to succeed, would be fatal to Craig's title.

2 See eg Combined Standard Clauses cl 16(f): 'Notwithstanding any other term within the Missives, this condition shall remain in full force and effect without limit of time and may be founded upon until implemented.'

years, are functionally very like feus, with the tenant being in effect a feuar, the landlord being in effect a superior, and the rent – or tackduty, the older term that is so often to be found in these deeds – being in effect feuduty. As with feus, inflation has generally reduced the real value of the rent to a small or nominal amount. As with feus, it is often neither tendered nor demanded. As with feus, it is sometimes nowadays unclear who the landlord is. As with feus, virtually the whole value of the property is attached to the tenancy, with the value of the landlord's interest being minimal. So when feudal tenure was abolished, there was an obvious logic in also purging the legal system of these quasi-feus by converting them into rights of ownership. For sound practical reasons this was not attempted in the project that led to the Abolition of Feudal Tenure etc (Scotland) Act 2000. But even before the 2000 Act was passed, the Scottish Law Commission (which was responsible for the feudal abolition project) had begun work on ultra-long leases.[1] Because of pressure of other work this project moved slowly, but culminated in the publication, in 2006, of a final Report on *Conversion of Long Leases*.[2] There was then a further delay until November 2010 when the Scottish Government introduced a Bill based on the Law Commission's draft. This Bill fell at the dissolution of the Scottish Parliament on 22 March 2011 but was reintroduced on 12 January 2012, and after completing its Parliamentary stages it received the Royal Assent on 7 August 2012. We do not yet have information on when it can be expected to be brought into force.

The broad outline of the scheme is, not surprisingly, based on that of the Abolition of Feudal Tenure etc (Scotland) Act 2000. Conversion of long leases into ownership will be automatic, just as under the 2000 Act the conversion of *dominium utile* into full ownership happened automatically: 'On the appointed day a qualifying lease becomes the right of ownership of the land.'[3] No conveyancing will be needed; the leasehold title automatically becomes an ownership title, and the current landlord loses ownership. As with the 2000 Act there are provisions for compensation, and as with the 2000 Act there are provisions for preserving certain rights by registered notices. But whilst the general picture is much the same as for feudal abolition, long leases are not the same as feus, and so many of the details are different. To some of these details we now turn.[4]

And some details

Convertible leases

What counts as an ultra-long lease? A twenty-five year lease obviously does not count, and a thousand-year lease obviously does. Precisely where one draws the line is to some extent arbitrary. The basic rule, to quote s 1(3), is that the Act applies to a lease:

---

1 Scottish Law Commission, *Thirty-Third Annual Report* (Scot Law Com No 167, 1998) p 13.
2 Scot Law Com No 204, 2006, available at www.scotlawcom.gov.uk.
3 Long Leases (Scotland) Act 2012 s 4(1).
4 Not all. The Act runs to 84 sections and there is a great deal of fine detail.

(a) which is registered,
(b) granted for a period of more than 175 years, and
(c) in respect of which the unexpired portion of that period is –

   (i) where the subjects of the lease wholly or mainly comprise a private dwelling house, more than 100 years,
   (ii) in any other case, more than 175 years.

There are some exceptions, listed in s 1(4).[1] One is where the rent is over £100 per annum (which would be unusual). Another is where the lease is 'for the sole purpose of allowing the tenant to install and maintain pipes or cables'.

In practice, ultra-long leases have often been divided, just like feus, so that, for example, a thousand-year lease of four acres in Ayrshire in 1820 may now consist of fifty separate units, all created between, say, 1825 and 1875, by partial assignations. In that case each of the fifty units is taken as a separate long lease for the purposes of the Act.[2]

Leases in layers

In feudal abolition, it was the estate that was the lowest unit of the feudal chain that was converted into full ownership, and all superiorities disappeared. The same principle applies to leasehold conversion. To quote the explanatory notes to the Bill:[3] 'If A, the owner of land, leases 10 hectares to B for 999 years and B in turn sublets 4 of these hectares to C for 920 years, C is the qualifying tenant in relation to the 4 hectares and B in relation to the remaining 6 hectares.' In this case, not only does A lose ownership, but B's intermediate lease is extinguished.[4] If, however, C's lease had been for 99 years then it would not be a qualifying lease, whereas B's would be, so it would be B who would become owner of all 10 hectares.

Leases with renewal and early termination provisions

In most cases the length of a lease is clear, but sometimes a lease has renewal provisions and a question may arise as to whether it is a convertible lease under the Act. The Act contains one or two significant provisions which, in borderline cases, make the lease a convertible lease. One is s 71 which provides, in part, that in calculating the period for which a lease is granted:

(a) any provision of a lease (however expressed) enabling the lease to be terminated earlier than the date on which it would otherwise terminate must be disregarded,
(b) where a lease includes provision (however expressed) requiring the landlord to renew the lease, the period for which any such renewed lease would, were that

1 There was lobbying to take certain leases outwith the ambit of the Bill. Some of this lobbying was unsuccessful (notably the attempt to exclude leases of common good property) while other lobbying was successful (eg the attempt by Peterhead Port Authority to keep its own arrangements outwith the ambit of the Bill).
2 LL(S)A 2012 s 1(5).
3 *Explanatory Notes* para 22. The *Notes* are detailed, clear and helpful.
4 LL(S)A 2012 s 4(1)(c).

provision complied with, be granted must be added to the period for which the original lease is granted. ...

Another is s 72, which says, perhaps rather cryptically:

Part 4 and s 71(1)(b) apply in relation to a lease which is continuing by tacit relocation as if any provision (however expressed) –

(a) included in the lease prior to it so continuing, and
(b) requiring the landlord to renew the lease,

had been complied with.

For example, suppose that there is a 200-year lease with a renewal option for a further period of 200 years, but the option has to be exercised before the expiry of the first 200 years. If the tenant does not exercise the option, but nevertheless stays in the property, what seems to be happening is that there is now a year-to-year lease by tacit relocation. Section 72 says that such a lease is treated as convertible.[1] In a year-to-year lease, almost all the capital value attaches to the landlord's interest, so if these leases are converted, the landlord will seemingly lose a great deal of money, for the compensation provisions of the Act do not give the landlord much. Accordingly, there might be a question whether s 72 is ECHR-compatible. However, the issues are admittedly not straightforward and differing views may be possible.

Opting out

The 2000 Act did not allow opting out: feudal tenure was abolished, lock, stock and barrel. By contrast, the 2012 Act does allow opting out, though since the opting has to be agreed to by the tenant, opt-outs are likely to be rare.[2]

Subordinate real rights

Conversion does not in general affect third-party real rights, such as servitudes, in respect of the *land* (ie the landlord's interest).[3] But if there is a standard security over the landlord's interest, that is extinguished;[4] such securities are presumably vanishingly rare.

Any subordinate real right affecting the *lease* (ie the tenant's interest) becomes, after conversion, a subordinate real right over the land itself.[5] For example, if a bank has a standard security over a 999-year lease, that automatically becomes a standard security over the land. Accordingly, if there is a standard security over the lease, granted in 2011, and the debtor defaults in 2016, what the lender sells will not be the lease but the land.

1 The provision was drafted with 'Blairgowrie leases' in mind.
2 LL(S)A 2012 s 64.
3 LL(S)A 2012 s 6(2).
4 LL(S)A 2012 s 6(4).
5 LL(S)A 2012 s 6(2).

Lease conditions

Under the 2000 Act, there was an elaborate scheme to deal with feudal conditions. Some of these converted automatically into non-feudal real burdens. Others were capable of being converted into non-feudal real burdens by the registration of a notice by the superior, in which case they survived if so converted, but otherwise died. Yet others were incapable of being saved. This scheme is applied by the 2012 Act to leasehold conversion, with appropriate adjustments.[1] For example, the system in the 2000 Act whereby certain feudal conditions could be converted into non-feudal real burdens by a neighbouring plot of land being nominated as the benefited property can also be found in the 2012 Act.[2] Normally the plot must contain a building used as a place of human habitation or resort and must lie within 100 metres of the land which was held on long lease.[3] Unsurprisingly, no leasehold condition can become a real burden unless it satisfies the requirements for real burdens under the Title Conditions (Scotland) Act 2003.[4]

Mineral rights and sporting rights

Reserved mineral rights are converted automatically into separate tenements, vested in the ex-landlords.[5] Reserved game rights are also to be kept by landlords, but with the difference that the conversion is not automatic, but requires the service and registration of a notice.[6]

Compensation

The 2000 Act had compensation provisions for superiors, and the 2012 Act has similar compensation provisions for landlords.[7] In feudal abolition, the vassal had to pay the superior a sum to compensate for the loss of any feuduty, and likewise the 2012 Act requires the tenant to make a 'compensatory payment' to compensate the landlord for loss of rent. Since, however, the Act excludes leases where the rent is over £100, such payments will range from the small down to the microscopic. And since the landlord has to serve a notice to claim this money, and do so within two years of conversion, it is likely that few such payments will in fact be claimed.[8]

In certain cases a landlord can, within two years of conversion, serve a notice claiming a further 'additional payment'.[9] This covers sources of loss to the landlord apart from the loss of rent, and is a mixed bag.[10] In relation to the

---

1 LL(S)A 2012 pt 2.
2 LL(S)A 2012 s 14.
3 LL(S)A 2012 s 14(4)(a).
4 LL(S)A 2012 s 11.
5 That the Act so says is perhaps not obvious at first glance, but this is the meaning and effect of s 6(5)(b).
6 LL(S)A 2012 s 8.
7 LL(S)A 2012 pt 4.
8 LL(S)A 2012 s 45.
9 LL(S)A 2012 s 50.
10 For the headings of possible loss see s 51.

'additional payment', as in relation to other matters, jurisdiction is given to the Lands Tribunal.[1]

The Land Register

Conversion happens automatically on the appointed day: those who drank their Horlicks the previous evening as tenants will sip their morning tea as owners. Thus the Land Register becomes inaccurate overnight. That is inevitable. Rectification of the Register will then be a matter for the Keeper,[2] although how long this will take is unclear.

UNFAIR MAINTENANCE ALLOCATIONS IN TENEMENTS

Frozen valuations

Missives standardly provide that maintenance liabilities should be equitably apportioned. Clause 15.1(a) of the Combined Standard Clauses is typical:

> Any part of the Property which is common or mutual with any adjoining property (including the roof and roof systems; rhones and downpipes; drains and boundary walls; fences or divisions) falls to be maintained, renewed and upheld by respective proprietors on an equitable basis.

Usually, of course, the apportionment is indeed equitable, whether the applicable provisions are found in the titles or, where the titles are silent, in the default rules set out in the statutory Tenement Management Scheme.[3] Certainly the TMS rules are equitable, providing as they do either for equality of contribution or, if the floor area of the largest flat is more than one and a half times that of the smallest, for liability on the basis of floor area.[4] And title provisions, although exhibiting a variety of techniques, also tend to achieve a basic fairness.

But it is not always so. Sometimes title provisions are unfair from the outset. A particular flat, for example, might be exempt from contributing to roof repairs, raising suspicions that in the mists of time it had been lived in by the original builder-developer. Equally, it is possible for provisions to begin fair but become unfair over time. Of this latter type the new case of *Patterson v Drouet*[5] is an important example.

First, some background. When domestic rates were abolished in 1989, the legislation provided that all existing maintenance obligations apportioned by reference to rateable value (or assessed rental or annual value) should continue to stand. But as there would be no new valuations, the valuation would be frozen

---

1 LL(S)A 2012 s 55.
2 Under the Land Registration etc (Scotland) Act 2012 s 80 (not yet in force but presumably in force by the appointed day) the Keeper must rectify a manifest inaccuracy if what is needed to do so is manifest.
3 The Tenement Management Scheme is set out in sch 1 to the Tenements (Scotland) Act 2004.
4 Tenement Management Scheme r 4.2.
5 20 January 2011 (first application), 2013 GWD 3-99 (second application), Lands Tribunal. The Tribunal comprised J N Wright QC and I M Darling FRICS.

as at 1 April 1989.[1] Today, more than twenty years on, some of these valuations might be seen to have become unfair, because there may have been changes to the *relative* values of the properties. And the unfairest case of all is where property that was in commercial use in 1989, and so had a high rateable value, has subsequently changed to domestic use and so should have a lower value.

That was exactly the position in *Patterson*. On the basis of the 1989 valuations, the two flats on the ground floor of an eight-flat tenement in Holland Street, Glasgow were liable for around three quarters of the maintenance costs. This is because they were used as shops and attracted a high valuation. Since 1989, however, the flats had reverted to residential use. If the valuation roll had continued to be updated, the position would have righted itself in the course of time. As it was, the ground-floor flats were subject to liability on a scale which had never been intended.

In theory, matters might have been put right by agreement among the proprietors. And since the maintenance provisions qualified as 'community burdens', the necessary deed of variation needed the agreement of the proprietors of a mere majority of the flats.[2] But in practice even a bare majority was unlikely to be attainable, for which upper proprietor would vote to pay more? Abandoning any idea of a consensual solution, therefore, the owners of the ground-floor flats applied to the Lands Tribunal for variation of the maintenance burdens. The application was opposed by the proprietors of some, but not all, of the upper flats.

The Lands Tribunal applications

The first application[3]

But there was a problem. While the Lands Tribunal can vary or discharge the burdens of those who apply to it, it cannot, in the normal case at least, vary or discharge the burdens of those who do not.[4] There is nothing surprising about this, for it would be a strange rule indeed which allowed an applicant to change the burdens on property belonging to a neighbour. In the present context, however, the result was undeniably awkward. The applicants requested a reduction in liability from 75% to 30%. But even if they succeeded, no corresponding increase in liability could be imposed on the owners of the upper flats. The result would be a liability shortfall. As it happens, the Tenements (Scotland) Act 2004 has a solution for cases of this kind. Where the figures for maintenance of 'scheme property' do not add up, the titles are disregarded and the relevant rule of the Tenement Management Scheme – rule 4.2 – applies instead.[5] In the circumstances of this particular tenement this would impose liability on the basis of floor area.

At this point, however, the Tribunal hesitated. On the merits it was satisfied that the application should succeed. The very first of the factors to which the Tribunal was required to have regard, under s 100 of the Title Conditions

---

1 The relevant provision is now s 111 of the Local Government Finance Act 1992.
2 Title Conditions (Scotland) Act 2003 s 33.
3 For discussion, see *Conveyancing 2010* pp 99–102.
4 Title Conditions (Scotland) Act 2003 s 90(1)(a)(i) (vary or discharge 'in relation to that property').
5 Tenements (Scotland) Act 2004 s 4(6).

(Scotland) Act 2003, was 'any change of circumstances since the title condition was created'. In the present case the change had indeed been striking:[1]

> Put shortly, the purpose of this title condition appears to us to have been to ensure that apportionment of common charges applicable to eight dwellinghouses would always be certain but would stay in line with current values. As we see it, three changes of circumstances in combination would make it reasonable in this particular case to vary the position which has now resulted: firstly, the change to commercial use of the applicants' properties; then the abolition of domestic rates and the resultant 'freezing' of values; and then the reversion back to residential use, resulting in frozen values bearing no relationship to current uses as intended by the deed of conditions. As a result of these changes in circumstances, the present apportionments produce gross disparities between two residential subjects and the other six residential subjects.

But the Tribunal had doubts as to competency. By s 90(5) of the Title Conditions Act a 'variation which would impose a new obligation' is not competent unless 'the owner of the burdened property consents';[2] and if the application in *Patterson* were to be granted, a new obligation would indeed be imposed on the other flats in the building. Yet there was no question of the owners of those flats giving their consent. The Tribunal continued the case for further submissions.

In our view, the application was competent. It is true that to grant the application would, in a sense, be to impose a 'new obligation' on the other flats. But there would be no new *real burden*, the obligation in question being imposed by the Tenement Management Scheme and not by the Tribunal. The significance of this distinction is brought out by the language of s 90(5) itself. The 'new obligation' to which that provision refers is one which is imposed on a 'burdened property' (the owner of which can give his or her consent); and 'burdened property' is defined in s 122(1) of the Act as land which is subject to a real burden or title condition. But if a 'new obligation' must thus be a title condition, it is evident that a (statutory) liability under the TMS does not qualify.[3]

The second application

As it turned out, however, there were to be no submissions as to competency. Instead there was a fresh application to the Tribunal,[4] and this time it was made, not in the 'normal' way, under s 90, but using the special procedure for community burdens set out in s 91. Less well known than it ought to be, this useful provision empowers the Tribunal to alter community burdens as they affect *all* the properties in the community provided that the application is brought by the owners of at least one quarter of these properties. In the present case the eight original flats had become nine following the division of one of the lower

---

1 *Patterson v Drouet* 20 January 2011, para 33.
2 This provision does not apply to applications under s 91, discussed below.
3 The official *Explanatory Notes* para 375 suggest that this provision (which was not in the Scottish Law Commission's draft Bill) is intended to cover the case where the application is made by a tenant and will have the effect of imposing an obligation on the property in respect of which the application is made, with the result that it will affect the owner of that property and should require his consent.
4 *Patterson v Drouet* 2013 GWD 3-99.

flats into separate ground-floor and basement units, and the application was brought by the proprietors of all three of the lower flats.[1]

As before and for much the same reasons, the Tribunal found for the applicants on the merits. A title provision which was once fair and equitable had, due to an unforeseen freezing of valuations, become unfair and inequitable. There was thus 'an unanswerable case based on material change of circumstances'.[2] Furthermore, although the provision benefited the upper proprietors in the obvious sense of substantially reducing their liability, there was also potential disadvantage in respect that the lower proprietors would be reluctant to agree to repairs when their own contribution was so high.[3] Indeed they could actually block the repairs, under the Tenement Management Scheme, due to the fact that their liability exceeded 75%.[4] The unfairness of the current apportionment was expressly accepted by the two proprietors who opposed the application, and must be taken to have been accepted by implication by the four proprietors who did not.[5]

The precise proposal was to change the basis of apportionment from annual value to floor area. This followed what would have been the default rule under the Tenement Management Scheme for a case like the present where the largest flat in the building (the undivided flat on the ground and basement) was more than one and a half times the size of the smallest. No doubt it would have been more fitting to propose a rule which, like the original, was based on valuation; but it was accepted by the Tribunal,[6] as it had earlier been accepted by the Scottish Law Commission in drawing up its reforms of the law of the tenement,[7] that no suitable rule could be found. As the following table shows, the overall change proposed was startling:

Flat	% Liability by annual value	% Liability by floor area
0/1	43.1	18
0/2[8]	32.6	17.2
1/1	3.76	9.9
1/2	4.42	11.7
2/1	3.64	9.9
2/2	4.42	11.7
3/1	3.64	9.9
3/2	4.42	11.7

1 The basement flat was owned in conjunction with a flat in the next-door tenement.
2 Paragraph 35. As previously mentioned, this is factor (a) of s 100 of the Title Conditions (Scotland) Act 2003.
3 Paragraph 37. This is factor (b) in s 100.
4 Tenement Management Scheme r 2.10. This point was not made by the Lands Tribunal.
5 Paragraph 46.
6 Paragraph 49.
7 Scottish Law Commission, Report on the *Law of the Tenement* (Scot Law Com No 162, 1998) para 5.62.
8 This aggregates the figures for what had become separate ground and basement flats.

As the case succeeded on its merits, and as no questions arose, this time, in respect of competency,[1] the Tribunal granted the application. The only remaining question was compensation.

Compensation

Under the legislation, the Tribunal, in granting an application, is empowered to order payment of compensation for any 'substantial loss or disadvantage' suffered by the benefited proprietors.[2] In *Patterson* the Tribunal declined to do so. 'Even … if it were established that the inequitable shares have had an effect on the value of any of the ground and basement properties at this tenement, so that variation will increase their value, it does not follow that the values of any of the upper flats would be reduced when their "generous" shares are increased to equitable shares.'[3] There was no evidence supporting such a reduction in values and, 'given the sums involved, and also the undoubted benefit to the tenement as a whole of replacing a scheme which has become inequitable with an equitable scheme', the Tribunal thought that a reduction was 'unlikely'. As for compensation for future additional liability, the Tribunal thought that it 'might possibly' be within its powers to award a capitalised sum[4] but that, in view of the benefit brought by the restoration of equitable apportionment, there had been no 'substantial loss' (as the statute required) to the upper proprietors.[5]

Wider applicability

Patterson v Drouet is a case of importance and of potentially wide applicability. The ready way in which the Tribunal found for the applicants, while refusing the claim for compensation, suggests that applications on the ground of inequitable apportionment are likely to be sympathetically received. Indeed the Tribunal's forthright views will have the welcome result of encouraging negotiated variations of unfair maintenance conditions.[6]

Some caveats, however, seem necessary. First, the burden in *Patterson* was inequitable, not in origin, but by supervening events. Absent the changes of circumstance (ie the statutory freezing of valuations followed by the switch from commercial to residential use), the application could hardly have succeeded. Importantly, *both* changes were needed. The statutory freeze produces inequitable results only where followed by significant changes in relative values. And if there is no change at all – if the position is simply that the apportionment

---

1 Paragraphs 25–28.
2 Title Conditions (Scotland) Act 2003 s 90(7). Although not relevant here, compensation can also be ordered 'to make up for any effect which the title condition produced, at the time when it was created, in reducing the consideration then paid or made payable for the burdened property'.
3 Paragraph 59.
4 The reason for the hesitation is unclear.
5 Paragraph 61. It may be added that the Tribunal was only willing to contemplate compensation to those proprietors who had troubled to oppose the application: see para 62.
6 As previously mentioned, community burdens can be varied by the owners of a majority of flats under s 33 of the Title Conditions (Scotland) Act 2003.

was unfair from the outset – then there is no basis for the Tribunal to interfere.[1] The change, however, could work either way. For if, as *Patterson* decides, a post-1989 change from shops to residential use makes apportionment unfair for the flats on the ground floor, so a change in these flats from residential use to shops would make apportionment unfair for those flats on the floors above.

Secondly, an application stands a better chance of success if brought under the special procedure for community burdens in s 91 rather than the standard procedure in s 90. But except in cases of unusual altruism, the 25% threshold required by the former is likely to be reached only if the owners of at least a quarter of the flats stand to gain from the proposed redistribution of liabilities.

Finally, and despite the decision in *Patterson*, it cannot be assumed that liability for compensation will always be avoided. Indeed the Tribunal was at pains to stress that the upper proprietors were not legally represented, that no valuation evidence was led on their behalf, and that 'compensation might be appropriate in some cases such as this'.[2] Depending on the circumstances, the compensation might even be large enough to induce the applicants to abandon their case.[3]

FRAUD

We do not usually cover English cases, because the English system is so different from the Scottish. But one area where it can be worth taking note of events south of the border is fraud, and below we deal with some English cases of 2012, two from the Court of Appeal and one from the Supreme Court, as well as one Scottish case.[4]

Mortgage forms and pork pies: enter the drugs squad

Playing POCA for profit

A loan application may not always be completed with the strictest regard for truth. What then? For the fraudulent borrower, there are normally no civil consequences. For once the loan has been advanced, the lender's right is simply to get it back, plus interest. If repayment in full takes place, the lender suffers no loss. If repayment in full does *not* take place, the lender does suffer a loss, for which the borrower is liable, but the borrower was liable anyway, simply by virtue of the loan contract.

What about criminal consequences? If someone obtains a loan by lies, that is fraud, and fraud is a crime. But in practice if the borrower successfully keeps up

---

1 As was shown in *Kennedy v Abbey Lane Properties* 29 March 2010, Lands Tribunal, discussed in *Conveyancing 2010* pp 97–99.
2 Paragraph 57. See also para 4: 'Although we are clear that the claims for compensation do not succeed in this case, it is a potentially difficult issue requiring deeper consideration.'
3 As they are entitled to do. Payment of compensation requires the agreement of the applicant: see Title Conditions (Scotland) Act 2003 s 90(9).
4 Further issues involving fraud are considered at p 88 above.

the payments, the fact of the lies is unlikely to come to light, and even if it does come to light, if the lender is suffering no loss the procurator fiscal is unlikely to be informed, and, even if informed, may not be very interested. If the borrower does default, the position may be different, but even here the procurator fiscal may not be told, and, if told, may not act. Fiscals have in their in-trays more crime than they can handle. They have to prioritise, and false loan applications are unlikely to be at the top of the list. Prosecutions cost money, and the penalties imposed are likely to be slight.

But this picture is changing. The change is happening only south of the border, or, at any rate, if it has been happening in Scotland we have not heard of it. But if it is not happening in Scotland at the moment, perhaps it will only be a question of time, because the relevant legislation is (with certain unimportant qualifications)[1] applicable both sides of the border: the Proceeds of Crime Act 2002 ('POCA').

We ordinarily think of the Proceeds of Crime Act 2002 – if we think of it at all, which no doubt most of us prefer not to – as the basis for stripping career criminals such as drug dealers of their ill-gotten gains. And so it is. The origins of the legislation were indeed about drug dealing.[2] But the legislation was later expanded so as to cover all forms of criminality. Sometimes the results can be startling and, indeed, of questionable fairness. The term 'draconian' has been used more than once by judges called upon to apply the legislation. *R v Waya*[3] illustrates the startling results. It also illustrates the impenetrable obscurity of the legislation, for the High Court produced one result, the Court of Appeal another, the majority of the Supreme Court a third, and the minority of the Supreme Court a fourth, with other reasonable possibilities also open to debate.

R v Waya

In 2003 Terry Waya applied for a mortgage loan to buy a flat in London. The price was £775,000, and the loan he sought, and obtained, was £465,000. The purchase went ahead in the ordinary way. In April 2005 he paid off the loan.[4] In November of the same year he was arrested for having obtained the loan by making untrue statements on the mortgage application form. Details are not known other than that 'he made false statements about his employment history and current earnings'.[5] Why the police took action against Mr Waya, especially

---

1 Many provisions of the 2002 Act apply only in England and Wales. But elsewhere in the Act substantially similar provisions exist which apply to Scotland.

2 The story begins with the Drug Trafficking Offences Act 1986. There have been numerous subsequent statutes, and the 2002 Act, which superseded most of the previous legislation, has itself been much amended. This interminable and rambling enactment will defeat most readers. Whether its policy is right or wrong, as a piece of legislation it is a blot on the statute book. Though vast, it does not even cover all the law: for instance parts of the Proceeds of Crime (Scotland) Act 1995 are still in force.

3 [2012] UKSC 51, [2012] 3 WLR 1188.

4 Though not relevant to the legal issue, we note that there was an early redemption fee of £58,000. Golly.

5 This is from para 7 of the judgment of Blake J when the case was in the Court of Appeal (Criminal Division): [2011] 1 Cr App R (S) 4. The Supreme Court notes that 'Waya's advisers may have encouraged him to make false statements' (para 36).

given that the loan had been repaid, is unknown. There is some mystery here to which the law reports provide no key.

Mr Waya was prosecuted and convicted.[1] His sentence was 80 hours of community service: evidently the court considered his offence to have been minor. But the prosecution also sought and obtained a POCA order. Mr Waya was condemned to pay the Crown £1,540,000. One can at once see why the 2002 Act has been proving so popular in England. From the Crown point of view, criminal prosecutions are generally loss-making enterprises. POCA is where the money is. Minor offences can bring to the Crown eyewateringly large amounts of money. Had £1,540,000 been labelled a fine, it would have been inconceivable and, if the inconceivable had actually happened, there would have been public uproar and questions in Parliament. But it was a 'forfeiture' of the 'proceeds of crime'. Change a label and all is changed.

How was the figure arrived at? The flat was, by the time of Mr Waya's conviction in 2007, worth £1,850,000. This was the property that he had been enabled to acquire by his fraud. From this sum fell to be deducted the amount that he had paid himself by way of deposit. So £1,540,000 was the figure that represented his ill-gotten gains. The main interest of the case to a Scottish audience has already been set out: false statements in loan application forms can result in spectacularly large forfeitures, so large that the result may be financial ruin for the client.[2]

Mr Waya appealed, and the Court of Appeal agreed that £1,540,000 was too much, and reduced the figure to £1,110,000.[3] The court reasoned thus: the fraudster had borrowed 60% of the purchase price, so 60% of the value of the property should be considered as being what he had fraudulently acquired. And 60% of the value of the property (at its current valuation) was £1,110,000. Clearly there was a strong logic about this way of looking at things.

Mr Waya appealed again, to the Supreme Court, which evidently found the case difficult, for it took about eight months to issue its decision, nine justices sat instead of the usual five, and, when the court did decide, it was a split decision. The court came up with yet another figure, £392,000, but the minority would have reduced this to zero. The majority reasoned thus:[4]

> The interest which fairly represented his original chose in action was 60% of the open market value of the flat from time to time, less the whole of the mortgage liability (£465,000). In other words it was 60% of any increase in the flat's market value over its acquisition price.

This 'interest' was Mr Waya's to keep, but anything beyond that interest constituted 'proceeds of crime'. Thus immediately after the purchase, the 'proceeds' element was nil, but as the value of the property increased, the

---

1 The conviction was under the Theft Act 1968 s 15A. In Scotland the offence would be common-law fraud.
2 Eventually, as will be seen, the sum was reduced to £392,000, but the point still stands.
3 [2011] 1 Cr App R (S) 4.
4 Paragraph 70.

'proceeds' element emerged and increased. The majority gave the following calculation to produce what they regarded as the correct result. It takes into account the new mortgage that Mr Waya took out and also a repayment he made of £23,400:[1]

Market value: £1,850,000
Mortgage: £862,000
Equity: £987,400
Original equity and repayment: £333,400
Appreciation: £654,000
60% thereof: £392,400

The minority (Lord Phillips of Worth Matravers and Lord Reed) disagreed.[2]

> It seems to us that the only benefit that Mr Waya obtained by his dishonesty was that the terms of the loan advanced to him may have been somewhat more generous than they would have been had he told the truth about his income. A confiscation order in the value of that benefit would plainly be proportionate. That, in effect, would make him pay the price that he should have paid for the finance that he obtained. ... In these circumstances we cannot accept that the real benefit that Mr Waya obtained by his dishonesty was any part of the increase in value of the flat. The real benefit was no more than the money value of obtaining his financing on better terms than might otherwise have been available. ... In theory the case could be remitted for determination of that benefit. But after the time that has elapsed and the stress that these proceedings must have involved for Mr Waya, we would not think it just to adopt that course. We would simply allow this appeal and quash the confiscation order.

There will be many who will consider this a more rational approach. But the truth is that POCA is hardly amenable to rational interpretation. It is not that criminals should not be stripped of their ill-gotten gains. Rather, it is that POCA is unable to do that job properly. That is so even without reference to the ECHR dimension. Though POCA post-dates the Human Rights Act 1998, it comes from a different world. The Supreme Court spent much time worrying about the need to interpret the Act in such a way as to ensure ECHR-compatibility.

We offer two final comments. One is that the approach of the majority results, we think, in an absurdity, which is that the 'offender' can minimise POCA liability by the simple device of increasing the mortgage debt. The other is that, to determine precisely what Mr Waya 'acquired', the Supreme Court found it necessary to enter into the technicalities of English property law. For example, it was said, in words barely comprehensible to a Scottish reader, that 'the mortgage advance remains in the beneficial ownership of the lender until completion, when it passes direct to the vendor'.[3] If the same type of case were to arise in Scotland, the courts would have to interpret POCA in the context of Scots property law.

---

1 Paragraph 80.
2 Paragraphs 123–25.
3 Paragraph 51.

Fake your own law firm

The CML *Handbook for Scotland* says:[1]

> If you are not familiar with the seller's solicitors or independent qualified conveyancers, you must verify that they appear in a legal directory or they are currently on record with the Law Society of Scotland or other supervisory body as practising at the address shown on their note paper. Check part 2 to see whether we require you to notify us of the name and address of the solicitors firm or licensed conveyancers firm acting for the seller.

Sensible advice no doubt. But the risks which caused this provision to be inserted are perhaps not sufficiently well known north of the border. In England, by contrast, fake law firms have been a problem for some years. We offer two cases from 2012, both of which reached the Court of Appeal, and which are interesting not only on their facts but also in legal terms.

Lloyds TSB Bank plc v Markandan & Uddin

In *Lloyds TSB Bank plc v Markandan & Uddin*[2] Victor Davies applied to Cheltenham & Gloucester plc[3] for a mortgage loan of £742,500 to buy a house at 35 Claremont Road, Hadley Wood, north London, at a price of £1,150,000. A law firm, Messrs Markandan & Uddin,[4] acted for both borrower and lender. A mortgage valuation was carried out, and the property was valued at £825,000.[5] The owners of the property were Gary and Monique Green. Messrs Markandan & Uddin were contacted by a law firm called Messrs Deen, who said that they were acting for the Greens. Messrs Markandan & Uddin checked the directory of law firms. They saw that the firm was a genuine firm but they also saw that the letter that had come in was from a branch not given in the directory. They raised this point, and were told that it was a new branch and would appear in the directory soon. They were satisfied with that explanation and went ahead with the transaction. When no signed transfer document was available at completion date, they accepted an undertaking from Messrs Deen to deliver it. On that basis they drew down the loan funds, and paid the price to Messrs Deen. Nothing further was heard from the latter. It turned out that the 'branch' was not a branch of the real Messrs Deen, who, indeed, knew nothing about it; it was simply the temporary address of a fraudster. It may be added that the owners of the property in question, the Greens, knew nothing about what was happening. What happened to Victor Davies, and indeed the possibility that he was part

---

1 Paragraph 3.2. The CML *Handbook for England and Wales* is in substantially the same terms: see p 148 below.

2 [2012] EWCA Civ 65, [2012] 2 All ER 884.

3 A subsidiary of Lloyds TSB Bank plc. How the present action could be competently raised by the parent company is unclear. However, the defendants did not raise the question of title to sue.

4 A search of the English Law Society's site (January 2013) fails to identify any firm with this name. It may be that as a result of this case the firm has been dissolved.

5 From the point of view of the fraudsters, this large difference was unwise, because it might have raised suspicions. But in the event it seems that no eyebrows were raised, and in the litigation nothing turned on this point.

of the fraud, and perhaps even the same person as the fraudster, is a question on which the report casts no light.

An unaccountable twist in the tale is that Messrs Markandan & Uddin settled the transaction *twice* in this way. In early September 2007 they paid the price against an assurance that the transfer document would be delivered shortly. When it was not delivered, they asked for the money back *and it was paid back*. We cannot offer any explanation as to why the fraudster did not simply pocket the money at this stage. Then in late September a second settlement happened, as set out above, and this time the fraudster did pocket the money.

One chilling aspect of the whole story is that the fraudster evidently had a substantial knowledge of English conveyancing practice, for otherwise it would not have been possible for him to deceive Messrs Markandan & Uddin so comprehensively. For example, here is the fax sent by the fraudster immediately before 'completion':

> Please refer to our telephone conversation of yesterday regarding the TR1. My clients are away until the 10th October 2007 and I undertake to forward you the duly signed TR1 on their return. Kindly remit the funds so that I may complete this transaction and forward you the DS1 as soon as I receive it. I can confirm that I have today spoken with my clients and they have agreed to let your client have possession today and the keys are to be collected from our offices.

The lender sued Messrs Markandan & Uddin to recover the loan funds. Its argument was that the advance, on being paid to the law firm, was held by the firm in trust, and that to pay the money over to a fraudster was breach of trust. The basis for this argument lay in the CML *Handbook for England and Wales*, which says: 'You must hold the loan on trust for us until completion.'[1] The High Court agreed, as did the Court of Appeal, that there could never be 'completion' in a fake transaction. Hence the firm had committed a breach of trust.

That was not, however, the end of the story. Under English law, a trustee who commits a breach of trust can be relieved of liability by the court:[2]

> If it appears to the court that a trustee ... is or may be personally liable for any breach of trust ... but has acted honestly and reasonably, and ought fairly to be excused for the breach of trust ... then the court may relieve him either wholly or partly from personal liability.

The defendants argued that if indeed they had been guilty of breach of trust, they should be relieved of liability under this provision. The High Court refused relief and the Court of Appeal confirmed that decision. Although the honesty of Messrs Markandan & Uddin was not in question, they had not acted with sufficient competence:[3]

---

1 Paragraph 10.3.4; in the current edition it is para 10.7. The CML *Handbook for Scotland* para 10.4 says the same: 'You must hold the loan on trust for us until settlement.'
2 Trustee Act 1925 s 61. The position is similar in Scotland: Trusts (Scotland) Act 1921 s 32.
3 Paragraph 61 of the Court of Appeal judgment.

Their material failings were: (i) to establish that Deen actually had an office in Holland Park, which constituted a breach of cl.A3.2 of s.3 (Safeguards)[1] of the *Handbook*; and (ii) to part for a second time with the money in late September when they knew that HPD[2] had breached their earlier undertakings.

So Messrs Markandan & Uddin were sunk because they had been insufficiently sceptical about the branch address. They were also sunk, as the passage above indicates, because they had 'part[ed] for a second time with the money in late September when they knew that HPD had breached their earlier undertakings'. This might be queried: the fact that the fraudster had actually (amazingly) returned the money after the first abortive settlement was surely good grounds for trust. We might add that it does not seem to have been regarded as negligent to settle against an assurance that the transfer deed would be delivered.

It will be noted that the action was based on trust law. What about simple contract law? Might Messrs Markandan & Uddin not have been liable simply for breach of their contract with the lender? After all, the firm was acting for both borrower and lender so the lender was a client. That issue was not really explored in that case, but it was explored in another Court of Appeal case, later in 2012, also involving a fake law firm.

Nationwide Building Society v Davisons

In *Nationwide Building Society v Davisons Solicitors*,[3] Kalpesh Kumar Hasmukh Patel wished to buy a house in Sutton Coldfield, Warwickshire. He obtained a loan from Nationwide Building Society, and the same law firm, Davisons, acted for both borrower and lender. The seller, Shamsun Naher Begum, was represented by a sole practitioner, Bipin Kumar Gill, who traded under the name 'Rothschild'. Davisons drew down the advance and paid the price to Rothschild.[4] In exchange they received a signed deed of transfer. But the executed discharge of the seller's mortgage, though promised, was not delivered. It then turned out that though Rothschild was genuine, Davisons had been dealing with a fake branch, and the fraudster running that fake branch had pocketed the money and disappeared.

Thus far the facts are much the same as in the previous case. But there were significant differences too. In the first place, Davisons had checked the branch address with the Law Society. It was indeed registered with the Law Society as a branch. How this situation arose is not clear, but this was a vital difference between this case and the previous case. Next, whereas in the previous case the owners, the Greens, knew nothing about the sale, and never signed anything, in the present case it seems that the owner, Shamsun Naher Begum, was intending to sell and did indeed sign the transfer deed.[5] The deed of transfer was in fact

---

1 This is substantially the same as the provision quoted above from the Scottish *CML Handbook* about verifying the identity of the other firm.
2 The Court of Appeal's shorthand for the fake branch.
3 [2012] EWCA Civ 1626.
4 In both this and the previous case one wonders how the fraudster had been able to set up an ostensibly valid solicitor's account with a bank.
5 This was never actually established in the litigation, but it is at least a reasonable inference.

registered, so that the buyer had acquired title to the property. But the seller did not move out and indeed carried on making his monthly mortgage payments.[1]

In an action by the lenders against Davisons, it was held that there had been no 'completion' and that accordingly Davisons had parted with the loan funds in breach of trust – a perhaps surprising conclusion given that what seems to have been a valid deed of transfer had been delivered in exchange for the price. The question then was, as before, whether Davisons should be relieved from liability under s 61 of the Trustee Act 1925. It was held that they should be relieved of liability, the key point being that the fake branch had appeared on the Law Society list.

But what about contract law? Could the lender not simply hold the law firm liable for damages for breach of contract, having failed to obtain a valid first charge over the property? This issue, which was not discussed to any significant extent in the *Markandan & Uddin* case, was given more attention in the *Davisons* case. The Court of Appeal held that the obligations set out in the CML *Handbook* are not obligations of strict liability:[2]

> The effect of the absolute undertaking for which counsel for Nationwide contended would be to impose on Davisons the equivalent of a guarantee that all existing charges would be redeemed and Nationwide would obtain a fully enforceable first charge by way of legal mortgage over The Property. If that was the intention of the parties almost all the rest of the CML *Handbook* would be redundant. In these circumstances I would hold that the obligation imposed by paragraph 5.8 goes no further than an obligation to exercise reasonable skill and care in seeking to procure the outcome it refers to, namely the redemption of all existing charges and obtaining a fully enforceable first charge by way of legal mortgage. ... There was no alternative claim for any failure to exercise reasonable skill and care. If there had been then it appears that Davisons would have relied on its allegations of contributory negligence.

This, of course, is an English decision. What about Scotland? As already noted, the terms of the two CML *Handbooks* are the same, apart from minor differences of wording, in relation to both (i) verifying the identity of the other law firm/branch and (ii) holding loan funds in trust. And the 'relief from liability' provisions of the trust legislation are again substantially the same. Of course, as an English decision the *Davisons* case would not be a binding authority in Scotland, but it would be a persuasive authority.

Finally, a few words about the fact (based on the CML *Handbook's* wording) that the loan money is held in trust until settlement. Presumably that means that the loan is not made until the trust ceases, at settlement. For if the client's

---

1 If, as the circumstances suggest, the seller was a genuine and honest seller, he would have been expecting to be paid the price (minus the amount needed to redeem the mortgage), and when this did not happen, because his 'solicitor' vanished, he may have reacted by simply staying in the property. But these issues are not explored in the case. If the seller is now a non-owning possessor, and the buyer is an owning non-possessor, and the seller's mortgage is undischarged, one wonders how the mess will be cleared up, especially when one considers that both the seller's and the buyer's lenders are unpaid.

2 Paragraphs 57 and 58 of the judgment of Sir Robert Morritt, with whom the other judges concurred.

obligation to repay the money arose before that time, the odd result would be that the bank would be owed the whole sum twice over (by the borrower and by the law firm). Hence it seems to be at settlement that the client is considered as having received the advance. That may make sense. But take the *Davisons* case. Here the law firm is not liable to the bank. Nor, it seems, is the borrower, Kalpesh Kumar Hasmukh Patel, because the advance was never actually made to him (because the court held that there had been no 'completion'). So who *does* owe the bank the money? The fraudster, presumably. And yet Kalpesh Kumar Hasmukh Patel is now the owner,[1] and thus seems to make a windfall gain.

The Scottish angle

Last year we discussed two connected fraud cases when they were in the Outer House: *Cheshire Mortgage Corporation Ltd v Grandison* and *Blemain Finance Ltd v Balfour & Manson LLP*.[2] In both cases, fraudsters impersonated the owners of residential properties, and borrowed money, granting standard securities over the properties. Having raised the money, they then vanished. In both cases, separate law firms acted for the lenders and borrowers. The two lenders then sued the two law firms that had acted for the fraudsters. The argument in both cases was the same. When one party (such as a law firm) purports to transact as the agent of another (such as a client), there is an implied warranty of authority. If that authority turns out not to exist, the purported agent is strictly liable. It should be added that the law firms acting for the fraudsters had carried out the usual ID checks. But high-quality fake ID can be fabricated or purchased.

The Lord Ordinary (Drummond Young) held that there had been no breach of the warranty of authority because the law firms had in fact been instructed. The problem was not lack of instructions but the fact that those giving the instructions had no title. The lenders reclaimed and the Inner House has refused the appeal, affirming the reasoning of the Lord Ordinary.[3] It may be added that in one of the two cases, but not the other, the claim was also based on the terms of the letter of obligation. This argument also failed, understandably.

The decision will be welcomed by the legal profession.[4] But when there is fraud there are often multiple legal issues. In these two cases the lenders were unsuccessful in their attempts to recover from the law firms that represented the fraudsters. But what would have happened if they were to sue the law firms that acted for them? That is the route that was explored in England in the cases discussed above, in which one action failed but the other succeeded. The argument would be that the firms held the loan money in trust 'until settlement',[5] that in view of the fact that the standard securities were forgeries

---

1 Or, to be precise, seized as tenant in fee simple.
2 [2011] CSOH 157, 2012 SLT 672: see *Conveyancing 2011* pp 118–21 where we discuss some details of the way the frauds were carried out which we will not repeat here.
3 [2012] CSIH 66, [2013] PNLR 3, 2012 GWD 30-609.
4 For a discussion with this angle to the fore, see Derek Allan, 'Who do you think they are?' (2012) 57 *Journal of the Law Society of Scotland* Dec/14.
5 CML *Handbook for Scotland* para 10.4: 'You must hold the loan on trust for us until settlement.'

there had been no true 'settlement', and that accordingly the trust money should be returned to the lenders, leaving the law firms out of pocket. If that argument were to be accepted, then the next issue would be whether the law firms could nevertheless escape liability on the basis of the 'relief' provision in the Trusts (Scotland) Act 1921.[1] There is also the question of whether the failure to obtain a valid first-ranking security constituted a strict-liability breach of contract: this issue too is explored in one of the English cases discussed above. These various issues remain to some extent open in Scots law.

There is also the 'which register?' question. These frauds both involved properties that were still in the Register of Sasines, and since the forged deeds were standard securities, first registration was not triggered. To what extent might matters have been different if these had been Land Register cases? So, to repeat: whilst this decision will be welcome to the legal profession, it should not be thought that the legal issues in this area are all now settled.

BOUNDARIES AND PRESCRIPTION

Contradictory elements in foundation writs

In its comfortingly familiar language, the Prescription Act requires, for Sasine titles, 'a deed which is sufficient in respect of its terms to constitute in favour of that person [ie the possessor] a real right in (i) that land or (ii) land of a description *habile* to include that land'.[2] And with positive prescription being fully restored by the Land Registration etc (Scotland) Act 2012, these words will in future apply to Land Register titles as well.[3]

But what do these words mean? And what, in particular, is a 'description *habile* to include' land?[4] Often the issue is analysed by reference to whether the description is 'bounding', on the basis that a bounding title will exclude anything which lies outside it. But this approach is simplistic and, often, unhelpful. It risks entanglement with the highly technical question of bounding descriptions; it seems to suggest what is not true, namely that a *non*-bounding title will necessarily be *habile* for prescription; and above all, it draws attention away from the central question for discussion, which is simply whether the description in the deed can be read as including the land which is targeted for acquisition.

A more sophisticated approach is to divide descriptions into four categories, as follows:

---

1 Trusts (Scotland) Act 1921 s 32.
2 Prescription and Limitation (Scotland) Act 1973 s 1(1).
3 Land Registration etc (Scotland) Act 2012 sch 5 para 18(2). This method of doing things is surprising. In s 86 of the Draft Bill accompanying its Report on *Land Registration* (Scot Law Com No 222, 2010) the Scottish Law Commission followed the existing law by focusing, not on the underlying deed, but on the actual entry on the Register. It is not clear why the 2012 Act has chosen to depart from this.
4 The initial discussion on bounding titles and types of description is drawn from *Conveyancing 2009* pp 170–71.

(a) *Uncontradicted inclusion.* The words or plan plainly include the targeted property and there is nothing else in the description to contradict that inclusion.

(b) *Ambiguity.* The words or plan might or might not include the targeted property.

(c) *Uncontradicted exclusion.* The words or plan plainly exclude the targeted property and there is nothing else in the description to contradict that exclusion.

(d) *Contradicted exclusion/inclusion.* The words or plan plainly exclude the targeted property but other words or plan in the description, equally plainly, include it.

In relation to the first three of these categories the law is well established. A description will found prescription where it includes the targeted property or where, though unclear and ambiguous, it is *capable* of being read as including the property.[1] Conversely, a description will not found prescription where there is an uncontradicted exclusion of the property.[2] This indeed is what is normally meant by a bounding description, ie one in which the targeted property falls on the wrong side of the boundary.

On the final category (contradicted exclusion/inclusion) there has until now been an unfortunate absence of authority. The issue, however, arose directly for decision in *Trustees of Calthorpe's 1959 Discretionary Settlement v G Hamilton (Tullochgribban Mains) Ltd.*[3]

By a disposition granted and recorded in 1977 there was disponed:[4]

ALL and WHOLE [A] that area of ground lying partly in the County of Inverness and partly in the County of Moray delineated in red and coloured pink on the said plan annexed and subscribed as relative hereto … [B] and which said last mentioned area of land is part and portion of all and whole those lands and others in the said counties extending to six thousand eight hundred and twenty one acres or thereby Imperial Measure delineated in red and coloured pink on the plan annexed and subscribed as relative to the Disposition granted by Ian Derek Francis Ogilvie-Grant-Studley-Herbert, Viscount Reidhaven in favour of Niall Hamilton Anstruther-Gough-Calthorpe dated twenty fourth September and recorded in the Division of the General Register of Sasines for the counties of Inverness and Moray for 1 November both in the year nineteen hundred and sixty eight. …

The description was in the two parts to be expected of a split-off writ. Part [A] described the land being disponed, in this case by reference to a plan; and part [B], through a part-and-portion clause, linked that land to the larger area from which it was broken off, being the area described in a disposition of 1968. But there was a problem, for while the subjects in dispute in the litigation were

---

1 The leading case is *Auld v Hay* (1880) 7 R 663.
2 Eg *Gordon v Grant* (1850) 13 D 1.
3 [2012] CSOH 138, 2012 GWD 29-599.
4 Paragraph 35; our lettering.

included within part [A], they were not included within part [B].[1] Further, these subjects, as it turned out, were not the property of the disponers at the time of the grant although they had subsequently been possessed by the disponees.[2] Could the 1977 disposition – and a subsequent disposition of 1991 which incorporated the 1977 description by reference[3] – found prescription in respect of the subjects?[4]

Lady Clark of Calton held that it could not. More than merely ambiguous – category (b) above – the 1977 description was 'internally inconsistent' and indeed 'self destructive'.[5] Lady Clark continued:[6]

> In my opinion it is impossible to make sense of the dispositive clause in the 1977 disposition as the description is totally contradictory. The disputed land is included in the 1977 plan but not included in the 1968 plan. This does not make sense.

The key question, however, is not whether the description 'makes sense' but whether it is *habile* for the purposes of prescription. The disputed subjects, after all, were included within *one* of the two descriptive elements, and the more important one at that, as being both the more recent and also the only one included in full in the disposition. There is nothing in Lady Clark's judgment to explain why that was not enough.

As it happens there is prior authority. In *Nisbet v Hogg*[7] a disposition from 1921 conveyed a property known as Raybank[8]

> [A] together with the whole rights and pertinents thereof, including all rights in any way competent to me in and to the triangular area of ground on the south side of the road or path in front of the said houses ... and in and to the washing-house erected thereon, lying the said subjects within the Parish of Melrose and County of Roxburgh [B] and which subjects are described in the title deeds thereof as follows, *videlicet*: all and whole that house and garden in Gattonside bounded as follows, namely ... on the south by the town street of Gattonside. ...

The dispute concerned 'the triangular area of ground' and, as in *Calthorpe*, the area was included within part [A] of the description but not within

---

1 This was because the 1968 disposition, it was held, did not include the disputed subjects: see paras 29–33.
2 No proof, however, has taken place.
3 Paragraphs 38–44.
4 The litigation concerned two rival titles to the same subjects, that of the pursuers being recorded in the Register of Sasines and reliant (as it turned out) on prescription, that of the defender being registered in the Land Register subject to exclusion of indemnity. The action was for reduction of the disposition in the defender's favour.
5 Paragraph 37.
6 Paragraph 37.
7 1950 SLT 289. *Rutco Inc v Jamieson* 2004 GWD 30-620 can possibly be read as another, although on one view the competing elements of the description could be reconciled. For a discussion, see *Conveyancing 2004* pp 111–12. The issue was also raised on one view of the facts in *Compugraphics International Ltd v Nikolic* [2011] CSIH 34, 2011 SC 744 but only if it was accepted, which it was not, that the airspace occupied by overhanging ducts could be owned as a separate tenement. For details, see *Conveyancing 2009* pp 171–73 and *Conveyancing 2011* pp 94–98.
8 The description is quoted at pp 295–96; our lettering.

part [B]. For Lord Carmont this contradiction was fatal to the running of the prescription:[1]

> It is, I think, a commonplace of conveyancing that a boundary descriptively set out in any part of the dispositive clause operates to make the subjects *ager limitatus*. When the description incorporated from the prior writs is really necessary to link a disposition containing a new description, with the earlier items in a progress of titles, the necessity for giving full effect to a limitation incorporated from earlier deeds is even more obvious. If in a deed there are disponed all and whole the lands of A with the parts and pertinents thereof, the title cannot be treated as non-bounding if the deed goes on in the dispositive clause to refer to the lands as described in another deed as (say) 'bounded by the River Esk on the north'. In my opinion, therefore, the subjects in question, Raybank, are held on a bounding title so far as the street of Gattonside is concerned, and the triangular area cannot be attached thereto as a 'right and pertinent thereof', as it is on the opposite side of the street forming the boundary.

On this approach, a description containing contradictory elements is governed, for the purposes of prescription, by the *more restrictive* of the two. The other two judges, however, were prepared to overlook the difficulty, if such it was, and to find the description a sufficient foundation for prescription. Although they do not say so, there is implicit in their decision the view that it is the *less restrictive* element which is to prevail.[2]

Nisbet v Hogg was cited to the court in *Calthorpe* but dismissed, for reasons which are barely explained, as being of no assistance.[3] Now it is certainly true that *Nisbet* is not as strong or as clear an authority as one might wish, for the majority opinions were preoccupied with a different issue from that which caused Lord Carmont to dissent.[4] And it may also be true that, due to the different bridging language used between parts [A] and [B], the descriptive weight to be given to the troublesome part [B] was less in *Nisbet* ('which subjects are described in the title deeds thereof as follows') than in *Calthorpe* ('which said last mentioned area of land is part and portion of all and whole'). But the fact remains that the majority of the court in *Nisbet*, unmoved apparently by Lord Carmont's doubts, was willing to treat a contradictory description as sufficient for the purposes of prescription.

There is another reason for suggesting that *Calthorpe* is wrongly decided. Suppose that the disponers' title had been good rather than bad. The question would then have been, not whether the description was *habile* for the purposes of prescription but whether it was capable of carrying to the disponees the disputed subjects. Now, contradictory elements in descriptions are more common than they no doubt ought to be, and the response of the courts is not to dismiss

---

1 At p 296.
2 Of course, it is possible to conceive of two elements, each of which is less restrictive in one respect and more restrictive in another.
3 Paragraph 25. The facts are misdescribed: it is not true that the 1921 disposition 'made no reference to the triangular piece of ground'.
4 Whether the words 'including all rights in any way competent to me in and to' were a sufficient conveyance of the triangular area.

such descriptions but to seek to discover their meaning by the process of interpretation. Indeed a whole set of rules has been developed for this purpose, so that for example verbal descriptions will usually prevail over plans.[1] If, then, a contradictory description is sufficient to carry land, it would be surprising if it were not also sufficient to found prescription; for of the two it is the prescriptive description that is invariably seen as the less demanding.

New boundary walls and the March Dykes Act 1661

That the March Dykes Act 1661[2] should be so neglected is one of the sadnesses of the modern epoch. A new case on this thoroughly useful little Act – the first for many years – is thus particularly to be welcomed.

The parties in *Corrie v Craig*[3] owned neighbouring farms. At one time the boundary at a certain point was marked by a double dry-stane dyke known as a 'consumption dyke', but this had fallen into a ruinous state half a century or more ago and been replaced, prosaically, by a fence. In this action the pursuer, founding on the March Dykes Act 1661, asked the court

> to remit to Roger Lewis, or such other person of skill as the court may think proper, to visit, inspect and report on the present state and condition of the march dyke between the pursuer's property of Little Park Farm ... and the defenders' property of Walton Park Farm ... and to report what works and repairs are necessary to put the same into a proper and sufficient condition as a march dyke and also to report on the probable expense thereof. ...

The 1661 Act is designed for cases where neighbours cannot agree on fencing or other boundary features. It allows either neighbour to apply for a court order for certain works of construction or repair to go ahead on the basis that each party must bear half the cost.[4] Much of the Act was repealed by the Statute Law Revision (Scotland) Act 1906, and the operative part of what remains is in the following terms:[5]

> wher inclosours fall to be upon the border of any person's inheritance, the next adjacent heritor shall be at equall paines and charges in building, ditching and planting that dyk which parteth their inheritance.

As the sheriff[6] noted in the course of a learned and valuable opinion, the Act applies to repair as well as to building of new[7] and, where the land is

---

1 W M Gordon and S Wortley, *Scottish Land Law* (3rd edn, 2009) para 3-08.
2 RPS 1661/1/348; APS vii 263, c 284.
3 2013 GWD 1-55.
4 K G C Reid, *The Law of Property in Scotland* (1996) para 216.
5 The text is taken from www.rps.ac.uk.
6 Alastair N Brown.
7 The sheriff derived this rule from the words 'building, ditching and planting' (para 52) and indeed there is ample previous authority, collected in Reid, *Law of Property* para 226(5). The sheriff was able to overcome doubts created by the repeal in 1906 of the Act's reference to repairing, but in fact the doubts were unnecessary. The text in question, which immediately follows on from the words quoted above, is: 'And [also] recommends to all lords, shirreffs and baillies of regalities, stewarts

agricultural, allows for a fence, hedge or wall which is stock-proof.[1] There are, however, some limitations. The Act does not apply in towns or cities, or to any plot of land of less than five acres.[2] More importantly for present purposes, it does not allow expenditure which is disproportionate or 'visionary and absurd'.[3]

It was this last point that proved fatal to the pursuer's application. The defenders, it turned out, had already erected a stock-proof fence at the relevant point. A replacement dry-stane dyke would be an unnecessary luxury as well as an expensive one, for the cost of the proposed dyke was £60 per metre as opposed to £5 per metre for a fence. It seemed that the pursuer saw farmers as 'custodians of the countryside' who had the duty of ensuring that dykes were replaced with dykes and not fences, both for aesthetic reasons and because dykes provided a shelter for wildlife.[4] Understandably, the sheriff was not persuaded:[5]

> The March Dykes Acts do not empower a sheriff to order a proprietor of land to provide a shelter for wildlife. So far as the materials produced to me go, the proposition that farmers are the custodians of the countryside is not demonstrated to be part of the law. ... The March Dykes Acts do not empower a sheriff to require a farmer to manage his land in a way which accords with any particular view of the aesthetics of the countryside. In my opinion I would be in error if I obliged a commercial farmer to join in a project which reflects a view of agriculture and of the countryside which he does not necessarily share and which forms no part of the law.

The pursuer's application was refused.

The application under the March Dykes Act concerned a boundary length of 100 metres. But by this time the pursuer had already incurred costs of £16,248 building a dry-stane dyke on the next section of boundary, covering a distance of 270 metres. This was done in the knowledge of the defenders but without their agreement. Nonetheless, as part of the same action, the pursuer sought to recover half of the cost, on the basis of unjustified enrichment. The claim was indeed a bold one. The pursuer had chosen to act without the permission of either the defenders or, under the March Dykes Act, of the court. And he had chosen an expensive form of barrier rather than a fence of the type which had been in use in recent years. In Scots law, claims for enrichment by 'imposition'[6] – by carrying out work for the benefit of another but without permission – are only

---

of stewartries and justices of peace, baillies of burrowes and other judges whatsoever, to sie this act put in execution, and to grant processe at the instance of the partie damnified, and prejudged and to sie them repaired after the forme and tenor of this act abovewritten in all points.' The word 'repaired' is used broadly here and the whole sentence is in general terms, applying to the whole Act much of which was not concerned with the erection of boundary walls.

1 Paragraphs 48–50.
2 *Penman v Douglas* (1739) Mor 10,481.
3 Hume, *Lectures* III, 415.
4 Paragraphs 6 and 56.
5 Paragraph 57.
6 As opposed to by 'transfer' and by 'taking'.

grudgingly conceded.[1] Nonetheless, following a full review of the authorities, the sheriff concluded that an enrichment claim did indeed exist.

The pursuer, however, failed on quantum. An enrichment claim is based on the defenders' gain and not on the pursuer's loss. Yet the claim in this case was for half of the cost of erecting the dyke. Differently pled, however, the claim would have succeeded. That there had been a gain for the defenders was not, the sheriff said, in doubt. The ruined dyke was either the 'joint' property – by which is presumably meant common property – of both parties, or each owned to the mid-point with an obligation, founded on common interest, to maintain his own part.[2] Either way the defenders were under a duty to contribute to the maintenance of a stock-proof fence.[3] The effect of the pursuer's unilateral act was thus to produce 'a saving to their patrimony in that they have not paid for a stock-proof barrier which the law would have obliged them to contribute'.[4] But their enrichment was much smaller than the pursuer's expenditure. An ordinary fence being perfectly adequate for the purpose, the defenders had only been saved one half of the cost of erecting one – a sum which the sheriff estimated at £675.[5] And as the pursuer had sued for a much larger sum (£8,124) and on a quite different basis, he was not entitled to recover.

CONVEYING TOO MUCH

Conveying more land than one or both parties intended is surprisingly easy to do and unsurprisingly difficult to sort out afterwards. In the first of the two cases discussed below, it was uncertain exactly what had been conveyed; in the second, it was all too clear that the disposition had been over-generous, but the buyer had promptly resold to an unyielding third party.[6]

Poor plans and proprietors in possession

Poor plans

In *Trustees of the Elliot of Harwood Trust v Feakins*,[7] the Trustees[8] sold Harwood Estate, near Bonchester Bridge, Hawick to a Mr Feakins. Missives were concluded

---

1 For enrichment by imposition of improvements, see J Wolffe, 'Enrichment by improvements', in D Johnston and R Zimmermann (eds), *Unjustified Enrichment: Key Issues in Comparative Perspective* (2002) p 384 and especially pp 404–11; H MacQueen, *Unjustified Enrichment* (2nd edn, 2009) pp 43–47.

2 Paragraph 23. Given that the dyke claimed for was new, it would have been more relevant to consider on whose land it was built. To the extent that it was built on the pursuer's land, and so was his property, there could be no question of an enrichment claim, since no claim arises for merely adventitious benefit.

3 And of course, as already seen, such an obligation would also arise under the March Dykes Act 1661.

4 Paragraph 23.

5 Paragraphs 41–44.

6 The issue also arose in a third case from 2012, *Mirza v Salim* [2012] CSOH 37, 2012 SCLR 460 (Case (53) above).

7 2012 GWD 10-194.

8 Together with some other parties.

on 30 August 2002, and the disposition was registered in the Land Register on 19 December 2002 under title number ROX 4028. This was a first registration.

Among other properties, the Estate included a lodge house known, to some at least, as Clocker Lodge.[1] This had been occupied since 1996 by Georgina Lauder, the former housekeeper of a previous owner of the Estate. A liferent in favour of Miss Lauder was granted by the Trustees in 1997 but had not been made real, the deed having been registered in the Books of Council and Session and not the Register of Sasines.[2] Although the sales particulars for the Estate were unclear on the point, apparently deliberately,[3] it was the Trustees' intention to exclude the Lodge from the sale. On 15 August 2002, while missives were still being negotiated, the Trustees' solicitors faxed the solicitors acting for Mr Feakins to the effect that the Lodge[4] was 'not to be included in the sale of the Estate'.[5] For some reason, however, this information seems not to have been communicated to Mr Feakins, who took for granted that the Lodge was part of the sale.[6]

Remarkably, this mutual misunderstanding continued for a number of years into the future. On the assumption that the Lodge was still theirs, the Trustees insured it and paid for its maintenance. Mr Feakins, too, insured the Lodge as part of a policy which covered the whole Estate. The truth did not come out until the day in November 2009 when Mr Feakins and his wife paid a courtesy call on Miss Lauder and discovered she thought the owners to be the Trustees. That view, Mr Feakins explained to her, was misplaced, for the Lodge lay within the boundaries shown on his title sheet. And indeed whatever the position ought to have been, there could be no doubt that, for the moment at least, the Lodge was his.

When they discovered what had happened the Trustees raised an action against Mr Feakins in which they sought a declarator that the Lodge was not included in the property transferred, and an order that the Land Register be rectified accordingly. Naturally, the case turned on the terms of the disposition granted in favour of Mr Feakins. This disponed:[7]

> ALL and WHOLE those parts and portions of the lands and estate of Harwood in the County of Roxburgh as also those parts of the lands at Shankendsiel in said County delineated and coloured red on the plan marked 'Plan 1' annexed and signed as relative hereto. . . .

---

1 It was also known as 'Harwood Lodge', which indeed was the name on the gate. The different names may have contributed to some of the misunderstandings: see para 22.
2 As is required: see now Abolition of Feudal Tenure etc (Scotland) Act 2000 s 65, a provision which will be replaced by s 51 of the Land Registration etc (Scotland) Act 2012.
3 Paragraph 26: 'The seeds for potential confusion were first sown when the draft Sales Particulars were drawn up in a manner which neither specifically included nor excluded Harwood Mill and Clocker Lodge. Savilles took the view that from a marketing point of view that might have deterred potential purchasers and was unnecessary since they were not within the body of the Estate.'
4 And another property lying outside the natural boundaries of the Estate and as to which there was no dispute.
5 Finding-in-fact 6.
6 Finding-in-fact 7.
7 Paragraph 11. There were certain exceptions with which the case was not concerned.

Plan 1 showed the whole subjects of transfer on a single sheet of A3 and on a scale (1:25,000) which was so astonishingly small that it was less than half the size of the smallest scale used on the Land Register (1:10,000), which itself is considered suitable only for mountain and moorland.[1] Why the Keeper was willing to accept such a plan, on which the entire description was periled, is unclear.[2] So small was the scale that it was no easy matter to determine whether the Lodge lay within or beyond the red boundary line. As the sheriff[3] explained:[4]

> There was perceived to be a minuscule kink or indentation in the red line in the Plan attached to the Disposition at about the point where the Lodge lies. While the inside edge of the line might be marginally indented, any indentation of the outside edge was less clear, with the result that it is difficult to determine whether a line of the same width is indented or the line is marginally widened at that point. Most witnesses saw this kink as involving the road.

If, however, the red line extended as far as the road, then, since the Lodge was reached *before* the road, it must follow that the Lodge was included within the red line. Making the best of a bad job, the sheriff concluded that the Lodge was included in the disposition and hence that the Register was perfectly accurate in showing Mr Feakins as owner. The defenders were assoilzied.

Defeated intentions

But was that what the parties had really intended? Plainly, the Trustees had not wanted the Lodge to be part of the sale, and although Mr Feakins thought otherwise, it is not clear that he could escape the knowledge of his agents, following the fax of 15 August 2002, that the Lodge was not included. It is true that, as the missives used substantially the same plan as the disposition, the Lodge must be taken to have been included in the contract. And it is also true that the missives sought to prevent any inquiry into earlier negotiations by an entire-agreement clause in the following terms:[5]

> The missives (including the annexations thereto) shall as at the date of conclusion thereof represent and express the full and complete agreement between the seller and the purchaser relating to the sale of the subjects and shall supersede previous agreements between the seller and the purchaser (if any) relating thereto.

Nonetheless if the parties had had a 'common intention' to exclude the Lodge,[6] then in principle it would be open to the Trustees to seek judicial rectification, under s 8 of the Law Reform (Miscellaneous Provisions) (Scotland) Act 1985,

---

1 I Davis and A Rennie (eds), *Registration of Title Practice Book* (2nd edn, 2000) para 4.22.
2 She would not do so today. For the current rules on plans, see Registers of Scotland, *Deed Plan Criteria: A guide for conveyancers and other legal professionals* (www.ros.gov.uk/pdfs/dpc.pdf).
3 Daniel Kelly QC.
4 Paragraph 28.
5 Paragraph 10. On the meaning to be given to such clauses, see para 30.
6 The sheriff's view, however, was that they had not: see para 31.

of both the missives and the disposition; and for this purpose 'all relevant evidence' – including, notwithstanding the entire-agreement clause, evidence of pre-missives negotiations – would be admissible.[1] Of course, such an application might not succeed; but if it did, it would lead to rectification of the Register to remove the Lodge from the registered title, and this would be so, under the legislation,[2] even if Mr Feakins was a 'proprietor in possession' – a subject to which we may now turn.

Proprietor in possession

Suppose that the Lodge had *not* been included in the disposition plan (as indeed was strenuously argued by the Trustees). In that case it would not have been carried by the disposition, and the Land Register would be inaccurate in showing Mr Feakins as its owner. But what then? Mr Feakins would remain owner unless or until the Lodge was removed from his title by rectification; yet, under the legislation, rectification is not usually possible to the prejudice of a proprietor in possession.[3] Mr Feakins was plainly the 'proprietor' of the Lodge because he was its registered owner. Whether he was in possession was, however, a much more difficult question.

The issue was much debated in the case and, although its relevance ceased when the Register was found to be accurate, the sheriff nonetheless offered his views on the topic. That Miss Lauder was in natural (ie direct) possession of the Lodge was not in dispute. Nor was it in dispute that Mr Feakins was in possession, natural or civil, of the rest of the Estate. In the light of these undisputed facts, might there be some basis for a finding that Mr Feakins was in civil (indirect) possession of the Lodge? The sheriff thought that there was. Among a number of reasons given for this view, two were of particular importance.[4] In the first place, in possessing the rest of the Estate, including the road beyond the Lodge, Mr Feakins must be regarded as possessing the Lodge itself; for possession of a part of what one owns can often be treated as possession of the whole.[5] In the second place, since she was not the owner, Miss Lauder must be taken to be holding her possession for the person who was, and that person was Mr Feakins. At any rate, 'the Trustees have no title to the Lodge and Miss Lauder could not have occupied it on their behalf'.[6] Admittedly, this would mean that Mr Feakins was in civil possession of the Lodge, not natural possession, but it seemed that the former was now accepted as sufficient for the purposes of the 1979 Act.[7]

---

1 Law Reform (Miscellaneous Provisions) (Scotland) Act 1985 s 8(2). By the same logic, the existence of a supersession clause in the missives does not prevent recourse to missives in an application to rectify the disposition.
2 Land Registration (Scotland) Act 1979 s 9(3)(b).
3 LR(S)A 1979 s 9(3)(a).
4 Many of the other reasons focus on what Mr Feakins must be taken to have intended and do not deal with the difficulty that the only person in occupation of the Lodge was Miss Lauder.
5 Paragraph 35. Some of the authorities are considered in para 34.
6 Paragraph 37.
7 Paragraph 33, founding on *Kaur v Singh* 1998 SC 233. That this is correct can hardly be doubted.

The sheriff's two grounds, however, are mutually irreconcilable. A person cannot at the same time be in both natural (direct) possession and in civil (indirect) possession. She must be one or the other (or neither). Yet the sheriff's first ground pointed to natural possession and his second to civil. It is the second ground which is the more plausible.[1] Let us trace the history of possession. When Miss Lauder first occupied the Lodge, in 1996, she did so by arrangement with the Trustees, as owners, and must be taken to have been possessing on their behalf.[2] And this civil possession by the Trustees may well have continued for several years after they ceased to be owners, in 2002, because so far as Miss Lauder was concerned the Lodge continued to be the property of the Trustees. But after the visit to her by Mr and Mrs Feakins, in November 2009, the position seems bound to have changed. Probably the change was a gradual one.[3] Miss Lauder's initial position may have been to disbelieve the Feakins and to persist in her view that the Trustees were the owners. But by the time of the litigation this position had ceased to be tenable. However the disposition plan fell properly to be interpreted – the main point of dispute between the parties – there could be no doubt that Mr Feakins had been owner of the Lodge since 2002; for the very act of registration would have conferred ownership regardless of the state of the disposition.[4] Once she realised that the Trustees did not own, Miss Lauder cannot readily be regarded as continuing to possess on their behalf. And unless she is to be supposed, in an act of rebellion, to have adopted the position of a squatter and so held for herself alone,[5] it must follow that she held the Lodge for the benefit of the person at whose pleasure she was now permitted to remain in occupation. In short, at some point civil possession seems to have passed from the Trustees to Mr Feakins, who thus became a proprietor in possession. It follows, therefore, that even if his disposition had been found to exclude the Lodge, the Register could not have been rectified against him.

Offside goals

Finally, it seems worth considering the position of Miss Lauder. She had failed to make her liferent real by registration. Nonetheless, for as long as the Trustees owned, her position was secure because she had a contractual right against them under the minute of agreement which granted the liferent. Mr Feakins, however,

---

1 For civil possession, see M Napier, *Commentaries on the Law of Prescription in Scotland* (1839) pp 174–89; K G C Reid, *The Law of Property in Scotland* (1996) para 121; W M Gordon and S Wortley, *Scottish Land Law* (3rd edn, 2009) paras 14-07–14-09. There is no indication that the sheriff was referred to any of the authorities on this topic.

2 We are unpersuaded by the view expressed in D Johnston, *Prescription and Limitation* (2nd edn, 2012) para 18.13 that: 'the fact that permission has been given does not always mean that the person permitting retains possession; there are plenty of contractual relationships in which this is not the case. If the effect of the informal permission is that possession is by licence, the general rule is that a licensee possesses for himself ...'.

3 A summary of Miss Lauder's evidence is given at para 18.

4 Land Registration (Scotland) Act 1979 s 3(1)(a). Title flows from the Register, through the Keeper's 'Midas touch', and not from the underlying deed.

5 This is the view taken in Robert Rennie, 'The lodge with three names: *Lubbock v Feakins*' (2012) 16 *Edinburgh Law Review* 438, 445.

was not a party to that agreement and was not bound by it. The sheriff's view was that Miss Lauder could 'acquire a liferent interest in the Lodge were the Minute of Agreement to be registered and the Land Register to be rectified', but as the Trustees had ceased to be owner, there was little or no prospect that the minute of agreement, now reduced in status to an *a non domino* grant, would be accepted for registration.[1] Instead the way forward seems to be by recourse to the offside goals rule.[2] The conditions for its application appear to be met. Thus Miss Lauder had a personal right which, as a potential proper liferent, was capable of being real;[3] the transfer of the estate free of the liferent is, arguably, a breach of the Trustees' implied obligation of warrandice to Miss Lauder; and Mr Feakins was in 'bad faith' in the technical sense that he knew of the existence of the liferent at the time of registering his disposition, and very likely at the time of entering into missives as well.[4] The precise remedy which would then arise – an obligation on Mr Feakins to grant the liferent? a right in Miss Lauder to reduce Mr Feakins' disposition? – is, however, unclear, as is the question of whether Mr Feakins would be protected, or not protected, as a proprietor in possession.[5] Fortunately, the issue is unlikely to matter for there is every sign that Mr Feakins will continue to honour the arrangements made for Miss Lauder by his predecessors.

The land to the west

A horrible history

McSorley v Drennan[6] concerned Station Cottages, Alloway, a terrace of three houses, just a stone's throw east of the Robert Burns Birthplace Museum (a fact wholly irrelevant to the legal issues at stake). Mr McSorley, the pursuer, owned the middle house, No 2. This had some garden ground attached. In addition, the title included a small detached area of ground a few metres to the west of the western end of the terrace. This additional ground was the focus of the dispute. What it was used for is unclear, but it may have been garden ground. Mr McSorley's title was in the Land Register, and the land certificate was clear in showing what property was included, ie it showed both (i) the house and attached garden, plus (ii) the detached additional ground.

In 2006 Mr McSorley sold the property to the defenders, Mr and Mrs Drennan. The missives, concluded on Valentine's Day, described the subjects of sale thus:

---

1 If it was accepted, then the rectification envisaged by the sheriff would not be necessary, because the liferent would already have entered the Register by registration.
2 For which see eg K G C Reid, *The Law of Property in Scotland* (1996) paras 695 ff.
3 This distinguishes the present facts from the personal right of occupancy which failed in the otherwise similar circumstances of *Wallace v Simmers* 1960 SC 255.
4 Finding-in-fact 7.
5 That would depend on whether, despite being a proprietor in possession, Mr Feakins had lost the protection that his status would normally confer by having been 'careless' within s 9(3)(a) of the Land Registration (Scotland) Act 1979.
6 [2012] CSIH 59, 2012 GWD 25-506. We are grateful to Eoghainn Maclean, counsel for the defenders, for sight of the closed record and certain other items of process.

> All and whole the mid-terraced cottage known as and forming 2 Station Cottages Alloway, Ayr, together with garden to front and rear, garden hut, outbuildings effeiring thereto, the parts privileges and pertinents thereof, free access and egress therefrom and thereto, the fixtures and fittings in and upon the said subjects all as inspected by our clients and per the schedule issued by you, the whole rights, common mutual or otherwise.

Given that the title included the additional ground, this was not the perfect way of identifying the property being sold. But it was a matter of mutual understanding that the additional ground was to be excluded from the sale, and it does not seem to have been suggested at any stage that the missives should be interpreted as including the additional ground. Unfortunately the disposition described the property simply by reference to the registered title, so that it included the additional ground. The disposition was duly registered and a land certificate issued accordingly. How all this came about is not known, but presumably it was simply a matter of oversight on the part of both law firms involved.

On 10 July 2006, the seller's law firm wrote to the buyers' law firm:

> We refer to the above transaction which was settled in February of this year. You may recollect that our clients sold only part of the subjects contained in their land certificate and accordingly we should be obliged if you can please return our client's land certificate to us just as soon as you receive same back from the Keeper with your clients' own land certificate.

We would observe that the letter presupposes that the disposition had excluded the additional ground, which was not the case. No reply was sent, and seemingly the issue was not chased up.

If the buyers had held the property in the longer term, matters might perhaps have been resolved – eventually. But as luck would have it, they decided to resell fairly quickly. A Mr McKie was the purchaser, and the disposition, duly registered, was again of the whole property. What the Drennan/McKie missives said, and what the mutual understanding of the parties was, is not known. On 8 May 2007, Mr McKie's law firm wrote to Mr McSorley:

> We acted for Mr McKie in his recent purchase of the above property. We enclose a copy of our client's plan which shows title to the property purchased, coloured pink, which includes the area of land also coloured pink. It has recently been brought to our client's attention that you may be under the impression that you own the piece of land currently purchased by our client...

What, specifically, prompted this letter we do not know, but at all events the result was that the problem came out into the open. We understand that the Drennans had not taken possession of the additional ground.[1] Whether Mr McKie did so is unknown to us.

---

1 Communication from the defenders' counsel.

The pursuer's case

Mr McSorley raised the present action against the Drennans for the value of the property, said to be £30,000.[1] We quote the pursuer's pleadings:[2]

> The Defenders sold the Property and area of land when it was known and accepted by them that the Pursuer had only entered into the Missives for the sale of the property and the gardens to the front and rear thereof. Accordingly the Disposition granted by the Pursuer in favour of the Defenders contained an error of expression which the Defenders have subsequently taken advantage of. As a result of the Defenders' wrong the Pursuer has suffered loss. As a third party has acquired title to the Property and area of land in circumstances unknown to the Pursuer but believed to be in good faith he is unable to seek reduction of the Disposition and rectification of the Land Register. ... The Pursuer having suffered loss in consequence of the unintentional error known to and taken advantage of by the defenders is entitled to reparation in respect of his loss arising therefrom.

The central issue was one of relevancy. Had the pursuer pled a relevant case? The word 'reparation' in the pursuer's pleadings suggests a case based in delict, but it is not apparent what delict the defenders were supposed to have committed against the pursuer. There is a suggestion in the pleadings that the fact of reselling the additional plot constituted a delict, but if so this approach seems not to have been taken further, for the pursuer's case came to be founded solely on contract law. The defenders had a contractual right to acquire only the main property, and accordingly the very contract itself meant that they should not have the additional ground, which, therefore, they were bound to return, which failing, they were bound to return its value.

The defenders' case

The defenders argued that the law of contract provided no basis for the action, and that if the pursuer had a remedy it lay in the law of unjustified enrichment. In other words, the real pith and substance of the pursuer's case was that land had been transferred by mistake, without any legal ground, and that accordingly it (which failing its value) should be returned. In the language of Roman law, this was an example of the *condictio indebiti*. It is somewhat like the textbook example of the absent-minded customer who pays a bill twice. The payee is bound to return the second payment, not under the law of contract (there is no contractual obligation to repay), nor under the law of delict (there has been no delict), but under the law of unjustified enrichment, for the second payment had no legal basis.

It might be thought that this line of defence was a mere delaying tactic. If the additional ground had been transferred by mistake, were not the buyers liable one way or another, so that even if the action as framed was to fail, a second

---

1 This seems a large amount for a small area of undeveloped ground. Perhaps there was the possibility of development. We have no information. The question of quantum has not so far been tested in court.

2 The extract which follows is taken from article 3 of the condescendence except that the final sentence is the second plea in law.

action, better framed, would succeed? But this was more than a mere technical argument. Under the law of unjustified enrichment there can be defences, such as 'change of position'. For instance, suppose that the buyers had conveyed the additional ground to Mr McKie without realising what had happened, it might well be that this conveyance would count as a 'change of position' sufficient to protect the buyers from an action under the law of unjustified enrichment.

The three decisions

The case was heard by the sheriff, who found in favour of the pursuer. The defenders appealed to the sheriff principal, who refused the appeal.[1] The defenders then appealed again, and the Inner House has now reversed the decision,[2] agreeing with the position taken by the defenders, and generally criticising the pursuer's pleadings:[3]

> [T]he pursuer's pleadings failed to identify any legitimate basis for a claim of damages. Neither contract nor delict was expressly relied on; if liability *ex contractu* was intended, no identifiable breach of obligation had been averred; the only averments of actual or imputed knowledge referred, not to the existence of the error, but to the intended scope of the original missives; there was no allegation of any such knowledge having arisen prior to the date at which the contract was fully performed; nor was there any relevant averment of such knowledge in advance of the resale to the third party.

The result was the pursuer lost the action, but the decree was dismissal, not absolvitor, and so the pursuer would remain free to litigate matters again, in a different form. What form might that take? Rather unusually, the Inner House offered the pursuer a series of suggestions, which we outline below, with comments. An additional remedy, rectification under the Law Reform (Miscellaneous Provisions) (Scotland) Act 1985, not mentioned by the court, will also be discussed.

Possible remedies (i): enrichment claim against the Drennans

The most obvious remedy would be an action under the law of unjustified enrichment. Property was transferred in error, and so should be returned, and, if, on account of the sale to Mr McKie, it cannot be returned, then its value must be returned. As already mentioned, there might be a defence here available to the Drennans, such as the 'change of position' defence.

Possible remedies (ii): enrichment claim against Mr McKie

The court thought that an enrichment claim might lie against the sub-purchaser, Mr McKie.[4] This would be an example of what is called 'indirect enrichment',

---

1 May 2011, Ayr Sheriff Court (*Conveyancing 2011* Case (14)).
2 [2012] CSIH 59, 2012 GWD 25-506. The Opinion of an Extra Division of the Court of Session was delivered by Lord Emslie.
3 Paragraph 7.
4 Paragraph 3.

and the starting point in Scots law is that indirect enrichment claims are not competent. There can indeed be exceptions, but it is not clear to us that this would be one of them.[1]

Possible remedies (iii): delictual claim against the Drennans

'[I]f the pursuer could have demonstrated bad faith on the part of the defenders at the time when the erroneous title was taken and sold on, a claim of damages might have been made on delictual grounds,'[2] said the court. Although this seems to require bad faith at both of two stages, only the second stage is probably relevant. As indicated earlier, it appears that this is what the pursuer did argue in the written pleadings, albeit he seems to have given up as the case went on. A delictual claim on these lines would be an example of pure economic loss. That fact would not necessarily be fatal to an action, but it would be a hurdle to surmount.

Possible remedies (iv): contractual claim against the Drennans

'Where the matter was not fully argued before us' said the court, 'we would be reluctant to hold that, with appropriate legal and factual averments, a claim focused *ex contractu* might not also be open.'[3] The sheriff principal had indeed been prepared to see the pursuer's claim as a contractual one 'in the broadest sense'.[4] Their lordships do not develop the point. Possibly the idea is that there is an implied term in a contract of sale that if too much is conveyed then the excess, which failing its value, must be returned. We merely speculate.

Possible remedies (v): reduction

The court said: 'Proceedings for partial reduction of the sale and sub-sale might have been instituted, so as to enable the error to be corrected and the pursuer's title to the additional plot restored.'[5] If the additional ground had still been owned by the Drennans, this might not raise eyebrows, though even then the efficacy of the remedy might turn on the question of possession, because a proprietor in possession is generally protected.[6] What is more remarkable is the suggestion that reduction could operate against Mr McKie. It is a familiar principle of property law that if X has a voidable title, and transfers to Y, who is a good faith buyer, then the title that Y acquires is not voidable.[7] The court adds by way of explanation: '[S]ome of the cases discussed by the House of Lords in *Anderson v*

1　On the law of indirect enrichment see N Whitty, 'Indirect enrichment in Scots law' 1994 *Juridical Review* 200.
2　Paragraph 3.
3　Paragraph 11.
4　Judgment of the sheriff principal (Charles Stoddart) para 39.
5　Paragraph 3.
6　Land Registration (Scotland) Act 1979 s 9(3)(a). See *Short's Tr v Keeper of the Registers of Scotland* 1996 SC (HL) 14. Land registration law is not mentioned in *McSorley*.
7　See eg K G C Reid, *The Law of Property in Scotland* (1996) para 692.

Lambie[1] might be thought capable of supporting a remedy along reductive lines notwithstanding the interposition of a third party.'[2] We will not in this place embark on a discussion of those cases, except to say that the principle we have just mentioned is, we believe, beyond dispute.

Possible remedies (vi): rectification

The court adds: 'For all we know there may be other potential avenues available to the pursuer beyond the examples already given.'[3] The obvious avenue would be rectification of the disposition under s 8 of the Law Reform (Miscellaneous Provisions) Scotland) Act 1985. Section 9 of that Act has rules about what happens where third parties are involved: in some cases they are protected, and in others not.[4] If rectification is ordered under the 1985 Act, there can be consequential rectification of the title on the Land Register, even if it prejudices a proprietor in possession.[5] Indeed, precisely this happened in another of this year's cases, *Mirza v Salim*,[6] where there had also been an over-conveyance and third parties were involved.

The Drennans' knowledge

The letter of 10 July 2006 has been quoted above. The pursuer had argued that this letter alerted the Drennans to the fact of the mistake. Whether such knowledge would make any difference to the legal position is a question that cannot be given any simple answer, for the answer depends on the type of remedy sought. At all events, the court rejected this interpretation of the letter:[7]

> [T]he terms of the letter of 10 July 2006 were perfectly consistent with all parties remaining unaware that the disposition had in error carried the additional plot to the defenders; it is a matter of speculation what the defenders' solicitors made of that letter, or whether they ever mentioned it to their clients; there is no averment as to when, in what circumstances or on what terms the resale took place; the averments of knowledge in articles 2 and 3 of condescendence expressly concern the (correct) missives rather than the (erroneous) disposition; and against that background we reject as untenable the notion that, as a matter of law and in all circumstances, purchasers like the defenders must be deemed aware of the technical details of dispositions, Land Certificates and related plans which they may never have seen.

---

1 1954 SC (HL) 43. In that case, as here, the deal was for the sale of only part of the seller's property. In that case, as here, the missives did not expressly exclude the area to be retained. In that case, as here, the disposition included the whole property owned by the seller. A major difference was that in that case there had been no subsale. The remedy sought by the pursuer was reduction, in which he was successful. Curiously, the action was to reduce the *whole* disposition. An action of partial reduction might have been thought more appropriate, but this issue seems not to have been explored, apart from a few *dicta* by Lord Reid at 60–61.
2 Paragraph 11.
3 Paragraph 11.
4 As to which see G L Gretton and K G C Reid, *Conveyancing* (4th edn, 2011) para 20-09. *Jones v Wood* [2005] CSIH 31, 2005 SLT 655 is the leading case, and one which also involved the conveyance of too much land.
5 Land Registration (Scotland) Act 1979 s 9(3)(b).
6 [2012] CSOH 37, 2012 SCLR 460 (Case (53) above).
7 Paragraph 9.

This seems to be saying (at least) two things. The first is that the letter of 10 July 2006 could not bear the weight placed on it by the pursuer. That seems correct. Indeed, the terms of the letter seem to presuppose that the disposition had been *correctly* drafted and that all that remained was for the Keeper to issue the two new land certificates, one of the main property, for the buyers, and one of the retained property, for the seller. In the second place, the court says that owners cannot automatically be deemed to know all the terms of their title. In one sense that is clearly right. In the present case it may well be (no proof has taken place, of course) that the Drennans were unaware that the additional ground had been included in the conveyance, and, when they resold, were still unaware of that fact, so that they may well have acted in perfect good faith throughout. If that is right, then the law relating to 'taking advantage of an error' may be irrelevant to the case.[1] But it may be added that it is also true that in some circumstances and for some purposes the knowledge of an agent may be treated as the knowledge of the principal, ie constructive knowledge.

SERVITUDES

Implied access rights

Almost always, servitudes are created by express provision in a deed (which nowadays requires to be registered in the Land or Sasine Register)[2] or by positive prescription. But a servitude can also be created by implication in a split-off conveyance, even if the courts have been understandably parsimonious when it comes to actual examples. One issue which sometimes arises is whether a servitude of access can be implied even where access is possible by other means. In principle the answer is yes, but in practice a servitude is likely to be recognised only where the existing access is seriously inadequate in some respect, for example as being confined to pedestrian use or as serving only one part of the property.[3] *Harton Homes Ltd v Durk*[4] is an illustration of the difficulties.

In 1985 two adjacent plots were feued in Dundee. Each was bounded on the south by a public road[5] and in due course the owners of one of the plots, having built a house, created an access to that road. The other plot remained undeveloped. In time both plots changed hands. This was an action by the owner of the undeveloped plot for declarator that a servitude existed allowing access to be taken to the public road over the access built on the developed plot. As neither feu disposition mentioned servitudes, and as there had not been sufficient use of the access to qualify for prescription, the pursuer's case rested on implied servitude.

---

1 For a valuable discussion of the case from the standpoint of the law of error, see Paul McClelland, 'McSorley v Drennan' (2013) 17 *Edinburgh Law Review* 68.
2 Title Conditions (Scotland) Act 2003 s 75(1).
3 D J Cusine and R R M Paisley, *Servitudes and Rights of Way* (1998) para 8.15.
4 2012 SCLR 554.
5 Dundee Road.

The action failed. Following a proof, the sheriff[1] found that there was no reason why the pursuer could not open up a direct access from its own plot to the public road in the same way as had already been done for the defender's plot.[2] Further, the larger area from which both plots were split off had the benefit of servitudes of access over private roads to the north leading to public roads, and it was 'eminently possible', though not certain,[3] that at least one of these roads touched the pursuer's land and so could be used for access.[4] Having regard, therefore, to the existence of alternative means of access, there was no basis for implying a servitude. The applicable test, that the servitude must be necessary for the comfortable use and enjoyment of the pursuer's plot, had not been met.

Given the findings in fact, the result reached comes as no surprise, and the main value of the decision lies in the discussion of the background law. One issue concerns chronology. Servitudes can be implied only when land is divided – when, for example, an area of land is split into two plots, A and B. But whether a servitude over plot A can be implied for the benefit of plot B depends to a considerable extent on which of the plots was broken off or, to put it another way, on which plot was disponed first. So if the owner disponed plot B and retained plot A, there would be implied into the disposition a *grant* of any servitude which was necessary for the convenient enjoyment of plot B. But if the chronology was reversed and plot A disponed first, any servitude for plot B would have been *reserved* rather than *granted*, and the courts have shown themselves unwilling to imply a reservation except in cases of actual or virtual necessity.[5] The novelty of *Harton Homes* is that neither plot was disponed first: on the contrary, both were disponed simultaneously, and both feu dispositions were registered on precisely the same day. For a servitude to have been created, therefore, it was necessary to suppose *both* (i) that the conveyance of the undeveloped plot contained an implied grant of the servitude and also (ii) that the conveyance of the developed plot contained an implied reservation. Which standard was then to be applied – the extremely restrictive one appropriate to reservation or the more generous one developed for grant? Although the point had not previously been decided, it seems not to have been seriously contested that the more generous standard should be used. No doubt it helped that Bell's *Principles* supported this line, although it may have escaped the sheriff's attention that the passage in question was not by Bell but by a later editor and that the authorities relied on were English.[6] Be that as it may, the approach adopted seems clearly correct.

Another issue is the role of prior use. In *Moncrieff v Jamieson*[7] the House of Lords had been willing to allow that a servitude of access, granted expressly,

---

1 John K Mundy.
2 Paragraph 48.
3 This was one of the issues on which the expert witnesses for each side, respectively Professor Roderick Paisley and Donald Reid, locked horns.
4 Paragraph 51. Even if it did not, there was the possibility of reaching one of the roads through the defender's plot, for which purpose an implied servitude might be available.
5 There may, however, have been some recent movement in this regard: see *Conveyancing 2005* pp 89–92.
6 Paragraph 26. See George Joseph Bell, *Principles of the Law of Scotland* (10th edn, 1899) § 992.
7 [2007] UKHL 42, 2008 SC (HL) 1.

might include by implication a right to park even though there was no practice of parking at the time when the servitude was created. But *Moncrieff* was about the existence of *ancillary* rights, not of the servitude itself (which had been expressly granted). And for the *creation* of servitudes by implication, as the sheriff in *Harton Homes* emphasised, there must normally be prior use, for the idea is that the grantee is to have the same use rights, post-severance, as existed when the plots were still one.[1] No prior use, however, had taken place in *Harton Homes* because the defender's access had not been in existence at the time of severance.

The sheriff accepted that the requirement of prior use was not an absolute one. As various commentators have pointed out, there can sometimes be exceptions, as for example where the need for a servitude becomes apparent only after severance.[2] The question was whether the present facts fell within these exceptions. The sheriff thought that they did not:[3]

> It could not be said that the supposed need only emerged after severance. ... Further, it is not in my view the sort of case postulated by *Cusine & Paisley*[4] where access is required for repairs to external surfaces which may be otherwise impossible or difficult to get at. I am not suggesting the category of such exceptions is closed, but it does not seem to me in the circumstances that this is a case where proof of prior use is unnecessary. As noted above, the pursuers have offered to prove use by them and their predecessors in title between 1985[5] and the commencement of these proceedings. There is therefore a tacit recognition of the requirement to establish use, whether or not the averment can be taken to encompass prior use. In the situation here, it seems to me that prior use is a critical component in this case for the constitution of an implied grant. The absence of use is in my view fatal to the pursuers' case and represents a separate ground for decision.

A final issue concerned the argument for the pursuer that, at the time of severance, there had been a common intention among all the parties – the disponer and the two disponees – that the access now sought should be made available to the pursuers. On the evidence, the sheriff found that no such common intention had been made out.[6] But even if the evidence had been more favourable, the sheriff would not have been prepared to regard common intention as a distinct ground for creation of a servitude:[7]

> As for common intention, while it may be relevant as potentially throwing light on whether the parties considered the access to be necessary at the time of severance, it should be recognised that it could not *per se* be a distinct ground for setting up an implied servitude. In that respect the position appears [to] be different in England and so the cases of *Stafford v Lee*[8] and *Pwllbach Colliery Company Limited v*

---

1 Paragraph 45. See *Conveyancing 2007* pp 114–15.
2 W M Gordon, *Scottish Law Law* (2nd edn, 1999) para 24.39; Cusine and Paisley, *Servitudes and Rights of Way* (1998) para 8.18.
3 Paragraph 54.
4 Cusine and Paisley, *Servitudes and Rights of Way* (1998) para 8.81.
5 The year of severance.
6 Paragraph 48.
7 Paragraph 42.
8 (1993) 65 P & CR 172.

Woodman[1] which refer to a class of cases (where easements may be implied where necessary to give effect to the common intention of the parties) should be regarded with a degree of caution in the present context.

Variation and discharge by the Lands Tribunal

Servitudes, like real burdens, can be varied or discharged by the Lands Tribunal. The procedure in both cases is the same except that, for servitudes, even unopposed applications must be considered on their merits, having regard to the statutory factors set out in s 100 of the Title Conditions (Scotland) Act 2003.[2] Applications in respect of servitudes seem to be on the increase: in 2012 as many as five such cases were decided by the Tribunal.[3]

In one of those cases, *McNab v Smith*,[4] the Tribunal helpfully set out a tripartite classification of the types of application encountered in respect of servitudes of way:[5]

> Firstly, and quite commonly, an application may simply be to vary the route of a defined right of access through the applicant's property, as for example where the applicant, the burdened proprietor, wishes to build an extension over the route and proposes an alternative route provided at his expense over his property. Secondly, an application may be for discharge on the basis that the benefited proprietor has another access (which perhaps did not exist when the servitude in question was created) so that, it is argued, it would be reasonable simply to bring the servitude to an end. Thirdly, an application may envisage the possibility that the benefited proprietor, although he has an alternative access available, might have to take steps to improve that alternative access in some way. It might be thought that depriving the owner of a servitude right of that right, on the basis that that owner should be expected himself to take steps to remedy the loss, ie the third situation, requires considerable justification.

Overwhelmingly, applications of all three classes are successful,[6] although it was said in another case from 2012, *Stirling v Thorley*,[7] that applications falling into the second and third classes 'require strong justification'.[8] Of the 19 applications made in respect of servitudes of way since the coming into force of the 2003 Act, all but four have been granted, although in a few cases subject to payment of compensation. Most – some ten in all – involved diversion of the route and so fell into the first of the three categories identified above. *McNab* itself, however, was a relatively rare, and successful, example of an application in respect of the third category.

---

1 [1915] AC 634
2 Title Conditions (Scotland) Act 2003 s 98. See further G L Gretton and K G C Reid, *Conveyancing* (4th edn, 2011) paras 16-07–16-12; A Todd and R Wishart, *The Lands Tribunal for Scotland: Law and Practice* (2012) ch 6.
3 See Cases (24)–(28) above.
4 15 June 2012, Lands Tribunal. The Tribunal comprised J N Wright QC and A M Darling FRICS.
5 Paragraph 47.
6 For a complete list, with summaries, see pp 191–93 below.
7 12 October 2012, Lands Tribunal.
8 Paragraph 27.

COMMON GOOD LAW

'Common good' is not a well-known branch of the law, though happily there is a book on the subject by Andrew Ferguson.[1] But it cannot be dismissed as unimportant, because the flow of cases, though not torrential, is persistent. And in 2012 there has been a major new decision.

In the old burgh system, some properties belonged to the burgh's 'common good', and if they had that status then the burgh was restricted in what it could do with them. The position was in some ways like a trust, with the burgh council being the trustee and the burghers being the beneficiaries. The duties of the burgh council were, like those of a trustee, fiduciary. But though trust-like, the common good was not a trust. It was a system on its own. Whether common good law should be regarded as part of private law or public law might be debated. Primarily it belonged to public law, but it seemed to have had private law qualities as well. We use the past tense, to indicate history, but in fact common good law did not perish when the burgh system was abolished by the Local Government (Scotland) Act 1973. That Act provides for the continuing existence of common good property, and for the way that the post-burgh local authorities are to deal with it. These provisions are, however, far from being a complete code of common good law, and much common law still applies. Some of that common law is uncertain, and some of the provisions of the 1973 Act are less than clear. A new decision, *Portobello Park Action Group Association v The City of Edinburgh Council*,[2] provides some welcome clarification, but a proper review of the whole subject, followed by legislation, is needed.

The fight for Portobello Park

Introduction

The issues at stake were not trivial. The case involved a decision by a local authority (Edinburgh) to take a large part of a public park (at Portobello) and to build a school there. Local authorities are usually impecunious and so buying property for a new school or other public buildings is not easy from a financial point of view. The use of public parks is a cheap option. Many would say that this approach is justifiable: parks and schools are both public goods, and perhaps a choice must be made, and who better to make that choice than the local authority? Others would say that public green space in urban areas is so precious that it should be preserved, that it matters little whether the bricks and concrete that spread across it are schools or shopping centres or affordable housing or relief roads or anything else, that if local authorities want property to develop they can do what everyone else has to do when they want property to develop, namely to go to the property market and buy such property, or alternatively go down the road of compulsory purchase, in which of course proper compensation has to be

---

1 Andrew Ferguson, *Common Good Law* (2006). There is also Andy Wightman, *Common Good Land in Scotland: A Review and Critique* (2005), a shorter work. For journal articles, see below.
2 [2012] CSOH 38, 2012 SLT 944 rev [2012] CSIH 69, 2012 SLT 1137.

paid for the land taken. Further, they might add, that if a park such as Portobello Park cannot be protected then no park can be protected, and all the city parks of Scotland are at risk of being concreted over, bit by bit, by cheapskate councils, who want property without paying for it. On this debate we offer here no view, but would note that the latter thoughts were not absent from the minds of the Inner House judges in the present case.

The first round

Portobello Park Action Group Association is an unincorporated voluntary association that was formed to protect the park from development. After the City of Edinburgh Council had decided on development, the association raised the present action for declarator that the development would be unlawful, since the park was common good property, and for reduction of the Council's decision. At first instance, before Lady Dorrian, the association lost on two counts.[1] The action, it was held, had been raised too late, in the sense that the association was barred by *mora* and taciturnity. If it had wanted to raise an action it should have done so earlier. But even apart from that, the Council was acting lawfully. Section 75 of the Local Government (Scotland) Act 1973 contained provisions whereby the power of 'disposal' of common good land was restricted, in that before such land could be disposed of the consent of the court was required. But s 75 contained no provisions restricting the 'appropriation' of common good land, and indeed s 73 of the same Act said expressly that 'a local authority may appropriate for the purpose of any functions, whether statutory or otherwise, land vested in them for the purpose of any other such function'.[2] This apparently straightforward view was supported by *South Lanarkshire Council, Petitioners*[3] and *North Lanarkshire Council, Petitioners*,[4] where petitions for authority to appropriate common good land were refused as unnecessary. Indeed, the second of these cases was similar to the present case in that a public park was involved and the local authority wished to use part of it to build a school.

The second round

The association's position looked bleak, but it reclaimed and it won.[5] On the first issue, *mora* and taciturnity, an Extra Division of the Court of Session decided, after reviewing the whole history, that there had been no unacceptable delay on the part of the association. This view is certainly persuasive.

On the other issue, as to whether the Council could appropriate the park, the Extra Division's decision is remarkable and will have surprised many. The court first sets out its view of the overall policy framework:[6]

---

1 [2012] CSOH 38, 2012 SLT 944.
2 Except land held for allotments. For discussion of the concepts of disposal and appropriation, see below.
3 CSIH, 11 Aug 2004.
4 2006 SLT 398. For commentary see Andrew Ferguson, 'Alienation and the appropriation of common good land' 2009 SLT (News) 235.
5 [2012] CSIH 69, 2012 SLT 1137. The Opinion of the Court was given by Lady Paton.
6 Paragraph 29.

If the Lord Ordinary were correct, of course, members of the local community would no longer have any legal right or title to prevent such encroachment; so long as a local authority's plans involved a transfer of the land from one of their functions to another, they could proceed unhindered and at will; and for practical purposes the future of every piece of inalienable common good land in Scotland, notably public parks and other open space recreational and amenity provision, would be in jeopardy. Subject only to planning constraints, local authorities would be free to appropriate open space common good land, even if nominally inalienable, away from dedicated recreational or amenity use. They could construct over the land housing, offices, schools or slaughterhouses, or use it for sewerage or waste disposal purposes. All or any of these would fall within the ambit of one or other of their statutory functions.

Clearly the result is already foreshadowed: only the most compelling legal argument is going to save the Council. So the court turned its attention to the 1973 Act. As indicated above, s 73 of that Act gives local authorities general powers of appropriation and disposal. Then s 75 imposes restrictions on the *disposal* of common good land, but is silent as to the *appropriation* of common good land. The inference drawn by the Lord Ordinary was that local authorities are free to appropriate common good land. But from the statutory silence the Extra Division drew the opposite conclusion. The common law restrictions on appropriation of common good land, not having been altered by the 1973 Act, remained intact. And under the common law the Council had no power to appropriate a public park for the building of a school. As the court put it:[1]

No statutory power to appropriate such land is conferred, nor has Parliament provided any mechanism whereby appropriation, with or without compensation, may be sanctioned by the court. There is thus nothing in the 1973 statute to remove, alter or diminish the relevant pre-existing common law rights and obligations as they apply to the appropriation of inalienable common good land.

As for the two decisions mentioned above, the court neatly sidestepped them.[2] '[B]oth applications were simply refused as unnecessary under section 75(2) on the ground that the relevant plans involved no disposal of inalienable common good land.' Although as a matter of form the court was merely distinguishing those decisions, as a matter of substance it was departing from them.

The Council had also invoked the Local Government in Scotland Act 2003. Section 20 confers on local authorities broad powers 'to do anything which it considers is likely to promote or improve the well-being of (a) its area and persons within that area; or (b) either of those'. This is qualified by s 22 which says that 'the power under s 20 above does not enable a local authority to do anything which it is, by virtue of a limiting provision, unable to do'. 'Limiting provision' is defined as meaning a provision in an enactment, so that common

---

1 Paragraph 33.
2 Although the earlier of them was an Inner House decision, no issued opinions appear to exist, so that its authority was inevitably weak.

good law would not be a 'limiting provision'. This argument looks strong, but it was firmly rejected:[1]

> [T]he reference to 'anything' in s 20(1) cannot in our view possibly be thought to mean what it appears to say. It cannot, for example, be understood as conferring on a local authority the right to act in breach of contractual or trust or title obligations, or to the detriment of established third party rights. It cannot constitute a blanket entitlement to disregard planning or other administrative constraints, or the general provisions of domestic or European law. By the same token, it is in our view inconceivable that s 20(1) can have been intended, while ss 73–75 of the 1973 Act remained in force, to sweep away all fiduciary restraints on a local authority's ownership of inalienable common good land. Even s 75(2), expressed as enabling a local authority to obtain the authority of the court for any disposal of such land, seems to us to constitute no more than an implied restriction, and thus to fall outwith the definition of a 'limiting provision' in s 22(2) of the 2003 Act. It cannot surely have been an intended (and unstated) effect of this legislation that, notwithstanding the provisions of s 75(2) of the earlier statute, a local authority in pursuit of 'well-being' could henceforth bypass any need for sanction and dispose of inalienable common good land without recourse to the court.

Some implications

A leading case

The *Portobello* decision is clearly a leading case. It marks a significant change in what had been thought to be the law, and it enhances the protection that the law gives to public parks around Scotland.[2]

An apparent oddity

The decision results in the oddity that local authorities have greater powers to *sell* common good land than to *change its use*. At all events, that is the implication that we see in the decision. For whereas sale is possible (albeit that it requires the consent of the court), change of use is generally impermissible, even with that consent. But if that is how the court interprets s 75 of the 1973 Act, that is not necessarily an objection to the decision. The real problem lies in the legislation, and we doubt whether *any* entirely satisfactory interpretation of the 1973 Act is possible.

Special legislation?

There has been speculation as to whether the Council might seek special legislation allowing the development to go ahead. At the time of writing we do

---

1 Paragraph 40.
2 For valuable discussions of the case see David Bartos, 'Old wine in new bottles: common good in the 21st century' 2012 SLT (News) 233, and Malcolm Combe, 'Lessons in Scots law: the common good school' (2013) 17 *Edinburgh Law Review* 63. And see also the pages on common good on Andy Wightman's website: www.andywightman.com/?page_id=1554. Here can be found the joint opinion of Malcolm Thomson QC and Sarah Wolffe QC given in 2008 to Edinburgh Council.

not know whether such an attempt will be made. If it is made, it would be an open question whether MSPs would support such legislation.

Alienation, disposal, appropriation

Part VI of the 1973 Act uses the twin concepts of 'disposal' and 'appropriation' but does not define them or lay down the distinction between them. The case law has interpreted 'disposal' as meaning not only transfer of ownership, but other acts as well. For instance in *Waddell v Stewartry District Council*[1] Lord Wylie said that 'what constitutes alienation must be liberally construed and would include any action which effectively deprives the community of something which, by custom or dedication by direct grant, they are entitled to have'. And in *East Lothian District Council v National Coal Board*[2] Lord Maxwell took the view that a 99-year lease would count as a 'disposal'. So 'disposal' is a broad concept, and its boundaries are not wholly certain.

Part VI of the 1973 Act also uses the term 'alienate'. This is not defined, nor is there any explanation of how it relates to the concept of 'disposal'. Do they mean the same, or is one concept wider than the other? If so, which one? The reason the Act uses the term seems to be an attempt to pin down common good property in the 'ordinary' sense, as property that a local authority cannot 'alienate'. This is contrasted with a broader sense of 'common good' which includes property which local authorities can do what they want with.

Actually, the relevant provision, s 75, is even less clear than that. For instead of drawing the line between common good property that can and cannot be alienated it draws the line between (i) 'land forming part of the common good with respect to which land a question arises as to the right of the authority to alienate' and (ii) 'land forming part of the common good of an authority with respect to which land no question arises as to the right of the authority to alienate'. This mixes up substantive questions with evidential questions and results in obscurity.

Conveyancing implications

The decision does not seem to have any direct implications for conveyancing in the ordinary sense, because it is a decision about 'appropriation' rather than 'disposal'. But it has made everyone much more aware of common good law. If land is common good land then a local authority does not have power to sell it. Long leases may also be prohibited, at any rate leases for 99 years or more, and quite possibly for shorter periods. To be precise, the local authority does have the power to sell or to lease but only if the court so consents. Do buyers or lessees have to worry about all this? Seemingly the answer is yes: an *ultra vires* act is void.[3] Hence those buying from local authorities, or taking long leases,

---

1 1977 SLT (Notes) 35.
2 1982 SLT 460.
3 In the case of companies, modern legislation means that buyers etc are usually protected from the *ultra vires* doctrine. But this protection has not been generally extended to transactions by other types of juristic person. For an example see *Piggins & Rix Ltd v Montrose Port Authority* 1995 SLT 418.

may wish to consider if there is any possibility that the land may be common good land, and, if there is such a possibility, may wish to insist that the consent of the court is obtained.

STAMP DUTY LAND TAX AND OTHER TAX ISSUES[1]

Devolution

In relation to tax in Scotland, particularly taxes affecting land, Scotland's taxpayers and their advisers are going to have to get used to the painful process of riding two horses. Stamp duty land tax will be fully devolved,[2] in that it will be disapplied from transactions involving land in Scotland in April 2015 and replaced with land and buildings transaction tax ('LBTT'). The same will apply to the rather more specialised area of landfill tax;[3] and these will be the first taxes to be administered (at least in part) by the new Scottish Government agency, Revenue Scotland. The two pieces of substantive tax legislation will be followed by a new Act devoted to tax administration.[4] From 2015–16 (perhaps dependent on what happens in the referendum in the autumn of 2014) income tax will also be partially devolved,[5] although on the current proposals this will continue to be administered by Her Majesty's Revenue and Customs. But pending all of these changes (and beyond them, given the need for transitional provisions), the UK tax system continues to evolve and increase its demands in an attempt to reduce the fiscal deficit. Thus a Scottish adviser on property tax will require to be triocular, with one eye focused on Holyrood, while the other two will be needed to watch developments from Westminster and the courts.

Land and buildings transaction tax

The Land and Buildings Transaction Tax (Scotland) Bill was introduced into the Scottish Parliament on 29 November 2012. When enacted, this legislation will form the basis for the replacement of SDLT with effect from April 2015. The block grant from the UK Government will be reduced to take account of the revenue that would have been raised from SDLT (and landfill tax) in Scotland.

Much work remains to be done on the Bill and indeed on the administration of the tax (the bulk of which will be carried out, at least as regards reporting and collection, by Registers of Scotland). The Scottish Government intends the new tax to adhere to four principles which, it says, will inform its tax policy: certainty, convenience, efficiency, and proportionality to the ability to pay. LBTT is intended to reflect Scottish law and practice, although there is work to

---

1 This part is contributed by Alan Barr of the University of Edinburgh and Brodies LLP.
2 Scotland Act 2012 ss 28–29, sch 3.
3 Scotland Act 2012 ss 30–31, sch 4. Legislation will be forthcoming in the Scottish Parliament: see *Protecting our Resources – Consultation on a Scottish Landfill Tax*, 25 Oct 2012 (www.scotland.gov.uk/Publications/2012/10/3524).
4 See *A Consultation on Tax Management*, 10 Dec 2012 (www.scotland.gov.uk/Publications/2012/12/5404).
5 Scotland Act 2012 ss 25–27, sch 2.

be done in this regard. Collection will rely to a significant extent on electronic efficiencies.

Perhaps inevitably, many of the Bill's provisions are drawn directly from existing SDLT legislation. Perhaps the most significant immediate change is to a progressive system as opposed to the 'slab' approach which applies to SDLT. Thus LBTT will apply at lower rates up to thresholds and at higher rates only on the amounts of consideration above those thresholds.[1] While rates will not be fixed until much nearer the time of introduction, it seems that for purchases there will be a 0% rate and at least two higher rates.

The tax on residential leases for less than 20 years (and thus effectively on all residential leases) will be abolished. The current rather complex method of charging non-residential leases is subject to consultation and the possibility of significant reform. The same applies to the impenetrable rules on partnerships. While most reliefs from SDLT are likely to continue in a revised form for LBTT, sub-sale relief is not at present included. Further omissions include a relief for relocation packages, insurance company demutualisations, and the time-limited SDLT relief for new zero-carbon homes.

Avoidance is to be tackled by a combination of supposedly clearer legislation, targeted anti-avoidance rules (TAARs) within the LBTT Bill and, subject to consultation, a general anti-avoidance rule (GAAR) to be included in the forthcoming Tax Management Bill.

Clearly, there is much legislative water to flow under the bridge before LBTT becomes a reality; the Scottish Government seems to be genuinely willing to engage in constructive consultation, so there may be a real opportunity to influence the new tax. This might improve the chances of its administration (likely still to be dealt with by solicitors) being as painless as possible. Of course, taxpayers may not feel the same about payment of the new tax.

Taxing the £2 million home

We return now from the future LBTT to the existing SDLT. The property market remains muted and receipts from SDLT are subdued. Despite or perhaps to some extent because of this, a package of measures was announced which was given the euphemistic title of *Ensuring the fair taxation of residential property transactions*.[2] These measures were directed at residential property valued at more than £2 million – and make it all the more important to consider in such high-value transactions whether what is being purchased is in fact 'residential' or indeed a 'dwelling'.[3] All measures other than the new 7% rate of SDLT were aimed at residential property held through non-natural entities, which is described as 'enveloping'. The notion is that once property is put into the 'envelope' of a

---

1 See Land and Buildings Transaction Tax (Scotland) Bill s 25.
2 HM Treasury, May 2012: www.hm-treasury.gov.uk/consult_ensuring_fair_taxation_residential_property_transactions.htm.
3 It seems that the definitions used for these measures will in general be those used for SDLT, found for 'residential property' in Finance Act 2003 s 116 and for a 'dwelling' in Finance Act 2003 sch 4A para 7, inserted by the Finance Act 2012 s 214, sch 35 paras 1, 4.

company or other entity, that envelope can then be transferred without the tax charges which would arise on a transfer of the property itself.

Two of the measures were enacted in Finance Act 2012. The first was the introduction of a 7% rate for purchases of residential property for more than £2 million on or after 22 March 2012.[1] This can be regarded simply as an increase in rates – a large one, but affecting relatively few people and not qualitatively different from any other change in rates. There are the normal transitional provisions for contracts entered into before that date.[2]

The other enacted change introduced what is in effect a penal charge at 15% for companies and certain other purchasers of 'higher threshold interests in dwellings'[3] – that higher threshold again being £2 million.[4] This applies to single dwellings, which include land occupied with or for the benefit of such dwellings;[5] and there is rather complex provision for apportionment where interests other than those in single dwellings are purchased.[6] The charge applies where the purchaser is a company, a partnership with a company among its partners, or a collective investment scheme.[7] There is an important (but limited) exemption for purchasers who are engaged in 'bona fide property development business'.[8] There is a requirement for the business to have been carried on for at least two years, which is a serious drawback for newly-established businesses, but this is to be removed, and limited further reliefs will be introduced, in Finance Act 2013. The most significant is a relief for property rental businesses. Generally, the reliefs will be subject to a three-year claw-back if the conditions are breached within that period.

A third part of ensuring the 'fair taxation' of residential property transactions is yet to be enacted. This is an annual residential property tax affecting dwellings owned by companies and certain other persons and valued at more than £2 million. This was initially described as a form of SDLT but is in fact a completely new annual tax. Importantly, it will continue to be due to the UK tax authorities even when SDLT has been replaced by LBTT for transactions in Scotland. Draft legislation for this new tax was published in December 2012, running to an intimidating 60 sections and two schedules.[9] The tax will be based on the value of the property on 1 April 2012. Tax will be charged in a series of broad bands, rising from £15,000 for properties valued between £2 million and £5 million up to £140,000 for properties valued at more than £20 million. As before, the affected owners will be companies, partnerships with at least one company member, and collective investment schemes. There will be a range of reliefs, including property development businesses, property rental businesses,

---

1 Finance Act 2012 s 213.
2 Finance Act 2012 s 213(3), (4).
3 Finance Act 2012 s 214, sch 35, inserting sch 4A into the Finance Act 2003.
4 Finance Act 2003 sch 4A para 4(1)(c).
5 Finance Act 2003 sch 4A para 7.
6 Finance Act 2003 sch 4A para 2.
7 Finance Act 2003 sch 4A para 3(3).
8 Finance Act 2003 sch 4A para 5(1).
9 HM Treasury, 'Finance Bill 2013 Draft Clauses', 11 Dec 2012 (www.hmrc.gov.uk/budget-updates/march2012/finance-bill-2013-draft.htm).

buildings conditionally exempt from inheritance tax, farmhouses occupied by working farmers, dwellings held by trading companies for use by employees, dwellings owned by a charity, and buildings owned by public or government bodies.

The final part of the attack on high-value residential properties is a first inroad into the UK principle that non-residents are not generally liable to capital gains tax on disposals, even of land located in the UK. This long-standing exemption will cease for certain non-resident, non-natural persons owning dwellings valued at more than £2 million with effect from April 2013. But the proposals have been heavily revised since they were first introduced.[1] Notably, the same range of exemptions as will apply to the annual residential property tax will apply to these provisions; and perhaps most importantly the charge (which will be at 28% with some reduction for properties with a disposal value just over £2 million) will only be applied to gains which accrue after 6 April 2013. While the properties affected are the same as those affected by other measures in the package, the persons affected will be extended to include trustees and executors; and the disposals affected will include shares in companies deriving more than 50% of their value from UK residential property (which seems almost impossible to enforce).[2]

It remains to be seen whether this package of what are essentially anti-avoidance measures will be extended to lower-value properties or, with much more impact, to commercial as well as residential property.

Land will always be an attractive source of taxation – it does not move and taxes affecting land are more readily capable of enforcement than many others. This fact may become increasingly relevant as governments of all kinds seek to increase or at least maintain their tax receipts.

Anti-avoidance

Anti-avoidance was also the theme of several other enacted and prospective measures. Sub-sale relief was (accurately) thought to be the basis of many of the most egregious SDLT-avoidance schemes. One, which HMRC did not consider worked in any event, involved the use of options, and the grant of options has now been excluded from the definition of relievable sub-sales.[3] A much more extensive reform of sub-sale relief is proposed for Finance Act 2013.[4] This purports to restore it to the more limited relief originally intended. As already mentioned, the Land and Buildings Transaction Tax (Scotland) Bill does not provide for sub-sale relief.

Part of the anti-avoidance agenda in recent years has included the enforced disclosure of promoted tax-avoidance schemes. This was extended in 2012 to

---

1 See HM Treasury, *Ensuring the fair taxation of residential property transactions: summary of responses*, Dec 2012 (www.hm-treasury.gov.uk/consult_ensuring_fair_taxation_residential_property_transactions.htm).
2 See HM Treasury, *Ensuring the fair taxation of residential property transactions* ch 3.
3 Finance Act 2003 s 45(1A), inserted by the Finance Act 2012 s 212.
4 See draft clauses published by HM Revenue and Customs in *Stamp duty land tax: transfers of rights*, Dec 2012 (www.hm-treasury.gov.uk/d/stamp_duty_land_tax_transfers_of_rights.pdf).

include schemes that had been notified under previous legislation before April 2012, so that such 'grandfathered' schemes will now require to be notified again.[1] Certain property valuation thresholds, below which notification was formerly not required, have now been removed.[2]

On a minor but complex note (and not concerned with tax avoidance), the relief from SDLT for acquisitions by certain health service bodies has been reformed in consequence of changes being made to the bodies concerned with the provision of healthcare.[3]

On tax avoidance more generally, work proceeds apace on the introduction of a UK General Anti-Abuse Rule, which is expected to take effect from the date when the Finance Act 2013 receives the Royal Assent.[4] And HMRC has had another success in challenging an SDLT avoidance scheme in *Vardy Properties v Revenue and Customs Commissioners*.[5] The scheme involved a purchase by an unlimited company and the distribution of its property by way of dividend; it failed because the dividend was unlawful and in any event the tribunal decided that the members of the company had provided the consideration for the purchase indirectly. HMRC considers that legislation passed since the scheme was used negates its effectiveness in all cases.

---

1 Finance Act 2004 s 308(6), inserted by the Finance Act 2012 s 215.
2 See Stamp Duty Land Tax Avoidance Schemes (Prescribed Descriptions of Arrangements) (Amendment) Regulations 2012, SI 2012/2395; Stamp Duty Land Tax (Avoidance Schemes) (Specified Proposals or Arrangements) Regulations 2012, SI 2012/2396. The information to be given to HMRC in relation to such schemes was consolidated in the Tax Avoidance Schemes (Information) Regulations 2012, SI 2012/1836.
3 See Finance Act 2012 s 216, which (*inter alia*) inserted Finance Act 2003 s 67A, defining the bodies benefiting from the exemption.
4 HM Revenue & Customs, *A General Anti-Abuse Rule: Summary of Responses*, 11 Dec 2012 (www.hmrc.gov.uk/budget-updates/11dec12/gaar-responses.pdf). See also three further consultations on aspects of the proposed Rule issued on the same date.
5 [2012] UKFTT 564 (TC).

PART V
TABLES

TABLES

CUMULATIVE TABLE OF DECISIONS ON VARIATION OR DISCHARGE OF TITLE CONDITIONS

This table lists all opposed applications under the Title Conditions (Scotland) Act 2003 for variation or discharge of title conditions. Decisions on expenses are omitted. Note that the full opinions in Lands Tribunal cases are usually available at http://www.lands-tribunal-scotland.org.uk/records.html.

Restriction on building

Name of case	Burden	Applicant's project in breach of burden	Application granted or refused
Ord v Mashford 2006 SLT (Lands Tr) 15; *Lawrie v Mashford*, 21 Dec 2007	1938. No building.	Erection of single-storey house and garage.	Granted. Claim for compensation refused.
Daly v Bryce 2006 GWD 25-565	1961 feu charter. No further building.	Replace existing house with two houses.	Granted.
J & L Leisure Ltd v Shaw 2007 GWD 28-489	1958 disposition. No new buildings higher than 15 feet 6 inches.	Replace derelict building with two-storey housing.	Granted subject to compensation of £5,600.
West Coast Property Developments Ltd v Clarke 2007 GWD 29-511	1875 feu contract. Terraced houses. No further building.	Erection of second, two-storey house.	Granted. Claim for compensation refused.
Smith v Prior 2007 GWD 30-523	1934 feu charter. No building.	Erection of modest rear extension.	Granted.
Anderson v McKinnon 2007 GWD 29-513	1993 deed of conditions in modern housing estate.	Erection of rear extension.	Granted.
Smith v Elrick 2007 GWD 29-515	1996 feu disposition. No new house. The feu had been subdivided.	Conversion of barn into a house.	Granted.

185

Name of case	Burden	Applicant's project in breach of burden	Application granted or refused
Brown v Richardson 2007 GWD 28-490	1888 feu charter. No alterations/new buildings	Erection of rear extension.	Granted. This was an application for renewal, following service of a notice of termination.
Gallacher v Wood 2008 SLT (Lands Tr) 31	1933 feu contract. No alterations/new buildings.	Erection of rear extension, including extension at roof level which went beyond bungalow's footprint.	Granted. Claim for compensation refused.
Jarron v Stuart, 23 March and 5 May 2011	1992 deed of conditions. No external alteration and additions.	Erection of rear extension.	Granted. Claim for compensation refused.
Blackman v Best 2008 GWD 11-214	1934 disposition. No building other than a greenhouse.	Erection of a double garage.	Granted.
McClumpha v Bradie 2009 GWD 31-519	1984 disposition allowing the erection of only one house.	Erection of four further houses.	Granted but restricted to four houses.
McGregor v Collins-Taylor, 14 May 2009	1988 disposition prohibiting the erection of dwellinghouses without consent.	Erection of four further houses.	Granted but restricted to four houses.
Faeley v Clark 2006 GWD 28-626	1967 disposition. No further building.	Erection of second house.	Refused.
Cattanach v Vine-Hall	1996 deed of conditions in favour of neighbouring property. No building within 7 metres of that property.	Erection of substantial house within 2 metres.	Refused, subject to the possibility of the applicants bringing a revised proposal.
Hamilton v Robertson, 10 Jan 2008	1984 deed of conditions affecting five-house development. No further building.	Erection of second house on site, but no firm plans.	Refused, although possibility of later success once plans firmed up was not excluded.
Cocozza v Rutherford 2008 SLT (Lands Tr) 6	1977 deed of conditions. No alterations.	Substantial alterations which would more than double the footprint of the house.	Refused.

Name of case	Burden	Applicant's project in breach of burden	Application granted or refused
Scott v Teasdale, 22 Dec 2009	1962 feu disposition. No building.	New house in garden.	Refused.
Rennie v Cullen House Gardens Ltd, 29 June 2012	2005 deed of conditions. No new building or external extension.	Extension of building forming part of historic house.	Refused.
Hollinshead v Gilchrist, 7 Dec 2009	1990 disposition and 1997 feu disposition. No building or alterations.	Internal alterations.	Granted.
Tower Hotel (Troon) Ltd v McCann, 4 March 2010	1965 feu disposition. No building. Existing building to be used as a hotel or dwellinghouse.	No firm plan though one possibility was the building of flats.	Granted.
Corstorphine v Fleming, 2 July 2010	1965 feu disposition. No alterations, one house only.	A substantial extension plus a new house.	Granted.
Corry v MacLachlan, 9 July 2010	1984 disposition of part of garden. Obligation to build a single-storey house.	Addition of an extra storey.	Refused.
Watt v Garden, 4 Nov 2011	1995 disposition. Use as garden only.	Additional two-bedroom bungalow.	Granted but with compensation.
Fyfe v Benson, 26 July 2011	1966 deed of conditions. No building or subdivision.	Additional three-bedroom house.	Refused.
MacDonald v Murdoch, 7 August 2012	1997 disposition. No building in garden.	Erection of 1½-storey house.	Refused.
Trigstone Ltd v Mackenzie, 16 Feb 2012	1949 charter of novodamus. No building in garden.	Erection of four-storey block of flats.	Refused.
McCulloch v Reid, 3 April 2012	2011 disposition. No parking in rear courtyard.	Parking of two cars.	Refused.

Other restriction on use

Name of case	Burden	Applicant's project in breach of burden	Application granted or refused
Church of Scotland General Trs v McLaren 2006 SLT (Lands Tr) 27	Use as a church.	Possible development for flats.	Granted.
Wilson v McNamee, 16 Sept 2007	Use for religious purposes.	Use for a children's nursery.	Granted
Verrico v Tomlinson 2008 SLT (Lands Tr) 2	1950 disposition. Use as a private residence for the occupation of one family.	Separation of mews cottage from ground floor flat.	Granted.
Whitelaw v Acheson, 29 Feb and 29 Sept 2012	1883 feu charter. Use as a single dwelling; no further building.	Change of use to therapy and wellbeing centre; erection of extension.	Granted subject to some restrictions.
Matnic Ltd v Armstrong 2010 SLT (Lands Tr) 7	2004 deed of conditions. Use for the sale of alcohol.	Use of units in a largely residential estate for retail purposes.	Granted but restricted to small units and no sale of alcohol after 8 pm.
Clarke v Grantham 2009 GWD 38-645	2004 disposition. No parking on an area of courtyard.	A desire to park (though other areas were available).	Granted.
Hollinshead v Gilchrist, 7 Dec 2009	1990 disposition and 1997 feu disposition. No caravans, commercial or other vehicles to be parked in front of the building line.	Parking of cars.	Granted and claim for compensation refused.
Perth & Kinross Council v Chapman, 13 Aug 2009	1945 disposition. Plot to be used only for outdoor recreational purposes.	Sale for redevelopment.	Granted.
Davenport v Julian Hodge Bank Ltd, 23 June 2011	2010 deed of conditions. No external painting without permission.	Paint the external walls sky blue.	Refused.

Flatted property

Name of case	Burden	Applicant's project in breach of burden	Application granted or refused
Regan v Mullen 2006 GWD 25-564	1989. No subdivision of flat.	Subdivision of flat.	Granted.

Name of case	Burden	Applicant's project in breach of burden	Application granted or refused
Kennedy v Abbey Lane Properties, 29 March 2010	2004. Main-door flat liable for a share of maintenance of common passages and stairs.	None.	Refused.
Patterson v Drouet, 20 Jan 2011	Liability for maintenance in accordance with gross annual value.	None, but, since the freezing of valuations in 1989, ground floor flats had reverted to residential use.	Variation of liability of ground floor flats granted in principle subject to issues of competency.
Melville v Crabbe, 19 Jan 2009	1880 feu disposition. No additional flat.	Creation of a flat in the basement.	Refused.

Sheltered and retirement housing

Name of case	Burden	Applicant's project in breach of burden	Application granted or refused
At.Home Nationwide Ltd v Morris 2007 GWD 31-535	1993 deed of conditions. On sale, must satisfy superior that flat will continue to be used for the elderly.	No project: just removal of an inconvenient restriction.	Burden held to be void. Otherwise application would have been refused.

Miscellaneous

Name of case	Burden	Applicant's project in breach of burden	Application granted or refused
McPherson v Mackie 2006 GWD 27-606 rev [2007] CSIH 7, 2007 SCLR 351	1990. Housing estate: maintenance of house.	Demolition of house to allow the building of a road for access to proposed new development.	Discharged by agreement on 25 April 2007.

Applications for renewal of real burdens following service of a notice of termination

Name of case	Burden	Respondent's project in breach of burden	Application granted or refused
Brown v Richardson 2007 GWD 28-490	1888 feu charter. No buildings.	Substantial rear extension	Refused.

Name of case	Burden	Respondent's project in breach of burden	Application granted or refused
Council for Music in Hospitals v Trustees for Richard Gerald Associates 2008 SLT (Lands Tr) 17	1838 instrument of sasine. No building in garden.	None.	Refused.
Gibson v Anderson, 3 May 2012	1898 disposition. No building other than one-storey outbuildings.	Two-storey house.	Refused; burden varied to allow limited building.

Applications for preservation of community burdens following deeds of variation or discharge under s 33 or s 35

Name of case	Burden	Respondent's project in breach of burden	Application granted or refused
Fleeman v Lyon 2009 GWD 32-539	1982 deed of conditions. No building, trade, livestock etc.	Erection of a second house.	Granted.

Applications for variation of community burdens (s 91)

Name of case	Burden	Applicant's project in breach of burden	Application granted or refused
Fenwick v National Trust for Scotland 2009 GWD 32-538	1989 deed of conditions.	None. The application was for the complete discharge of the deed with the idea that a new deed would eventually be drawn up.	Refused.
Patterson v Drouet, 2013 GWD 3-99	1948 deed of conditions apportioned liability for maintenance in a tenement on the basis of annual value.	Substitution of floor area for annual value.	Granted; compensation refused.

Servitudes

Name of case	Servitude	Applicant's project in breach of burden	Application granted or refused
George Wimpey East Scotland Ltd v Fleming 2006 SLT (Lands Tr) 2 and 59	1988 disposition. Right of way.	Diversion of right of way to allow major development for residential houses.	Granted (opposed). Claim for compensation for temporary disturbance refused.
Ventureline Ltd, 2 Aug 2006	1972 disposition. 'Right to use' certain ground.	Possible redevelopment.	Granted (unopposed).
Graham v Parker 2007 GWD 30-524	1990 feu disposition. Right of way from mid-terraced house over garden of end-terraced house to the street.	Small re-routing of right of way, away from the burdened owner's rear wall, so as to allow an extension to be built.	Granted (opposed).
MacNab v McDowall, 24 Oct 2007	1994 feu disposition reserved a servitude of way from the back garden to the front street in favour of two neighbouring house.	Small re-rerouting, on to the land of one of the neighbours, to allow a rear extension to be built.	Granted (opposed).
Jensen v Tyler 2008 SLT (Lands Tr) 39	1985 feu disposition granted a servitude of way.	Re-routing of part of the road in order to allow (unspecified) development of steading.	Granted (opposed).
Gibb v Kerr 2009 GWD 38-646	1981 feu disposition granted a servitude of way.	Re-routing to homologate what had already taken place as a result of the building of a conservatory.	Granted (opposed).
Parkin v Kennedy, 23 March 2010	1934 feu charter. Right of way from mid-terraced house over garden of end-terraced house.	Re-routing to allow extension to be built, which would require a restriction to pedestrian access.	Refused (opposed).
Adams v Trs for the Linton Village Hall, 24 Oct 2011	Dispositions of 1968 and 1970 reserved a servitude of access.	Re-routing to a route more convenient for the applicant.	Granted (opposed).

Name of case	Servitude	Applicant's project in breach of burden	Application granted or refused
Brown v Kitchen 28 Oct 2011	1976 feu disposition reserved a servitude of pedestrian access. 1944 disposition reserved a servitude of pedestrian access.	Re-routing to the edge of the garden.	Granted in principle (opposed) subject to agreement as to the widening of the substitute route. Granted (opposed).
Hossack v Robertson, 29 June 2012	Servitude of access.	Re-routing to end of garden to allow building of conservatory.	Granted (opposed).
Cope v Ms X, 19 Nov 2012		Substitute road.	Granted (opposed).
ATD Developments Ltd v Weir, 14 September 2010	2002 disposition granted a servitude right of way.	Narrowing the servitude so as to allow gardens for proposed new houses.	Granted (unopposed).
Stirling v Thorley, 12 Oct 2012	1994 and 1995 dispositions granted a servitude of vehicular access.	Building a house on half of an area set aside for turning vehicles.	Refused (opposed).
Colecliffe v Thompson 2010 SLT (Lands Tr) 15	1997 disposition granted a servitude of way.	None. But the owners of the benefited property had since acquired a more convenient access, secured by a new servitude.	Granted (opposed).
G v A, 26 Nov 2009	1974 disposition granted a servitude of way.	None. But the owners of the benefited property had since acquired a more convenient access (although not to his garage).	Granted (opposed) but on the basis that the respondent should apply for compensation.
Graham v Lee, 18 June 2009	2001 disposition granted (a) a servitude of way and (b) of drainage.	None.	(a) was granted provided the applicants discharged a reciprocal servitude of their own, and compensation was considered. (b) was refused.

Name of case	Servitude	Applicant's project in breach of burden	Application granted or refused
McNab v Smith, 15 June 2012	1981 disposition granted a servitude of vehicular access for agricultural purposes.	None. But the owner of the benefited property could access the property in a different way.	Granted (opposed) but, because works would be needed to improve the alternative access, on the basis of payment of compensation.
Stephenson v Thomas, 21 November 2012	1990 disposition granted a servitude of vehicular access.	None. But the owner of the benefited property could access the property in a different way.	Refused (opposed) on the basis that there were safety concerns about the alternative route and the benefited proprietors were proposing to revert to the original route.
McKenzie v Scott, 19 May 2009	Dispositions from 1944 and 1957 granted a servitude of bleaching and drying clothes.	None. But the servitude had not in practice been exercised for many years.	Granted (opposed).
Chisholm v Crawford, 17 June 2010	A driveway divided two properties. A 1996 feu disposition of one of the properties granted a servitude of access over the driveway.	None. But the applicant was aggrieved that no matching servitude appeared in the neighbour's title.	Refused.

CUMULATIVE TABLE OF APPEALS

A table at the end of *Conveyancing 2008* listed all cases digested in *Conveyancing 1999* and subsequent annual volumes in respect of which an appeal was subsequently heard, and gave the result of the appeal. This table is a continuation of the earlier table, beginning with appeals heard during 2009.

Aberdeen City Council v Stewart Milne Group Ltd
[2009] CSOH 80, 2009 GWD 26-417, 2009 Case (6) *affd* [2010] CSIH 81, 2010 GWD 37-755, 2010 Case (9) *affd* [2011] UKSC 56, 2011 Case (13)

AMA (New Town) Ltd v Finlay
2010 GWD 32-658, Sh Ct, 2010 Case (8) *rev* 2011 SLT (Sh Ct) 73, 2011 Case (1)

Blemain Finance Ltd v Balfour & Manson LLP
[2011] CSOH 157, 2012 SLT 672, 2011 Case (69) *affd* [2012] CSIH 66, [2013] PNLR 3, 2012 GWD 30-609, 2012 Case (70)

Cheshire Mortgage Corporation Ltd v Grandison; Blemain Finance Ltd v Balfour & Manson LLP
[2011] CSOH 157, 2012 SLT 672, 2011 Case (69) *affd* [2012] CSIH 66, [2013] PNLR 3, 2012 GWD 30-609, 2012 Case (69)

Compugraphics International Ltd v Nikolic
[2009] CSOH 54, 2009 GWD 19-311, 2009 Cases (22) and (90) *rev* [2011] CSIH 34, 2011 SLT 955, 2011 Cases (21) and (74)

Co-operative Group Ltd v Propinvest Paisley LP
17 September 2010, Lands Tribunal, 2010 Case (36) *rev* [2011] CSIH 41, 2011 SLT 987, 2011 Case (38)

Cramaso LLP v Viscount Reidhaven's Trs
[2010] CSOH 62, 2010 GWD 20-403, 2010 Case (58) *affd* [2011] CSIH 81, 2011 Case (57)

EDI Central Ltd v National Car Parks Ltd
[2010] CSOH 141, 2011 SLT 75, 2010 Case (5) *affd* [2012] CSIH 6, 2012 SLT 421, 2012 Case (4)

Euring David Ayre of Kilmarnock, Baron of Kilmarnock Ptr
[2008] CSOH 35, 2008 Case (82) *rev* [2009] CSIH 61, 2009 SLT 759, 2009 Case (93)

Christie Owen & Davies plc v Campbell
2007 GWD 24-397, Sh Ct, 2007 Case (53) *affd* 18 Dec 2007, Glasgow Sheriff Court, 2007 Case (53) *rev* [2009] CSIH 26, 2009 SLT 518, 2009 Case (82)

Martin Stephen James Goldstraw of Whitecairns Ptr
[2008] CSOH 34, 2008 Case (81) *rev* [2009] CSIH 61, 2009 SLT 759, 2009 Case (93)

Hamilton v Dumfries & Galloway Council
[2008] CSOH 65, 2008 SLT 531, 2008 Case (37) *rev* [2009] CSIH 13, 2009 SC 277, 2009 SLT 337, 2009 SCLR 392, 2009 Case (50)

Hamilton v Nairn
[2009] CSOH 163, 2010 SLT 399, 2009 Case (51) *affd* [2010] CSIH 77, 2010 SLT 1155, 2010 Case (44)

Holms v Ashford Estates Ltd
2006 SLT (Sh Ct) 70, 2006 Case (40) *affd* 2006 SLT (Sh Ct) 161, 2006 Case (40) *rev*
[2009] CSIH 28, 2009 SLT 389, 2009 SCLR 428, 2009 Cases (19) and (52)

Hunter v Tindale
2011 SLT (Sh Ct) 11, 2010 Case (16) *rev* 2011 GWD 25-570, Sh Ct, 2011 Case (19)

Kerr of Ardgowan, Ptr
[2008] CSOH 36, 2008 SLT 251, 2008 Case (80) *rev* [2009] CSIH 61, 2009 SLT 759,
2009 Case (93)

L Batley Pet Products Ltd v North Lanarkshire Council
[2011] CSOH 209, 2012 GWD 4-73, 2011 Case (62) *rev* [2012] CSIH 83, 2012 GWD
37-745, 2012 Case (43)

Luminar Lava Ignite Ltd v Mama Group plc
[2009] CSOH 68, 2009 GWD 19-305, 2009 Case (91) *rev* [2010] CSIH 1, 2010 SC 310,
2010 SLT 147, 2010 Case (77)

McGraddie v McGraddie
[2009] CSOH 142, 2009 GWD 38-633, 2009 Case (60), [2010] CSOH 60, 2010 GWD
21-404, 2000 Case (48) *rev* [2012] CSIH 23, 2012 GWD 15-310, 2012 Case (38)

McSorley v Drennan
May 2011, Ayr Sheriff Court, 2011 Case (14) *rev* [2012] CSIH 59, 2012 GWD 25-506,
2012 Case (6)

Mehrabadi v Haugh
June 2009, Aberdeen Sheriff Court, 2009 Case (17) *affd* 11 January 2010 Aberdeen
Sheriff Court, 2010 Case (15)

*Moderator of the General Assembly of the Free Church of Scotland v Interim Moderator
of the Congregation of Strath Free Church of Scotland (Continuing)*
[2009] CSOH 113, 2009 SLT 973, 2009 Case (96) *affd* [2011] CSIH 52, 2011 SLT 1213,
2012 SC 79, 2011 Case (77)

Morris v Rae
[2011] CSIH 30, 2011 SC 654, 2011 SLT 701, 2011 SCLR 428, 2011 Case (39) *rev* [2012]
UKSC 50, 2013 SLT 88, 2012 Case (41)

Multi-link Leisure Developments Ltd v North Lanarkshire Council
[2009] CSOH 114, 2009 SLT 1170, 2009 Case (70) *rev* [2009] CSIH 96, 2010 SC 302,
2010 SLT 57, 2010 SCLR 306, 2009 Case (70) *affd* [2010] UKSC 47, [2011] 1 All ER
175, 2010 Case (52)

Orkney Housing Association Ltd v Atkinson
15 October 2010, Kirkwall Sheriff Court, 2010 Case (21) *rev* 2011 GWD 30-652,
2011 Cases (22) and (41)

Pocock's Tr v Skene Investments (Aberdeen) Ltd
[2011] CSOH 144, 2011 GWD 30-654, 2011 Case (40) *rev* [2012] CSIH 61, 2012 GWD
27-562, 2012 Case (36)

R & D Construction Group Ltd v Hallam Land Management Ltd
[2009] CSOH 128, 2009 Case (8) *affd* [2010] CSIH 96, 2010 Case (4)

Royal Bank of Scotland plc v Wilson
2008 GWD 2-35, Sh Ct, 2008 Case (61) *rev* 2009 CSIH 36, 2009 SLT 729, 2009 Case
(75) *rev* [2010] UKSC 50, 2011 SC (UKSC) 66, 2010 SLT 1227, 2010 Hous LR 88, 2010
Case (66)

Scottish Coal Company Ltd v Danish Forestry Co Ltd
[2009] CSOH 171, 2009 GWD 5-79, 2009 Case (9) *affd* [2010] CSIH 56, 2010 GWD
27-529, 2010 Case (3)

Sheltered Housing Management Ltd v Bon Accord Bonding Co Ltd
2007 GWD 32-533, 2006 Cases (24) and (35), 11 October 2007, Lands Tribunal, 2007
Case (21) *rev* [2010] CSIH 42, 2010 SC 516, 2010 SLT 662, 2010 Case (25)

Smith v Stuart
2009 GWD 8-140, Sh Ct, 2009 Case (2) *affd* [2010] CSIH 29, 2010 SC 490, 2010 SLT
1249, 2010 Case (10)

Tuley v Highland Council
2007 SLT (Sh Ct) 97, 2007 Case (24) *rev* [2009] CSIH 31A, 2009 SC 456, 2009 SLT
616, 2009 Case (48)

Wright v Shoreline Management Ltd
Oct 2008, Arbroath Sheriff Court, 2008 Case (60) *rev* 2009 SLT (Sh Ct) 83, 2009
Case (74)

TABLE OF CASES DIGESTED IN EARLIER VOLUMES BUT REPORTED IN 2012

A number of cases which were digested in *Conveyancing 2011* or earlier volumes but were at that time unreported have been reported in 2012. A number of other cases have been reported in an additional series of reports. For the convenience of those using earlier volumes all the cases in question are listed below, together with a complete list of citations.

Aberdeen City Council v Stewart Milne Group Ltd
[2011] UKSC 56, 2012 SC (UKSC) 240, 2012 SLT 205, 2012 SCLR 114

Cheshire Mortgage Corporation Ltd v Grandison; Blemain Finance Ltd v Balfour & Manson LLP
[2011] CSOH 157, 2012 SLT 672

Edinburgh Tours Ltd v Singh
2012 Hous LR 15

Frank Houlgate Investment Co Ltd v Biggart Baillie LLP
[2011] CSOH 160, 2012 SLT 256

Landmore Ltd v Shanks Dumfries and Galloway Ltd
[2011] CSOH 100, 2012 SCLR 46

Moderator of the General Assembly of the Free Church of Scotland v Interim Moderator of the Congregation of Strath Free Church of Scotland (Continuing) (No 3)
[2011] CSIH 52, 2011 SLT 1213, 2012 SC 79

Scott v Muir
2012 SLT (Sh Ct) 179, 2012 Hous LR 20